300
St. Louis

D0810444

Florissant Valley Library
St. Louis Community College
3400 Pershall Road
Ferguson, MO 63135-1499
314-513-4514

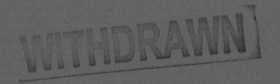

GONE WITH THE GLORY

THE GLORY

The Civil War in Cinema

GONE WITH THE GLORY

The Civil War in Cinema

BRIAN STEEL WILLS

ROWMAN & LITTLEFIELD PUBLISHERS, INC.
Lanham • Boulder • New York • Toronto • Oxford

ROWMAN & LITTLEFIELD PUBLISHERS, INC.

Published in the United States of America
by Rowman & Littlefield Publishers, Inc.
A wholly owned subsidiary of The Rowman & Littlefield Publishing Group, Inc.
4501 Forbes Boulevard, Suite 200, Lanham, Maryland 20706
www.rowmanlittlefield.com

PO Box 317
Oxford
OX2 9RU, UK

Distributed by National Book Network

Copyright © 2007 by Rowman & Littlefield Publishers, Inc.

All rights reserved. No part of this publication may be reproduced,
stored in a retrieval system, or transmitted in any form or by any
means, electronic, mechanical, photocopying, recording, or otherwise,
without the prior permission of the publisher.

British Library Cataloguing in Publication Information Available

Library of Congress Cataloging-in-Publication Data

Wills, Brian Steel, 1959–
    Gone with the Glory: The Civil War in Cinema / Brian S. Wills.
      p. cm.
    Includes bibliographical references and index.
    ISBN-13: 978-0-7425-4525-0 (cloth : alk. paper)
    ISBN-10: 0-7425-4525-3 (cloth : alk. paper)
    1. United States—History—Civil War, 1861–1865—Motion pictures and the war. 2. War films—
United States—History. I. Title.

E656.W55 2007
791.43'658—dc22   2006004554

Printed in the United States of America

⊗™The paper used in this publication meets the minimum requirements of American National
Standard for Information Sciences—Permanence of Paper for Printed Library Materials,
ANSI/NISO Z39.48-1992.

For Elizabeth Smiddy Wills

CONTENTS

CONTENTS

PHOTOGRAPHS

ACKNOWLEDGMENTS

I HAVE BEEN WATCHING movies since I was a boy. I always preferred the historical epics to other genres, partly because of my interest in history and partly because these films were what I thought movies should be—that is, big and entertaining depictions of another place and time. Through films such as *Ben Hur*, *The Ten Commandments*, and *El Cid*, I became a Charlton Heston fan. Sword and sandal epics were particular favorites, although nothing beat a Civil War film. It is certainly true of me, as Mark C. Carnes observed in an essay on "Hollywood History," "Historians love movies about the past."[1]

Simple segments or references to the war would suffice, but films that featured the conflict were an especial delight. *Shenandoah* profoundly moved me. The doxology has never been the same since I saw how the James Stewart classic ended with the missing son returning to the arms of the loving father who had already lost so much in a war he had tried so desperately to avoid.

Our family made it a Sunday ritual to see whatever happened to be playing at the Chadwick Theater or the drive-in at Suffolk. Those were great days and left powerful memories. My parents surely thought that I watched too much television when I was growing up, although I did so just as often to catch a film I could not have seen in the movie theaters as to watch *Star Trek*, *Bonanza*, or *Hawaii Five-0*. Indeed, I kept a record of the films I had seen and the actors and actresses featured in them.

In completing this project, I particularly would like to thank the colleagues at the University of Virginia's College at Wise who lent their support. I am appreciative of a faculty research grant that made time available for research and writing that I otherwise would not have had.

Robin Benke of the College's Wyllie Library has been especially helpful with this project. He is not only a great library director, but a great friend as well. Rhonda Bentley has also offered tremendous support. A student and an actor in his own right, H W. "Bill" Smith read the manuscript and offered helpful suggestions and additions. Another former student and colleague, Brian McKnight, read the manuscript in the later stages and provided his excellent insights. My profound gratitude goes to both of them.

I want to express my appreciation for the extraordinary patience and good spirit exhibited by Matt Hershey at Scholarly Resources. Thanks also to Laura

Gottlieb, Andrew Boney, and Laura Wynn at Rowman & Littlefield, who took on this project when that publishing house acquired Scholarly Resources.

To my wife, Elizabeth Smiddy Wills, to whom this book is dedicated, I owe the greatest appreciation. Foremost among the many things she has done to encourage my work and make it easier for me to find time and space to research and write is her own love of the movies. It has been enormously beneficial that all the members of our family truly enjoy film, even if our youngest prefers scary ones.

Finally, a few brief notes with regard to the style used in this book are in order. To aid in distinguishing between discussions of history and the portrayal of history in film, I have used the present tense when dealing with the films themselves and the past tense while discussing the historical events and personalities. In addition, the names of characters in the films appear with the identities of the principal actors or actresses who portrayed them in parentheses when their cinematic counterparts first appear. Readers interested in obtaining information concerning anachronisms, inconsistencies, and other imperfections in many of the films discussed here will benefit from the Internet Movie Database, which can be found at www.imdb.com. Finally, dialogue from the motion pictures considered in these pages comes from the films themselves and not from screenplays or scripts. Any failures in transcription are the author's.

If I have accomplished my goal, this book will not only serve as a useful reference tool for the Civil War in cinema, but will also supply some historical connections and corrections for what has appeared on the motion picture screen. Finally, and probably most importantly, I hope that it helps to bring back a few pleasant movie memories as well.

Note

1. Mark C. Carnes, "Hollywood History," American Heritage (September 1995), 74.

Hollywood's Civil War

The biggest event in our history belongs on the biggest canvas humans can devise.

—historian and author William C. Davis

There is an old Hollywood axiom that motion pictures about the Civil War never succeed.

—author Jack Spears

Every filmmaker, like every historian, has an agenda.

—director John Sayles

SOME OF THE nation's best actors, actresses, and directors have taken the Civil War as a movie screen canvas upon which to display their talents and skills. The impressive list includes actors John Wayne, William Holden, Richard Widmark, James Stewart, Clark Gable, Clint Eastwood, Denzel Washington, and Morgan Freeman; actresses Vivien Leigh, Gene Tierney, Elizabeth Taylor, Yvonne De Carlo, Anne Bancroft, Susan Hayward, and Nicole Kidman; and directors D. W. Griffith, John Ford, John Huston, Sam Peckinpah, William Wyler, Raoul Walsh, John Frankenheimer, and Ang Lee.[1]

The body of work that such talented professionals have produced has always reflected the dual nature of history in film, including the entertainment value of the stories and the accuracy of the depictions being rendered on-screen. In the case of the American Civil War, the tableau is rich in color, conflict, and character. Yet some producers, directors, and performers have less interest in, or knowledge of, the demands of history than others. Many will use the war as a mere backdrop or context rather than seek to inform audiences of the issues and complexities of the conflict itself. Others cast the struggle in the simplest forms. Thus, even in the best of situations,

1

there is always a tug of war between two powerful poles: entertainment value and historical accuracy.

In the early years of the twentieth century, silent films followed the lead of literature and theatrical productions and employed Civil War themes with regularity.[2] As historian Edward D. C. Campbell has asserted, "What postwar romantic literature had so popularly begun, the movies ratified."[3]

Producers and directors intended some of these film depictions to convey historical reality, at least as the people of the times understood it. Others simply used the war as a familiar backdrop for audiences that still contained veterans of the Late Unpleasantness and witnessed constant reminders of the veneration of the Lost Cause. Perhaps because of their proximity to those aging warriors and the reunion or memorial celebrations associated with them, moviegoers of the period seemed to be drawn to the depictions of divided families and personal loyalties that the Civil War provided.[4]

Famed pioneering film director David W. Griffith used the Civil War as a motif in a number of his short works with the American Mutoscope and Biograph Company. In 1910, the year of his most active use of the war, these included *In the Border States*, *The House with the Closed Shutters*, *The Fugitive*, *His Trust*, and *His Trust Fulfilled*. Griffith produced two more Civil War–oriented projects, *Swords and Hearts* and *The Battle*, the following year.[5]

The Birth of a Nation was the great Civil War film of its generation. The images blasted onto the screen with a power that the movie's silence only emphasized. Its elements—the brave and heroic Southern family beset by the conditions of war, defeat, and reconstruction, a benevolent Abraham Lincoln taken too soon by an assassin's bullet, corrupted Northern politicians and their ravenous African American compatriots, and the Ku Klux Klan as defenders of social and racial order—for decades became the centerpieces of a portrait of the conflict that maintained credibility for many of the viewers in mainstream America. Griffith had been concerned with telling the truth about the war, at least as he saw it, because in his estimation the history books had failed to do so.[6]

Another silent movie classic, *The General*, employed the war as a backdrop for the comedic genius of Buster Keaton. Using the pursuit of Union raiders in a thinly disguised version of the James J. Andrews raid in North Georgia as his foil, Keaton labored mightily to reclaim his captured train and retrieve his kidnapped fiancée from Northern hands.

Other Civil War comedies would follow, such as *A Southern Yankee* (1948), with the incomparable Red Skelton as a spy, and *Advance to the Rear* (1964), featuring a usually serious Glenn Ford (although the film also cast Jim Backus) as the leader of a misfit Union unit. But no such film has ever rivaled the mastery of the Buster Keaton silent classic.

In the sound era, light musicals featured Shirley Temple and Bill "Bojangles" Robinson in a variety of settings, including the Civil War. *The Littlest*

Rebel (1935) and *The Little Colonel* (1935) contained the precocious youngster amidst the familiar Civil War and reconciliation themes so prominent in late-nineteenth- and early-twentieth-century America.

The Birth of a Nation had established the parameters in the silent era, but *Gone with the Wind* (1939) set the standard thereafter for Hollywood's big-screen impression of the Civil War. Films since that time have tried to match the pageantry and splendor of the David O. Selznick spectacle. Television followed suit with soap opera–style imitations such as *Love's Savage Fury* (1979) and *Beulah Land* (1980). It was the Old South as it should have been—picturesque and elegant, even as it is buffeted and eventually swept away by the harsh winds of war.

Despite the enormous commercial and critical success of the 1939 classic, Hollywood failed to capitalize on the groundwork that *Gone with the Wind* had laid in the following decade. World War II represented a disconnect between the movie-going public and the American Civil War. There was enough to do to focus on the conflict at hand without people concentrating on the one that now lay eighty years in the past. Thus Brian Donlevy had to celebrate American determination on *Wake Island* (1942). Humphrey Bogart was busy thwarting Nazi intentions in *Casablanca* (1942). John Wayne needed to help the Chinese (*Flying Tigers*, 1942), escape the Nazis in France (*Reunion in France*, 1942), and resist the Japanese (*Back to Bataan*, 1945; *They Were Expendable*, 1945; *The Fighting Seabees*, 1945; and *Sands of Iwo Jima*, 1949) rather than lead Union raiders through Confederate Mississippi as he would a decade later.

The great era of Civil War cinema seems to have been the 1950s, when dozens of films reached the screen portraying the nation's most bitter conflict. Again, influenced by the times, they usually sought to de-emphasize the struggle between Northern and Southern Americans by introducing common opponents or focusing on the tragedy of war for all participants.

The heyday of Civil War cinema continued into the 1960s as the nation celebrated the centennial of the conflict. At least half a dozen films enjoyed releases during this period, including the ultimately uplifting Jimmy Stewart classic, *Shenandoah* (1965), and the film that Charlton Heston had hoped would serve as his Civil War epic, *Major Dundee* (1965).[7]

Some producers of Civil War films sought to satisfy demographics, and draw viewers into the theaters, by diluting the lines between recognizable names in other areas and those in film. Thus, while screen icons John Wayne and William Holden headlined *The Horse Soldiers* (1959), they shared billing with African American tennis star and Olympic champion Althea Gibson. Ten years later, Wayne and Rock Hudson worked with professional football greats Roman Gabriel and Merlin Olsen in *The Undefeated* (1969). Later, character actors Jack Elam and Woody Strode supported sports legend Joe Namath in *The Last Rebel* (1971), a cinematic vehicle as notable for its poor history as for the regrettable performance of the National Football League quarterback.[8]

3

But it was also clear in the latter 1960s that Hollywood filmmakers were exploring darker issues, or certainly embracing darker characters, suggesting the worries of the time even in their treatment of the Civil War. William Holden's *Alvarez Kelly* (1966) was largely (although not entirely) an amoral capitalistic entrepreneur. Jack Palance's character in *The Desperados* (1969) was nothing short of a homicidal psychopath, while Max Baer Jr. (television's beloved Jethro in *The Beverly Hillbillies*) displayed a similar personality disturbance in *A Time for Killing* (1967).

Choices were obviously becoming harder to make, sacrifices more severe, and the consequences of war more devastating, as evidenced by the disintegration of James Stewart's clan in *Shenandoah* (1965). It was hardly accidental that a Confederate sentry caused the death of one of the Anderson party, while a Union soldier and a Union officer proved instrumental in saving the missing youngest son's life and helping the father in his search for the lad. This war, perhaps unlike others, appeared to have no easy boundaries between right and wrong, good and evil, in a conflict that pitted Americans against each other.[9]

The late 1960s and early 1970s also brought reactions to Vietnam onto the big screen. *Journey to Shiloh* (1968) was less the story of young Texans bound for a war in distant Tennessee than an allegory for the waste of war, particularly when the sacrifices being offered seemed to have no justifiable cause.

The Beguiled (1971) blurred the lines between civilians and soldiers, allowing the Southern women of a small private academy to exact revenge on their Northern tormentor. This ambiguity also reflected the uncertainty people in the United States felt about the war in Southeast Asia, where eighteen-year-old All-American boys with Bic lighters were turning Vietnamese villages into ashes and massacres were no longer always those things perpetrated by others on Americans or their supporters.

The late 1980s and 1990s gave film audiences a new social consciousness, although *Glory* (1989) could not help but provide the black soldier perspective through the eyes of its young white officer. Still, for a Civil War film to depict the African American experience for a larger audience, Hollywood was making strides from the days of the stock figures and racist imagery of *The Birth of a Nation* and *Gone with the Wind*.

Late twentieth-century filmmakers also presented their subjects in starker, more realistic terms. *Pharaoh's Army* (1995) offered an unvarnished examination of the war in the divided Appalachians. *Ride with the Devil* (1999) was much more graphic than its Civil War film predecessors, and thus more true to life in its portrayal of the violence of warfare. *Gangs of New York* (2002) depicted the savagery of urban warfare in mid-nineteenth-century New York City, culminating in the bloody confrontations that filled the streets during the draft riots of July 1863.

Beyond the portrayal of combat violence in *Ride with the Devil*, it remains to be seen how the heart-wrenching depiction of the Normandy Invasion in

Steven Spielberg's *Saving Private Ryan* (1998), the brutal action of the bloody Somali gauntlet U.S. soldiers ran trying to rescue fallen comrades in *Black Hawk Down* (2001), or the harrowing Vietnam firefights depicted in *We Were Soldiers* (2002) will translate into future Civil War films. Already, there is evidence of the trend toward realism, in such historically suspect films as *The Patriot* (2000), and in the re-release of material cut earlier from *Spartacus* (1960) as being too violent or too suggestive for public consumption or moral sensibilities when the film was first released.

In many ways, *Gods and Generals* (2003) and *Cold Mountain* (2003) can be said to straddle the line between older conventions and newer sensitivities. The former sought to remind audiences that great individuals could become heroic commanders leading soldiers into battle, yet tried to raise the consciousness of viewers to the existence of slavery and the contradictions of a slave society that stressed its fight for its own freedom while holding others in bondage. Yet the latter could not resist an obligatory scene of slaves harvesting cotton that might as well have been cut from footage of *Gone with the Wind*, while emphasizing the important role and capabilities of women in the midst of war and deprivation.

Historians have also begun to examine film and its influence on the viewing public's understanding of history in a much closer, more systematic fashion. Two works have focused on the South in film. In 1978, Jack Temple Kirby looked at *Media-Made Dixie*, and in 1981, Edward D. C. Campbell Jr. examined *The Celluloid South*. Both of these studies discussed the social milieu of film and other forms of popular expression relating to the American South. Later in the decade, writer and self-described "film fan" John M. Cassidy wrote a fine pictorial history of *Civil War Cinema*.[10] Then in 1996, writer Roy Kinnard outlined *The Blue and the Gray on the Silver Screen*.[11]

In the mid-1990s, a number of academically oriented studies concerning Civil War cinema appeared. In 1995, Jim Cullen examined the conflict in the context of American popular culture with a substantial examination of films on the subject, including *Glory* (1989).[12] In the same year, Catherine Clinton "revisited" Tara and explored "women, war, and the plantation legend."[13] The next year, prolific author William C. Davis examined Civil War cinema in a chapter of *The Cause Lost*.[14]

The trend of analyzing Civil War films continued into the next decade as well. Some of these analyses dealt with the larger issue of public memory, such as Carol Reardon's *Pickett's Charge in History and Memory*, which contained a brief reference to the movie *Gettysburg*.[15] Neil Longley York chose to analyze the film *The Horse Soldiers* in popular memory in his 2001 study, *Fiction As Fact*. The following year, authors Paul Ashdown and Edward Caudill assessed *The Mosby Myth*.

Of course, not all studies of history and film have dealt with the Civil War. Robert Brent Toplin examined eight feature films, none of which related to the war, as case studies in *History by Hollywood*.[16] However, such examinations of popular culture and its reflection upon and shaping of the understanding of American history in general, and the Civil War in particular, will certainly continue.

Just as surely to continue is the parallel between Civil War cinema and Civil War fiction. From Thomas Dixon's *The Clansman*, through Margaret Mitchell's *Gone with the Wind*, to modern adaptations of Michael Shaara's *The Killer Angels* and Charles Frazier's *Cold Mountain*, film producers have seemed to take their lead, and their ideas, from what popular audiences have read on the written page. If that pattern continues, Civil War film will always be only as good and as historically accurate as the material from which it springs. Since the primary purpose of fiction is to entertain, this purpose is likely to work its way onto the big-screen adaptation as well, provided that the script is even an adequate translation of the novel.

The time-honored convention of adapting literature to the screen is part of any film genre, but especially of American Civil War cinema, and this brings us full circle. The film industry drew heavily upon literature and theater in its inception, and it has continued to do so under the assumption that fiction readers will become moviegoers. We also return to the notion that the movies have always been meant for entertainment, first and foremost. Their function as educational tools has generally taken a secondary, and often un-witting, role that has served as corollary to the box office dollars that a film could generate.

Yet, whether done overtly, as with directors such as D. W. Griffith, or more subtly and even unexpectedly, cinema has educated everyone who entered a darkened theater or turned on their television sets to participate. "Millions of Americans have had their vision of the South, race relations, and even the en-tire panorama of our past shaped if not wholly defined by the movie business," according to one observer.[17] As William Davis so aptly puts it, "The biggest event in our history belongs on the biggest canvas humans can devise."[18]

In assessing Charlton Heston as an interviewee, biographer Michael Munn concludes, "It is as though he is in control of the interview and you can be sure that he'll tell you exactly what he wants you to know."[19] The same could be said for Civil War cinema. The celluloid will only reveal what we want it to reveal, and in the process will tell us much more about ourselves than we can ever learn about the past it is attempting to display, even so im-portant a part of our collective past as the American Civil War.

CHAPTER 1

The *Birth* of Civil War Cinema

In this view from *The Birth of a Nation*, the "Little Colonel," portrayed by Henry B. Walthall, stands ready to lead his men against the Union lines in a forlorn charge during the siege of Petersburg.

We do demand, as a right, the liberty to show the dark side of wrong,
that we might illuminate the bright side of virtue.

—*The Birth of a Nation*

It is like writing history with lightning.

—President Woodrow Wilson's reported
reaction upon seeing *The Birth of a Nation*

I N MANY RESPECTS, *The Birth of a Nation* ushered in a new era of
filmmaking; it also brought a historical interpretation of the pivotal events
of the middle period of the nineteenth century to the big screen for a national audience and shaped the way a generation of filmgoers came to see
a volatile period in American history.[1] Yet, at the time of its release and despite the popular reception it received, the movie was not without its detrac-
tors. Subsequent assessments have taken the film to task for its historical sim-
plicity, flawed interpretations, and patent racism.[2] Even so, *The Birth of a
Nation* remains powerful cinema in its own right.

The movie's creator, D. W. Griffith, was an undisputed film innovator and
cinematic visionary. *The Birth of a Nation* would bring him extraordinary
fame, but it was not the beginning of Griffith's examination of the war on celluloid. The film was actually the culmination of a life's work, much of which
had involved short subjects, many of these touching upon or directly examining the American Civil War.

Historian Jack Temple Kirby has noted, "Griffith's greatest paean to paternalism and the faithful darky was an ambitious two-reeler which Biograph
Company officials released in January, 1911, as two separate but sequential
movies, *His Trust* and *His Trust Fulfilled.*"[3] The director clearly wanted to en-
dow the central black figure in these short films with characteristics he viewed
as essential: devoted service and unwavering loyalty to the master and that
master's family. Through his consistent displays of devotion to the interests of
others, the servant embodies the traits of self-sacrifice and dedication that the
movie audience is expected to appreciate and applaud.

The first reel depicts events during wartime as a Confederate colonel sets
off with his command for the battlefield. This necessitates parting with his
wife and child, whose care he turns over to his body servant, George. With
the Southern Cross flag flying above the immaculately appointed troops and
the slaves dancing and waving joyously, Colonel Frazier takes his leave.

On the battlefront, the colonel directs his men while a subsequent shot
shows the wife and child going about their daily routines at home, the young
girl riding the back of the servant George as he pretends to be a horse, to the
delight and amusement of all.

In the meantime, on that distant (and unidentified) battleground, the husband and father realizes that his Federal opponents are bringing up artillery

and orders a charge to overrun the Union position. The attack comes in the face of heavy fire, and the Federals repulse it easily. Braving a hail of gunfire, the colonel reaches the Union lines, only to be struck down.

Confederate reinforcements advance in a second wave, carrying the works and the day. But Colonel Frazier has sustained a mortal wound. Fellow officers reach his side as he expires, leaving his sword to them to return to his loved ones at home. The weapon becomes the symbol of the sacrifice he has made to the Cause for which he has fought and perished.

Back at home, life has continued, but the arrival of the news of the husband's sacrifice shatters the tranquillity. The grief-stricken widow grasps the sword, but again with George's help, accepts the fate of her husband stoically. A storyboard informs the audience, unless they are allowed to miss the point of the human cost of the conflict, "When war winged its wide desolation— The Southern woman's heavy burden." The distraught widow has the servant place the sword above the mantel, and the treasured memento takes its honored spot in the home. He, too, is visibly shattered by the master's loss.

Unhappily, the intrusions of war continue. Union raiders approach the home and ransack it, despite the faithful servant's attempts to prevent them from entering. Not content to loot, the Federals gleefully set fire to the structure. The servant composes himself enough to realize that the Colonel's sword and daughter both remain inside the burning building. "George risks his life to be faithful to his trust," the audience learns, and they watch anxiously from their seats as he dismisses the danger to himself and enters the home amid smoke and flames to retrieve the endangered sword and girl.

Despite these heroics, the family can only stand by as helpless victims and witness the destruction of their home. The war has turned the wife and child out into the world, destitute and homeless. Yet, once more, George "gives his all" by offering his own cabin for their use. As he does so, he contentedly pulls a covering from the wall and spreads it on the ground outside his former home, to sleep at the doorstep.

The second reel opens with a summary of the earlier story and projects the audience four years into the future, "After the war." Emancipation has come, but the servant George disdains all suggestions that he abandon the trust of his fallen master and leave the family that he has served so devotedly through the years. Now, a much older George finds that his burdens increase when the widow's health fails and she leaves both her daughter and the husband's sword to his care as she dies.

George accepts these responsibilities, employing his life's savings for the purpose of boarding the orphaned child when there is no other money available. He swears to secrecy the attorney who will make the arrangements, so that the young girl will think the money came from her estate. The attorney agrees, serving as the intermediary for providing the $3.00 a year tuition for her enrollment in the Woodbury Seminary.

In the meantime, the daughter flourishes while the ex-slave's conditions deteriorate, as he continues to sacrifice his resources on her behalf. Even so, reality threatens to expose the arrangement when she reaches maturity and desires to attend a finishing school, but the attorney acting as her agent informs her that she cannot do so since there is no more money. Again, George deprives himself in order to help his former master's daughter by offering the last of his meager savings. The juxtaposition becomes obvious as the girl's dress contrasts with George's rags.

After the first term, even this support evaporates. "I regret to inform you that it will be impossible for you to return to school there being no money available," the attorney writes the daughter. All seems to be lost until a wealthy relative arrives from England. As the English cousin meets with the attorney, the servant appears and "George's love for the child leads him into temptation." He considers pilfering the rich man's wallet and decides better of it. But, as he reaches to place it back, the men discover his presence. Learning of the girl's plight, the cousin concocts to meet her and falls in love. The old servant's task is nearly complete, as the audience is told, "After the happy wedding, his trust fulfilled." George returns to his destitute cabin, pulls the sword from its place on the wall and holds it, satisfied that he has met his obligation.

Clearly, Griffith found the story of the faithful servant who stands behind the white family, literally and figuratively, as a powerful icon for the screen. Not surprisingly, he would present similar themes several years later on a grander scale in *The Birth of a Nation*, exploring in much greater detail the master/slave relationship, as he understood it, and the impact of that relationship on life in the South during and after the Civil War. As such, the 1915 Griffith epic solidified his notions of social order and racial stratification and perpetuated those views before mass film audiences.

Interestingly, given the context of the Great War then raging in Europe, Griffith opens *The Birth of a Nation* with a statement pertaining to armed conflict, not racial or social order. "If in this work we have conveyed to the mind the ravages of war to the end that *war may be held in abhorrence*, this effort will not have been in vain" (emphasis in the original). Of course, the ravages of war in this case are those felt by white Southerners, symbolized by the Cameron family of South Carolina and, to a lesser extent, the Stonemans of Pennsylvania. No thought is offered on the effects of this upheaval on black Americans, except to present the first African slave arrivals as planting the "seed of disunion" and as exhibits for abolitionists in the prewar North.

The crux of the story is the relationship between two families. The foreshadowing is clear, as a storyboard informs us that life in Piedmont, South Carolina, the home of the genteel Camerons, "runs in a quaintly way that is to be no more." Here, the "kindly master" rules his domain with a benevolence that is interrupted only by the "hostilities" between a kitten and a puppy.

White actors in black face makeup portray the key house servant roles, while black actors perform the duties of field hands. Cotton, dancing, and frivolity mark the life of these slaves on this plantation.

In the meantime, a presidential election threatens to bring the nation to the brink of conflict. Even as the Stoneman sons visit the home of their Southern friends, newspaper headlines promise secession if the "North" wins the coming election.

The indication that war has arrived comes not by a depiction of the Confederate firing on Fort Sumter in nearby Charleston Harbor, South Carolina, but through a depiction of President Lincoln's call for seventy-five thousand volunteers to suppress the Southern rebellion. Griffith employs the device of a "historic facsimile" for this scene, basing it upon John G. Nicolay and John Hay's 1890 study, *Abraham Lincoln*. Although the director will create a highly sympathetic Union leader, whom he dubs later as "the Great Heart," he sees the fight to come as a war on state sovereignty.

When the conflict comes, the Cameron and Stoneman boys choose their respective sides and march off to war. Each of the warriors bids farewell to the loved ones at home. In the case of the Southerners, the departure comes at the conclusion of a ball that lasts through the night, amid the news of victory at "the first battle of Bull Run" (not Manassas, as the Confederates would have referred to it). As Colonel Ben Cameron (Henry Walthall) prepares to take his leave, he points out a patriotic banner emblazoned with the stirring phrase, "Conquer we must, For our cause is just," surrounding an ominous declaration, "Victory or Death."

While the young men of the families spar on the battlefield, the war reaches Piedmont. "An irregular force of guerillas raids the town," a placard explains as it adds by way of historical reference, "The first negro regiments of the war were raised in South Carolina." Black Union soldiers under a "scalawag white captain" raid the Cameron home, wrecking the property and forcing the women into hiding. The Federals shoot down anyone who resists, until word reaches a "company of Confederate state troops," who rush to the town's defense. In a scene that will be repeated in the second half of the film with members of the Ku Klux Klan, "The Confederates [come] to the rescue."

In the meantime, on the frontlines, "*War* claims its *bitter, useless, sacrifice*," when the two youngest sons of the competing families die side by side. The scene depicting the deaths of the two young men, as well as the images of dead soldiers—"War's Peace"—and distraught women and children are clearly what Griffith has in mind when he expresses the hope that the film will make war "abhorrent." Again, the victims are white Southerners, as the interspersion of scenes of weeping civilians and troops engaged in William T. Sherman's "March to the Sea" indicate. The "bombardment and flight" of a burning Atlanta adds to the image of devastation and serves as the background for the death of a second Cameron son. Only the "little Colonel," as

Ben Cameron was known, remains of the three children who had gone off to war in 1861.

But such sacrifices do not bring the conflict to an end. More destruction awaits as the scene of warfare shifts to the "last grey days of the Confederacy" on "the battle lines before Petersburg." The Southerners have already been reduced to living on parched corn as "their only rations," when a supply train takes the wrong road and gets lost behind Union lines. For the hungry Confederates there is but one hope, and General Robert E. Lee turns to the "little Colonel" to accomplish the retrieval of the wayward wagons.

Griffith appropriately fills the screen with smoke in the battle scenes that follow, but the earthworks of Petersburg are hardly as elaborate as they would have been by this point in the siege. Still, under the Confederate Third National flag, the Southerners surge forward. "The little Colonel leads the final desperate assault against the Union command of Capt. Phil Stoneman," we learn in a scene depicting a charge that will not be confused with Lee's historic last grand offensive against Fort Stedman on March 25, 1865.

Against great odds, the Confederates succeed in capturing two lines of the Union entrenchments. But a third remains beyond their reach. Colonel Cameron prepares to lead his men on this forlorn mission when he pauses to assist a stricken Union soldier with a drink of water. The Federals cheer the "heroic deed," then turn back the final, fateful charge. Alone, the little colonel staggers toward the objective, plants a Southern banner in the tube of a Union artillery piece, and collapses. His friend, Phil Stoneman, pulls the severely wounded Southerner into the Union lines.

Hospitalized by his captors, Ben slowly recovers under the watchful eye of Elsie Stoneman, the woman he has loved from afar and whose image he has carried with him. But the colonel's prospects are not altogether good. Inexplicably, except as a device to further the story, the commissioned officer who has fallen at the head of his troops on a conventional battlefield is threatened with hanging "as a guerrilla." Fortunately, the arrival of Cameron's mother and the assistance of his beloved Elsie prove decisive when the women turn to Abraham Lincoln, "the Great Heart," for mercy. The president is busy with affairs of state and war; but moved by the mother's plight, he pauses to scribble a letter of clemency, and the Confederate is spared.

Colonel Cameron will have the opportunity to recover, but the prognosis of the South as Confederacy is grave. General Lee meets with his counterpart, Ulysses S. Grant, in Wilmer McLean's parlor at Appomattox Courthouse, Virginia, and the conflict comes to an end. Again, Griffith employs the historical facsimile to lend the scene historical veracity, turning to Horace Porter's *Campaigning with Grant* (1897) as the authority. Lee is appropriately subdued as Grant writes out the terms on a table that looks authentic to the scene and Colonels Charles Taylor and Ely Parker attend to their respective chiefs. Whatever may happen to other commanders, such as Joseph E. Johnston,

Richard Taylor, Edmund Kirby Smith, or Stand Watie, the war has closed for Griffith and his audience.

The ordeal of Reconstruction now begins with the assassination of the one man Griffith clearly feels might have contained its excesses, Abraham Lincoln. The scene at Ford's Theater, recreated with another historical facsimile, is effectively rendered. Amid cheers from the theatergoers for the long-sought victory, Lincoln arrives to watch *Our American Cousin*. John Wilkes Booth appears in dark hues, as he prepares to complete the task he has set for himself, of killing Lincoln. As the shot rings out and the assassin jumps to the stage from the president's box with a shout of "sic simper tyrannis," pandemonium erupts. News quickly filters to distant South Carolina, where the Cameron patriarch laments, "Our best friend is gone. What will become of us now?"

Certainly, Griffith shared the sentiment, as the remainder of the film depicts a South beset by Radical Republicans bent on punishment and ex-slaves who wish to test the limits of their freedom and find that under Republican auspices those freedoms are essentially limitless. Excesses under these circumstances are inevitable.

Ben Cameron recognizes the risk this set of conditions poses to his world and determines to combat it. Thus the Ku Klux Klan is born as a protective and defensive organization of former Confederates embroiled in a struggle with the Radical Republicans, and the former slaves who assist them, for the survival of Southern whites such as Cameron and his compatriots. It is the Klan that rides to the rescue of a beset white population, and its triumph is the Klan's as well. The Confederate States of America may have lost the war, but with Griffith in the director's chair, the battered and broken South that emerges from it is on its way to winning the peace.

Jack Temple Kirby describes D. W. Griffith as "self-consciously southern." The son of a former Confederate cavalryman, the film director "absorbed the lore of the Old South and [the] Lost Cause from his flamboyant father."[4] *The Birth of a Nation* illustrates the extent to which this was true.

Kirby also recognizes that Griffith "had a sense of historical mission, too, which he often emphasized along with his concern with 'authenticity' of detail."[5] The film director certainly seemed to pride himself on the accuracy of his facsimiles, based upon historical works that he cites in the film. The director used as many other resources as he could bring to hand as well, including Matthew Brady photographs that he obtained when an assistant won the favor of a librarian with a box of chocolates.[6]

Indeed, the demands of presenting a historically accurate film in this sense were significant for Griffith. In order to give the film the feel of the battlefield, he "rented a plot of land in Burbank, a few miles north of Los Angeles, and ordered the construction of trenches and breastworks. He contacted Civil War veterans and asked them to help lay out the set so that it resembled as closely as possible the actual Petersburg, Virginia battlefield." Griffith also called upon a couple of West Pointers for their military expertise.[7]

Yet in other important respects the film trod on less firm historical ground. As Kirby explains, "Griffith and [Thomas] Dixon rode a historiographical and political juggernaut which swept all before it." They were also the beneficiaries of long-held racial views and sectional prejudices carried by significant portions of their audiences.[8] As one writer explains, the film simply "magnified convictions already there."[9] Thus Griffith's story of the South in the crucible of war and reconstruction represents the popular version for white conservatives in the period in which he produced the film.

The Birth of a Nation included all of the stereotypes of Claude Bowers's *The Tragic Era*. Reconstruction was not the attempt to bring equality that later historians such as Eric Foner have viewed as a noble, if failed, experiment.[10] Instead, by Griffith's account, it was a Radical Republican power grab made possible by the death of Lincoln, with the aid of the former slaves. To put credibility to such an interpretation the characters in the film had to be stock figures who represented the kind of society and interpretation of history that white audiences generally expected in this era of Jim Crow segregation. Thus, in his opening credits, at least three black figures bear descriptions that make their roles impossible for anyone to miss. There is Silas Lynch, the "mulatto lieutenant governor"; Gus, "the renegade Negro"; and Mammy, "the faithful servant." This is the extent to which such roles are subsequently developed in terms of motivation or nuance of characterization.

Black reaction proved much stronger and understandably less accepting of the product that Griffith presented his audiences than he surely expected. The National Association for the Advancement of Colored People organized protests of the depictions of such "faithful servants" and "renegade Negroes." Griffith could point to his employment of black actors and actresses for some of the background scenes as mitigation for their dissatisfaction, but little else.[11]

Whatever could be said of it historically, *The Birth of a Nation* was a cinematic masterpiece. Edward D. C. Campbell has lauded the technical aspects and innovations of the film. "Griffith developed or refined the close-up, cross-cutting, rapid editing, the split screen shot, plus realistic and impressionistic lighting." He also understood the difficulty of separating these positive features of filmmaking from the negative messages of the final product itself. "As cultural illusion, it has no equal," he concludes. "In one momentous stroke, the bigotry and conservatism which had been so strongly suggested in the earlier silent stories was ratified."[12]

Historian David Blight also sees both the technical superiority and the historical inferiority of the film, noting, "With its stunning battle scenes and suspenseful chases, *The Birth of a Nation* made cinematic history. But it was the racial dramas that Griffith foisted on to the semicentennial that left the deepest impact."[13]

That impact lasted for at least another forty years. Other films followed in the footsteps of the Griffith extravaganza in their presentations of racial stereotyping. Humorist Will Rogers played a former Confederate who had returned to the bench in *Judge Priest* (1934). Henry B. Walthall, the little colonel from the Griffith film, also held a prominent role. Lincoln Theodore Monroe Andrew Perry, best known as Stepin Fetchit, provided comic relief as a simpleminded laborer employed by the judge. In this sense in particular, *Judge Priest* continued and reemphasized the racial portrayal that *The Birth of a Nation* made universal in American cinema.

Of course, just exactly what the effect of the Griffith movie has been, outside of its affirmation of the social and racial mores of its times, may never be fully understood. The most famous quotation that was supposed to have been uttered about it, President Woodrow Wilson's comment, "It is like writing history with lightning," has been disputed almost from the moment it was said to have been made.[14]

Even so, in February 1915 Thomas Dixon expressed tremendous enthusiasm for the president's graciousness with regard to the private viewing of the film that had taken place in the White House.[15] A subsequent communication with Griffith by Wilson in early March betrayed no particular sense of discomfort or outrage, and indeed promised whatever assistance the director might need, provided the president's busy schedule permitted it.[16] Only later, as a firestorm of protest erupted, particularly among African American communities, did Wilson begin to step back from any real or perceived endorsement of the film. As a side comment in response to concerns from a New York resident made on March 27, the Virginia-born chief executive instructed simply two days later, "Please say I have expressed no opinion about it."[17]

By April, pressure was mounting for a formal statement on the controversial motion picture. But when Wilson's secretary, Joseph Tumulty, urged him to "write some sort of a letter showing that he did not approve" of the film, the president demurred.[18] He could see no means by which any statement would be useful in the heated atmosphere that surrounded Griffith's production.[19] Finally, with two years of perspective and with the backdrop of a world at war to influence him further, Woodrow Wilson explained to his secretary, "I have always felt that this was a very unfortunate production."[20]

For his part, Griffith had continued to produce films and was more recently turning his considerable talents to the "Great War" itself. He also still understood the power of the images being set forth to shape the public mind. "We must hit them hard to touch them," he explained to Edith Galt Wilson in June 1918 about the propaganda work he was doing at that time.[21]

Subsequent historians and biographers have tried to assess the validity of President Wilson's positions on *The Birth of a Nation*. Arthur Link addressed the matter in his 1956 study, *Wilson: The New Freedom*, stressing both the virulent racism of the motion picture and the ambivalence of the president toward it.[22] In a more recent examination, Anthony Gaughan focused on the theme of reconciliation, noting that the president, who "never quite put the Civil War behind him," expended his energies "evangeliz[ing] for reunion."[23] Thus, Gaughan concluded, "Although Wilson would belatedly attempt to distance himself from the film, *The Birth of a Nation* illustrated in graphic fashion Wilson's own vision of national reunion."[24]

Historian Leon Litwack asserts, "Few if any films in the history of the cinema had such tragic and far-reaching consequences."[25] Some students of the film have suggested that its influence can be seen in any number of subsequent social issues and expressions. Robert Brent Toplin observes that the "most suggestive evidence of *Birth of a Nation*'s impact" was the rebirth of the Ku Klux Klan on Stone Mountain, Georgia, in 1915.[26] Joan L. Silverman links the film to the coming of Prohibition due to its depiction of former slaves turned to barbarity by the alcohol they consumed in their first taste of freedom.[27]

Indeed, such influences may have existed, though surely not as directly as suggested by these writers. In any case, *The Birth of a Nation* had an enormous effect on social attitudes already prevalent at the time. Portions of white America believed that they would be better served when the former sectional opponents discarded their differences, reconciled with each other, and returned to the work of leading the nation together. They expected black Americans to return as well to those happy days of paternalism and adherence to benevolent white authority. As depicted in the film, it would only take the undoing of a symbolic few recalcitrants by the Ku Klux Klan as the defenders of white womanhood and virtue to bring the world back to its appropriate order, with its consequent security and happiness for Southern whites.

This racial ideal was Griffith's vision. Its achievement on-screen embodied the real birth of a new nation that, although not necessarily a Confederate one, would be a recognizably Southern one, arising from the ashes of war and reconstruction. Here was the justification that the famed film director himself spelled out in answer to those who criticized that vision: "These facts are based on an overwhelming compilation of authentic evidence and testimony. My picturisation of history as it happens requires, therefore, no apology, no defence, no 'explanation.'"[28]

Later historians have justifiably decried that "picturisation" as deeply flawed. One historian labels it, "incongruously the most technically innovative yet ideologically retrograde film of its day."[29] Indeed, modern instructors who have used the images of Griffith's movie to foster genuine debate about popular depictions of slavery, war, and Reconstruction have often found themselves trying to undo the effects of what the students have just witnessed, given that the images produced are so powerfully and indelibly ingrained, even in the minds of sophisticated modern audiences.[30] In this regard, *The Birth of a Nation* continues to strike, as it did in the early twentieth century, with the force of a lightning bolt that scorches history as it flashes past.

CHAPTER 2

Victory Rode the Rails

Buster Keaton demonstrates his comedic genius here in *The General* by using a railroad tie to prevent being stopped by Union raiders in the pursuit of his stolen engine.

Armies came to depend on the railway for their maintenance without
realizing how dependent they had become.

—soldier and author B. H. Liddell Hart

Victory rode the rails.

—historian George E. Turner

RAILROADS AND TRAINS have had an almost magnetic attrac-
tion, especially on film. Whether it is the image of billowing smoke and
churning power racing along sleek rails or the rhythm of cars swaying
as they pass from section to section of track, something about the images of trains captivates the imagination of film audiences. Indeed, placing
railroads in the context of the Civil War in cinema provides the best of two
worlds: the image of industrial progress and the evocation of military power.

No film in Civil War cinema purports to be a documentary on railroads
during the conflict. Yet, several of them employ trains or railroads as a device
to further their stories. The 1951 motion pictures *Drums in the Deep South* and
Santa Fe feature different aspects of railroading, with Confederates trying to
disrupt Union supply lines in the former and an ex-Confederate attempting to
build a railroad line in the latter. In *The Horse Soldiers* (1959) and *Rio Lobo*
(1970), John Wayne's characters experience this dichotomy when as a railroad
builder he leads men in the destruction of a Confederate line in the former
and when he tries to stop a Southern attempt to rob the payroll from a Union
train in the latter. *Shenandoah* (1965) demonstrates the function railroads
played in transporting prisoners of war. While two films, *The General* (1927)
and *The Great Locomotive Chase* (1956), adapt the story of an actual military operation, the James J. Andrews raid, to the big screen, they do so in dramatically different ways. Buster Keaton, a master of comedy, turns the mission into
a series of pratfalls and sight gags, with the historic events as mere background. Disney tries a more conventional approach, with popular television
star Fess Parker as Andrews and Jeffrey Hunter as the Southern engineer who
thwarts him virtually single-handedly.

The setting for *Drums in the Deep South* is wartime Georgia as William T.
Sherman presses Joseph E. Johnston back upon the defenses of Atlanta. Yet, as
the Union forces advance, they become increasingly dependent upon a single
rail line for supply and communication. The Confederates realize that the sole
railroad line along which supplies can be moved is vulnerable to artillery
placed on a steep mountain adjacent to the track.

A Confederate major concocts a scheme to mount artillery pieces on this
high point to interrupt the flow of supplies upon which Sherman must depend
for the success of his offensive. The Southerners manage to move the guns
into place at the base of the mountain without being spotted and follow a

18

pathway through the heart of the edifice to the top. Setting the cannon into place, they wait for the moment when they can do the most damage and open fire on a passing Union train. The destructive results close the line, but expose their position. The Federals immediately take steps to silence the threat and reopen the vital supply line.

When an initial attack fails to dislodge the Southerners, the Federals try unsuccessfully to force them from the peak with light artillery pieces of their own. Frustrated, the Union major calls for heavier ordnance, and a fifteen-inch Dahlgren gun that will offer greater range arrives by rail. Warned of the heavy weapon's arrival, the Confederate major determines that only with double charges of powder and reinforcement with piano wire will his lighter artillery be able to respond effectively to the big gun's fire.

The Union's heavy artillery piece conveniently remains silent while a party of Southerners works its way to a local plantation, strips the piano of its wire, and uses the material to reinforce the tubes of the Confederate field pieces to allow them to withstand greater charges of powder. Still, when the Union gun finally opens fire, it does so with devastating effect. Only the double charges and the strengthened tubes of their guns save the Southerners from total annihilation.

Still, time is running out for the Confederates. The Union commander decides to gather barrels of gunpowder in the chambers below the summit and silence the guns in one dramatic blast. Although informed that given the slope of the peak, any blast will fill the gorge of Snake Gap and close the line, he pushes forward with his plan. Fortunately for the Confederates most of them leave their positions before the blast and survive to become prisoners. But the resulting explosion sheers off the top of the mountain, obliterating the Southern artillery position and blocking the pass with debris as predicted. The viewer will not know whether the rail line was ever reopened or the campaign against Atlanta ended successfully.

Railroads figure prominently in the reconciliation film *Santa Fe* (1951). The building of a rail line serves as the basis for setting aside the bitterness of the recent war. As he promotes his line, a railroad executive explains, "There are many who come from the North and the South. I ask you all now to put aside your differences for all time in the interest of a good and common cause."

Captain Britt Canfield (Randolph Scott) is the only one of four brothers from war-torn Virginia who accepts the challenge. Veterans of "White's Raiders," the Canfield brothers have traveled West to start anew, but the prospects do not seem good. "A man who rode with Confederate guerrillas might have a little trouble making friends up here," Captain Canfield worries.

But Britt Canfield's task is not simply to find a way to fit into his new community. He also has to convince his brothers that their war is over, however much hostility they continue to harbor. "You've got to stop fighting a war that doesn't exist. You've got to forget it," he tells them. But the brothers are not ready to accept their sibling's logic or his conclusion.

"Forget it?" one snaps back. "I'll always remember what the Yanks did to the South. To us," another explains. "For that I'll hate 'em all my life," the first adds. Britt: "We all fought for something we believed in and lost. Now we've got to mend our fences. Hate won't help us any."

Despite the fact that he had fought "at Parson's Creek," against his boss on the railroad when the latter was a major with Federal troops under General Sheridan, Britt Canfield makes friends with the railroad executive, who is prepared to put the past behind them. Canfield is similarly successful in winning the affection of an assistant whose husband was killed at the same battle "in the charge that you led." He is not as fortunate with his brothers. They continue to clash, literally taking up arms against each other. But the railroad will not be stopped. In the case of *Santa Fe*, at least, it seems that it is reconciliation that rides the rails.

Union raiders in *The Horse Soldiers* (1959) target a key Confederate railroad in Mississippi by capturing and destroying Newton Station. The film offers an illustration of some of the techniques the historical raiders used to disable such lines. The Federals pull the rails from the ties, heat them, and dump them into water to warp the metal. They take down the telegraph wire strung adjacent to the track and apply the torch liberally to depot buildings, boxcars, and anything else of military value at Newton.

In one of the more affecting scenes of the film, Colonel Marlowe stands in a saloon converted into a makeshift hospital to treat those who have been wounded in the fighting for possession of the station. He "closes" the bar and listens as explosions ring out from the demolition of the railroad facilities. He sends a whooping trooper out of the door and laments loudly that at a former time in his life he had made his living building railroads instead of destroying them.

Virtually everything involving the Civil War in the film *Rio Lobo* (1970) relates to the rails. The opening sequence features a remarkable effort on the part of Confederate raiders to steal a Union payroll. The elaborate scheme begins with the Southerners locating a steep grade in the line that will force the locomotive to strain at its heaviest. By applying grease to the rails, the Confederates plan to cause the engine to lose traction. Others wait at the bottom of the grade, stretching stout ropes across the tracks to break the speed of the train as it slides downward toward them. To ensure that the soldiers guarding the shipment are neutralized, the Southerners drop a nest of hornets into the car to drive the Union guards out.

Union Colonel Cord McNally (John Wayne) waits at the next station for the train to arrive. When word reaches him that the telegraph is no longer working, McNally realizes that something has gone amiss. He orders his command into the saddle and races for the point of trouble.

In the meantime, the Southern plan for snaring the train and its cargo unfolds essentially as drawn up. The only hitch is the speed at which the train descends once it has hit the greased tracks. Still, once it has reached the ropes, the train's progress is finally arrested. The hornets force the Union guards to jump, leaving the Confederates to smoke the insects out of the car and make off with the Union gold.

Colonel McNally happens upon the injured commander of the guard detachment, a soldier he has known since the beginning of the war. His neck broken from the fall, the soldier implores his commander to catch the Rebels before they can escape.

By the time McNally reaches the scene, the Southerners are already gone. Inexplicably, he and a small number of troopers trail the raiders. When the trail splits, McNally rides on himself, until two of the Confederates waylay him.

Although a prisoner, the Union colonel learns that a spy in his own ranks had leaked word of the shipment to the Southerners, enabling them to hijack the train. He determines to seek out the traitor. When the Confederates try to bypass a Union camp with their prisoner, McNally seizes upon an opportunity to sound the alarm and escape from his captors. He returns the favor by capturing the Confederates, who are then consigned to a prison camp, after having refused to give him the name of their Union contact.

At the end of the war, McNally goes to the camp to interview the Confederates, who are now free to describe the man for him. The remainder of *Rio Lobo* consists of McNally and his Southern compatriots, with the aid of a cantankerous old man (Jack Elam) and a young woman (Jennifer O'Neill), tracking down the traitor.

Shenandoah's brief depiction of trains in the Civil War occurs when the Anderson party, in its search for the youngest Anderson sibling, halts a train transporting prisoners of war. Charlie Anderson (James Stewart) scours the countryside looking for his son after learning that he has been taken by Union soldiers. After briefly conferring with a sympathetic Federal officer (George Kennedy), he travels to the nearest depot where prisoners of war are being gathered for transportation. The captain there is much less cooperative, dismissing the anxious father with the comment that he has a schedule to keep.

Anderson leaves the station more determined than ever to inspect the train. Setting a bonfire of rails and sitting behind them atop a stack of railroad ties on the tracks, he blocks them so that when the engine comes into view it has to stop. Soldiers dash up, insisting that the tracks be cleared immediately. The Anderson sons convince them otherwise at the point of their weapons. The incredulous officer who had earlier refused to assist the father suddenly realizes that this is the man who has been searching for his son, and Charlie reminds him of the importance he had given to maintaining his schedule. The Andersons send the troops off and begin to search the converted cattle cars for the "boy."

They do not succeed in locating him, but the effort yields a captured Sam (Doug McClure), the husband of Anderson's daughter. A brief reunion and the release of the other prisoners follows. Charlie has threatened to burn the train, since "It's not the kind of a train I favor," but understandably, the engineer (Strother Martin) tries to change his mind. "Sir, I've been the engineer on this train for ten years," he explains plaintively. "She's been a good train all that time. Well, it ain't right to burn her just because she come on to hard times."

Anderson ponders the request. "You run a sad kind of train, Mister," he tells him, "It takes people away when they don't want to go and won't bring them back when they're ready." Then he puts the decision to the Confederate prisoners. They decide to burn the engine and cars. Sam orders the men to disperse, saying that the war is over. The Anderson party, with its new addition, rides off into a night lit by the flames that engulf a train that will carry no more captives to Union prisons.

The engine in *Shenandoah* is named the *Genl. Gault,* and the fuel car is marked "U.S. Military R.R.," for the organization that supervised the railroads that served the needs of the Union armies. It specialized in helping to convert Southern tracks into useful tools of transportation and supply for Union forces, under the able, if often troublesome, leadership of Henry Haupt.[1]

Buster Keaton's silent film classic, *The General,* opens in 1861 Marietta, Georgia. Johnny Gray, an engineer with the Western and Atlantic Railroad, whose name is appropriately used here, calls on his ladylove, Annabel Lee. As he courts her, Annabel's brother bursts in to tell the family that Fort Sumter has been fired upon and to proclaim his intention to enlist in the service of the South. Annabel's father offers to join as well, and he gives a reluctant Johnny an ultimatum that his courtship will end if he does not do likewise.

Johnny tries to enlist, but when the recruiters learn that he is a railroad engineer they determine that he would serve the South better continuing in that capacity. No one bothers to inform him of this assessment, and thinking that he has been rejected Johnny is crestfallen. "If you lose the war, don't blame me," he blurts out at the recruiting officer who has refused his services, and he returns to his civilian occupation.

A year later, he is still at the controls of his beloved engine, the *General.* Unbeknownst to Johnny, the war is about to converge on him. On board the train is a band of Union raiders led by Captain Anderson. As the train, its passengers, and Johnny stop to eat, the raiders seize the train and head North toward Union lines with it.

Yet the Union agents have more than Johnny's train in their possession, for Annabel is present on it and ends up in their clutches as well. Johnny dashes off on foot in pursuit. He soon acquires a handcar and uses it to chase his locomotive until it derails at a place where the raiders have disabled the track.

Johnny soon locates a locomotive with which to take up the chase, although he inadvertently leaves behind the troops he was supposed to carry with him. Nevertheless, at the controls of the locomotive, *Texas*, Johnny valiantly forges ahead. Along the way, he amazingly finds a mortar and uses it to fire at the raiders, barely missing himself and his train in the process. The Northerners release a boxcar and drop cross-ties on the rails, succeeding only in derailing the boxcar and giving Johnny additional opportunities to display his comedic and acrobatic abilities, as he uses one tie to flip another from the track while balancing himself on the machine's cowcatcher.

In another move consistent with the events of Andrews's Raiders and the historical locomotive chase, the Northerners attempt to burn a key bridge by leaving a burning boxcar on it. Once again, Johnny saves the bridge and the day, remaining in pursuit of the *General* and his girl.

From this point, however, the story departs from any semblance of historical reality. As Johnny continues the chase, the Confederate forces begin to retreat in the face of a Union advance. Shortly, the Federals arrive and the raiders reach the safety of Union lines. Conveniently, he finds refuge behind the Northern lines in a Union headquarters, to which Annabel is brought as a prisoner. Johnny determines to rescue her and then absconds with his train. The locomotive chase now occurs in reverse, with Johnny doing all he can to delay the pursuit of Anderson's raiders.

When Johnny, Annabel, and the *General* reach Rock River Bridge, the bewildered Southerner decides to burn the structure. The Federals close on him by rail and over land. Johnny takes the train into Marietta, where he warns the Southerners that the Union troops are advancing against them and returns with the Confederates to defend the bridge.

Brashly, the Union commanders decide to press the attack. The pursuing Union train attempts to cross the bridge and wrecks in spectacular fashion. In the meantime, the Confederates have arrived with artillery and pummel the Federal forces as they try to ford Rock River. Despite a tremendous amount of pyrotechnics, there never seem to be any actual casualties.

Again unwittingly, Johnny helps the cause by misfiring an artillery piece that strikes a dam and floods the Union forces, forcing them into retreat. Johnny returns a hero and receives his coveted enlistment and promotion to lieutenant. As the film ends, he is reunited with his train and his love, only slightly inconvenienced by the promotion, which requires him to salute every soldier who walks by, even as he tries to kiss his beloved Annabel.

While Buster Keaton was less concerned with history than humor in *The General*, *The Great Locomotive Chase* presents itself as a reflection of what Andrews and his raiders actually tried to accomplish in 1862. From its opening, the Disney story's producers make every effort to validate the historical foundation of the film. "This true life historical adventure is based upon a real incident of the American Civil War," the scripted narration assures the viewer.

"Names and places have not been changed." To lend further legitimacy, the story is told from the vantage point of one of the raiders, Corporal William Pittenger.

The film opens with Secretary of War Edwin Stanton bestowing the newly minted congressional Medal of Honor to the men before him. "You gentlemen are to have the first ever given." Pittenger then relates his story, explaining the reason for the medal ceremony through the mechanism of the flashback.

The viewers learn that Andrews (Fess Parker) is a smooth-talking Union spy who has succeeded in winning friends among the Southerners. He meets with Union Brigadier General Ormsby M. Mitchell (Richard Cutting), who has developed an elaborate scheme to capture Chattanooga and shorten the war. Andrews plans to take a handpicked team and infiltrate Confederate territory, seize a train, and use it to incapacitate the Western and Atlantic Railroad in Northwest Georgia.

In the course of his briefing, Mitchell makes an interesting reference to Robert E. Lee in Virginia and Pierre Gustave Toutant Beauregard in West Tennessee. "And here's Beauregard who's bringing everything he's got to fight Grant at Shiloh," he tells Andrews, although it is unclear how he knew what Beauregard intended and curious that he made no mention of the principal Confederate commander in the battle, Albert Sidney Johnston.

But with his task laid before him, Andrews selects his compatriots, predominantly from the Twenty-first and Thirty-third Ohio Infantry. He instructs them to make their ways to Marietta, Georgia, where in three days they will rendezvous and begin the operation. Many of these men rather conveniently gather at a boardinghouse. On at least two occasions, the raiders narrowly avert exposure, particularly when obliged to sing "Dixie" or when confronted by a boisterous Rebel sergeant (Morgan Woodward).

Even so, the men gather at the Marietta Hotel. They purchase tickets for various destinations, the names of which are accurately related (Allatoona, Kingston, Calhoun, Resaca, and Chattanooga). Perhaps the best touch of authenticity comes from a bit player who responds to a query from Andrews about the possibility of rain by replying that it "might could."

The raiders climb aboard the passenger train, pulled by the *General*, and head for breakfast at Big Shanty, a small station on the route. Andrews has determined to steal the train at that point and succeeds in doing so. Unfortunately for the raiders, not much else goes their way. The most significant piece of misfortune is the determination of the conductor, William A. Fuller (Jeffrey Hunter), to reclaim his train. Together with engineer Anthony Murphy (Kenneth Tobey) and another hand, they inaugurate the pursuit.

Andrews and his men stop to dismantle track and cut telegraph wire, but Fuller and Murphy remain hot on their trail. The Southerners first impress a handcar and then a small engine, the *Yonah*, before meeting and commandeering a standard train engine, the *Texas*. The engineer of the *Texas*, Pete Bracken (Slim Pickens), backs his train along the track. The raiders drop off boxcars, dismantle track, and toss rails and ties onto the track to slow the pursuit, but to no avail.

Fuller's dogged pursuit frustrates the raiders' intent. They cannot gain the breathing space necessary to wreck the principal bridges and trestlework that will disable the railroad for an extended length of time. Finally, with the train running short of fuel and Confederate cavalry and the *Texas* closing in, Andrews orders the men to scatter. The exuberant Southern cavalry capture many of the men, and Fuller reclaims the *General*.

The Confederates shift Andrews and his raiders from prison to prison as a court-martial meets to decide their fates. As spies, their fate is certain. They will be hanged. Then, in a final twist, the captives stage a prison break. Some escape, others are recaptured, including the leader. The film scrupulously avoids showing any of the executions, returning full circle to the Medal of Honor ceremony in the War Department. Secretary Stanton tells the recipients that with the exception of Andrews, who was a civilian and thus ineligible, their fallen comrades will receive Medals of Honor posthumously.

Just before his death, Andrews asks to speak to Fuller. The conductor reluctantly agrees. The men reconcile as warriors of a kind, symbolic of the reconciliation to come one day between the North and the South. Each has done his duty, and there are no regrets or apologies. The antagonists end with grudging respect and a handshake.

Unlike *The Great Locomotive Chase*, and to a much lesser extent *The General*, *Rio Lobo* does not purport to detail an actual historical event. The historical references are vague and general, the action more a backdrop for the efforts of John Wayne and his compatriots to avenge the betrayal of greedy Union soldiers who have leaked information regarding gold shipments to the Confederates. The train robbery might just as easily have been the work of more traditional "Western" bandits, although the effort was cinematically more effective as a Civil War caper than it might have been otherwise.

Once the gold is secure, the action strains credulity, with Wayne pursuing the Southerners almost single-handedly, despite his rank as a colonel. His capture is predictable, his escape certainly not less so, and the Civil War segment of the film ends early. Still, if only because of *Rio Lobo*'s opening sequence, the motion picture is worth watching, even for the Civil War aficionado who might wish the film related more to the war itself.

Railroads contained more than symbolic value in the era of the Civil War. Not only was the railroad an "emblem of progress" for nineteenth-century Americans, as one historian has called it, but it was also critical to the demands of modern war.[2] The movement of men and materiel across vast reaches of territory provided Civil War logisticians with obstacles that must have seemed insurmountable without rail transportation. At the same time, the relative ease with which troops and supplies could be transported must have seemed deceptively simple. British veteran and author B. H. Liddell Hart notes that in the Civil War, "armies came to depend on the railway for their maintenance without realizing how dependent they had become."[3] The North could mitigate this dependency somewhat through use of naval assets and, as William T. Sherman ably demonstrated, living off the land as they advanced, but even Union armies often found themselves tied to long lines of supply and communication.

Rail transportation played a fundamental role in the grand strategies of both sides in the war. The Confederate plan for achieving and maintaining independence rested upon the ability to concentrate troops located at significant distances from each other against invading Union columns. President Jefferson Davis saw the "offensive defense" as the best way for his nation to offset Northern advantages in manpower and resources.[4]

Federal authorities realized the benefits to be derived by securing a rail system that could be altered and improved to support a modern war effort. Ultimate Union victory "rode the rails," as historian George Turner observes.[5]

Northern engineers became particularly adept at restoring their own broken lines. When not repairing damaged lines, these men worked to extend rail connections as the Federal armies advanced, often converting captured Southern lines to a common gauge for use by Union forces penetrating deep into the Confederacy.

Early in the war, individuals on both sides recognized the advantages to be gained by disrupting transportation and communication lines through various means. In pro-Union East Tennessee, civilians sought to contribute to the war effort by destroying key bridges at points along the Tennessee Railroad. Although only partially successful, the operations illustrated the vulnerability of long lines to sabotage.

Not coincidentally, both sides in the conflict targeted depots, track, and bridges with deep penetrating cavalry raids. One of the most successful practitioners of such raids, Confederate cavalry commander Nathan Bedford Forrest, made something of an art of wrecking rail lines, trestles, culverts, and depots. In an address near the end of the war, following Confederate general John Bell Hood's disastrous 1864 Tennessee campaign, Forrest sought to boost his men's morale. He listed the capture or destruction of forty blockhouses, thirty-six railroad bridges, and two hundred miles of railroad as proof of their collective exploits and as inspiration for staying the course through what was left of the fighting.[6]

Forrest's earlier destruction of the rail system in West Tennessee and Earl Van Dorn's destruction of Ulysses S. Grant's forward supply base at Holly Springs, Mississippi, thwarted the Union general's first effort to march against the Confederate stronghold of Vicksburg on the Mississippi River. James Ewell

Brown "Jeb" Stuart, John Hunt Morgan, and John S. Mosby enjoyed success against Union railroads and communications lines for the South as well.[7]

General Forrest also became famous for defending a critical rail line from destruction when he thwarted a raid by Union colonel Abel Streight across northern Alabama into Georgia. Had he been successful, Streight would have damaged the Western and Atlantic Railroad, which connected Atlanta and Chattanooga. Forrest's exploits in running the Union raiders to ground and capturing their numerically superior force won further notoriety for the Southern cavalry commander and saved the vital line from destruction.

Benjamin Grierson, Philip Sheridan, and James Harrison Wilson wreaked havoc on Southern rail lines and facilities for the North. Grierson won fame (and movie exposure of a sort) for cutting a swath over the length of Mississippi in 1863; Sheridan conducted operations into central Virginia that resulted in Jeb Stuart's death in 1864; and Wilson decimated the Confederate heartland in a final dramatic sweep in 1865.[8]

For all of their dash and élan, Confederate cavalry, with few exceptions, failed to knock Union railroads out of commission for substantial periods. Similarly, Federal raids often proved more nuisances than anything else, even when the damage wrought was extensive. To be sure, the Confederate rail system broke down as the war progressed, but this was as much due to the South's inability to maintain what it controlled as to the North's ability to disrupt it with raids and sabotage.

On operations carried out deep behind enemy lines, raiders from both sides risked becoming trapped themselves, before they could complete their missions successfully and return to safety behind their own lines. Usually, this meant falling victim to converging columns of pursuing cavalry. But in the instance of James J. Andrews and his small Union squad of raiders, the effort and the pursuit were carried out by rail. Eventually, the Southerners ran their quarry to ground, capturing and hanging Andrews and seven of his compatriots for their part in the operation.

In the aftermath of the war, railroads took on even greater significance and meaning as the nation attempted both to rebuild and expand. Men such as Bedford Forrest who had built reputations for destroying railroads now sought new ones for constructing them. Yet cinema seemed less interested in chronicling this reconstruction in the South than in celebrating the westward movement of rails and the effect this had on the reconciliation of the former antagonists, such as in *Santa Fe*.

The use of railroads in these films mirrors the importance of railroads for transportation and supply in the Civil War and offers spectacular images for film audiences amid the backdrop of that war. Victory, in this case, seems to have ridden the rails into the box office.

CHAPTER 3

The Romantic Era
of Civil War Cinema

Scarlett O'Hara (Vivien Leigh) is nearly lost in a sea of distressed humanity as she works her way through rows of wounded soldiers in Atlanta while searching for a doctor in *Gone with the Wind*.

> *Gone with the Wind* reigns uncontested as the most popular American
> historical film ever made.
>
> —historian Catherine Clinton

NO CIVIL WAR FILM exudes romance like the MGM classic *Gone with the Wind*. If indeed imitation is the sincerest form of flattery, *Gone with the Wind* has been consistently "flattered" since it first appeared in 1939. The producers of *Raintree County* (1957) and television's *Love's Savage Fury* (1979) and *Beulah Land* (1980) have sought to replicate the successful formula of strong-willed Southern woman, roguish Southern man, and their relationship amid the turmoil of civil war.

The proof of this obsession to recapture the romance of the 1939 film is in the miles of celluloid thus produced. Yet a winning formula is much more than the duplication of a particular story line. It is the combination of timing, writing, acting, and directing associated with the original production that is unique. There will never again be another *Gone with the Wind* because there cannot be. The mixture of audience expectations and popular impressions about the period being portrayed, the world events that affected the mind-set of the audience and the filmmakers, the on-screen chemistry between Clark Gable and Vivien Leigh, and so on all combine to make the film one of a kind. Add to the mix the writing that pressed the norms of accepted screen utterances and the "burning" of Atlanta itself, and it is difficult to imagine that anyone could succeed in duplicating this movie.

The historical matter that the film explores, insofar as the American Civil War is concerned, rests on three phases: the opening features the heady days of secession, nationhood, and war; the middle depicts the dawning of reality as the conflict develops into a "hard war" phase represented by William Tecumseh Sherman's taking of Atlanta and his "March through Georgia to the Sea"; and the end carries into the Reconstruction period following the Confederacy's demise.

Gone with the Wind covers the middle period of the nineteenth century in epic style. Based upon Margaret Mitchell's best-selling novel, it opens with a glimpse of the popular conceptions of the Antebellum South. Although the initial images are prewar ones of large plantations and slaves in the cotton fields, *Gone with the Wind* is not long in bringing the crisis of secession and war to this idyllic world. Boasts of how few Southerners it will take to defeat any number of "Yankees" suggest the innocence of ignorance about the nature of the conflict about to descend upon them.

Despite warnings by the sophisticated visitor, Rhett Butler, the gentlemen continue in their illusions of Southern invincibility. Reality wears slowly away at the illusion. Shunned by Ashley Wilkes, Scarlett marries, only to have her husband die early in the war. As a widow, she presides over a lavish ball. Draped in mourning black, but little concerned with the fate of a husband she did not love, Scarlett dances with Rhett. The scene is exquisitely filmed, fresh uniforms vying with flowing gowns for Technicolor's attentions. It is all a treat for the senses, as the antebellum world retains its grip on the participants and the audience alike for a few moments longer.

Trisha Curran has observed that the "contrast in color between Scarlett's black dress and the pastels of the other women at the Atlanta ball expresses her nonconformity with them and prefigures her union with Rhett, his black tuxedo equally expressive of his nonconformity and equally conspicuous amid the grey and gold of the Confederate uniforms."[1] Certainly this is a valid point. Yet it should be noted that the contrast was also used to draw the eye to the two key figures in the scene, who after all do adhere to the strictures of the Virginia reel along with everyone else.

Still, if the partying ignores the gusts in the larger world at war, the wind is blowing, and so it will be too strong for the Old South as Confederacy to endure. For the audience, the most powerful imagery expressive of this reality comes in Atlanta when Scarlett goes in search of the doctor to assist in the delivery of Melanie's baby.

As she reaches the train station, jammed with seemingly numberless wounded, the camera pulls back to catch a tattered Confederate battle flag presiding over the dismal scene. Atlanta is in its death throes, as is the world represented by Tara and the slaveholding South. Soon the city will be consumed in flames.

Rhett manages to take Scarlett out of the burning mass that had once been Atlanta, dodging flaming warehouses and explosive-laden trains. Near the end of the first part of the film, the buggy carrying the refugees lumbers alongside the remnants of the retreating Confederate army, the glow of destruction illuminating the night sky behind them. Much to Scarlett's chagrin, Rhett decides to throw his lot in with the dying nation's military fortunes. It is a noble gesture to a lost cause.

Scarlett will return to Tara only to find that her world has been radically transformed. With the stubborn determination that has marked her pursuit of Rhett Butler, she decides that there is nothing more important than the land and that she will "never be hungry again."

The remainder of *Gone with the Wind* follows Scarlett and Rhett through Reconstruction. The impression of that volatile era on-screen is as typical of the time period in which the film appeared as the views of slavery and the war. Actor Charlton Heston recognizes the historical weaknesses of the film in his autobiography. "*Gone with the Wind* all but ignores that watershed in American History [the Civil War]: it contains no battle scenes, and neither secession, states' rights, nor emancipation is mentioned."[2] Historian William Davis agrees. Chiding the film for depicting "almost nothing of the Civil War itself," he concludes, "It tells nothing of the causes, presents a distorted and one-sided view of the consequences, and barely hints at a few events in the conduct of the war. It is a love story to which the war and the Confederacy are quite peripheral."[3] When it comes to the film's rendering of history, it may be Clio as the muse of history as much as Scarlett who Rhett Butler has in mind when he utters the immortal screen line, "Frankly, my dear, I don't give a damn."

Certainly in terms of offering an examination of the causes of the sectional conflict looming over the nation, *Gone with the Wind* does little more than provide visual and verbal references to slavery. The Southerners who gather early on to discuss the fate of their section in any war that might occur exhibit an overconfidence based on their parochialism. Only Rhett Butler (Clark Gable) demonstrates any awareness of and realism about what is coming, and it isolates him from the others when they refuse to heed his warning. In frustration tinged with disgust, Rhett leaves the room for a quiet smoke. Yet his subsequent departure from the discussion serves as the cinematic device by which he can be introduced to Scarlett O'Hara (Vivien Leigh).

The dependence upon slavery was despite the fact that slaveholding white Southerners were less than 30 percent of the white population. Most white Southerners did not own even one slave, although the "peculiar institution" was central to the South's being and undoubtedly shaped its priorities and mind-set for slaveholders and nonslaveholders alike.[4]

Of course, other issues divided the North and South, too, not the least of these being divergent economic interests and policies and the development of competing ideologies or worldviews that put the sections increasingly at odds with each other. But slavery remained the most divisive and immediate issue. Besides, it was also what movie audiences expected to see in the Antebellum South.

As with most Civil War films, *Gone With the Wind* mentions the Confederate firing upon Fort Sumter, without referencing Abraham Lincoln's subsequent call for seventy-five thousand volunteers to suppress the "rebellion." Interestingly for a film that employs war as its primary backdrop, *Gone with the Wind* is Scarlett's story. Historian Catherine Clinton maintains, "O'Hara's tempestuous emotional upheavals, which drive the plot of *Gone with the Wind*, are, of course, central to the novel and film's popularity."[5]

In terms of its racial composition, *Gone with the Wind* is cut from much the same cloth as *The Birth of a Nation*, although with less emphasis on the "renegade" aspect of black (or black-faced) people compared with the Griffith silent film. The absent-minded Prissy knows nothing about "birthing" babies or much of anything else, reinforcing the dependency upon which paternalism rested for its justification of the master's or mistress's dominance and superiority. Mammy is the stereotypical black housekeeper, loyal and loving, but stern with her charges when she feels she has to be. This personality endears her to the white audience, but clearly does not represent a meaningful departure from Griffith's "faithful souls." Yet the selectors for the Academy Awards demonstrated a measure of enlightenment when they chose Hattie McDaniel for best supporting actress and made her the first black performer to be so recognized.[6]

The military elements of the film come and go with little direct influence on the story line or the principal characters except for the occasional oblique reference or the appearance of casualty lists or hospitals. Despite the powerful imagery of wounded Confederates gathered along the railroad tracks or the fiery race through Atlanta of Rhett Butler and Scarlett O'Hara, *Gone with the Wind* does not focus on the battles in the Atlanta campaign. It is not until the fighting reaches the environs of the city that the war begins to take center stage in the film. Using the movie as a guide, little can be learned concerning the opening phases of the 1864 Atlanta campaign. Joseph Johnston's futile efforts to resist William T. Sherman's advance receive no mention, from his initial positions around Dalton, Georgia, to his bloody repulse of Union advances at Kennesaw Mountain. Not until the Federals are at the doorstep of the city itself do the characters or the viewers understand they are in mortal danger.

Like its illustrious predecessor, *Drums of the Deep South* (1951) is not a film about the Atlanta campaign or any significant historical aspect of it. The premise of the motion picture is that by putting a small force on a mountaintop with artillery the Confederates could close the railroad upon which Sherman's forces depend for their supplies, at least for a time. There is no historical basis for such an effort by the Southerners in North Georgia. Confederate cavalryman Nathan Bedford Forrest's real-life frustrations in disrupting the supply lines that supported Sherman's Federals amply illustrate that the task was not as simple as the movie suggests.[7]

If the Atlanta campaign of 1864 represented the "last chance of the Confederacy," as historian Richard McMurry has asserted, *Drums of the Deep South* illustrates the futility that such a chance embodied.[8] The juggernaut that William T. Sherman unleashed in heading an army group of three—the Army of the Cumberland under George H. Thomas, the Army of the Tennessee under James B. McPherson, and the Army of the Ohio under John M. Schofield—would prove virtually unstoppable, certainly given the Fabian style of warfare Confederate general Joseph E. Johnston chose to undertake. Giving ground to Sherman to buy time cost the Confederates valuable real estate. As the Federals pressed closer to Atlanta, Georgia governor Joseph Brown and others increased their demands that something be done to disrupt Sherman's supply lines. The answer seemed to be available in Mississippi, in the person of Confederate cavalry commander Nathan Bedford Forrest. If he were to be turned loose to smash Sherman's supply lines, the outcome could be strategically significant.

Sherman understood the stakes, too. He ordered troops out of Memphis to advance toward the Mississippi breadbasket. Although these strikes met with disaster at Brice's Cross Roads in June, a mixed victory at Harrisburg or Tupelo in July, and a retreat after a sensational Confederate raid on Memphis in August, they served their strategic purpose. Forrest stayed in Mississippi, where he would not threaten Sherman's supply lines until it was too late to have any strategic effect.[9]

In the meantime, Johnston had been weighed in the balance and found wanting. Confederate commissary head Josiah Gorgas reflected the general concern about the state of military affairs in North Georgia in his diary in May: "Johnston verifies all our predictions of him. He is falling back just as fast as his legs can carry him. . . . Where he will stop heaven only knows."[10] Yet the South's chief supply officer also understood the odds the Confederacy faced. "What the issue will be is in God's hands," he wrote resignedly in June, "nothing but an unforeseen event can it seems to me save us from the gradually rising strength of our opponents; or rather, from the defeats our waning strength must entail."[11]

Exasperatedly, Gorgas confided in his journal what most Southerners must have felt by July, as the Federals seemed to push inexorably toward Atlanta: "Everybody has at last come to the conclusion that Johnston has retreated far enough."[12]

President Davis, who had never had much faith in Johnston to begin with and harbored a dislike of the man, certainly agreed. With no prospect of turning affairs around under his leadership, he opted for another, more aggressive commander. Army command thus passed from Johnston to John Bell Hood.

Kentuckian by birth and Texan by choice, Hood had established for himself a reputation for courageousness and combativeness that few could match. Horribly wounded at Gettysburg, where he lost the use of an arm, and at Chickamauga, where he lost a leg, Hood was living evidence of his pugilistic approach to war. The important thing for Davis was that he would not abandon Atlanta without a fight. At the gates of the city, Hood had the task of doing what his predecessor had been unable to do: defeat and turn back Sherman's blue-coated hosts. Hood proved unsuccessful, although he smashed his army against the Federals repeatedly in the process. Virtually nothing of this military process appears in the David O. Selznick film classic.

Although flawed in its stereotypical depiction of its characters and limited in its historical vision, *Gone with the Wind* has nevertheless served as the introduction of the Civil War era to generations of moviegoers. If Margaret Mitchell used the war in her novel and proved to be the inspirational force behind the film based on it in many ways, the same may be said of Ross Lockeridge Jr. and his 1948 novel, *Raintree County*. Less than a decade later it, too, would be featured on the big screen, with notable stars amid a powerful setting.

The film *Raintree County* was obviously meant to cash in on the success of *Gone with the Wind*. The idea seems to have been to create a film of epic proportions, fill it with the beauty of Elizabeth Taylor and the splendor of the

Old South, toss in the Civil War, and a blockbuster would be a certainty. It did not quite work out that way.

Unlike *Gone with the Wind*, *Raintree County* is set in the North, in Indiana, although some of the action in the film is connected through Susanna Drake (Elizabeth Taylor) to New Orleans and Louisiana. She refers to plantations in New Orleans and Savannah, Georgia, and appears quite comfortable with the institution of slavery (or at least the concept of personal servants).

The protagonist is John Shawnessy (Montgomery Clift), a teacher with decidedly pro-Northern, but generally antiwar, notions. Johnny loves Susanna and marries her when she pretends to be pregnant. They travel to New Orleans and engage in a philosophical discussion concerning slavery. "You ever read *Uncle Tom's Cabin*?" she asks. But, perhaps out of a sense of the fragility of their relationship, Johnny expresses his concern "about all the talk of secession." He does not share her position on slavery, and she responds by asking if he prefers the wage slavery of the North.

Clearly, their relationship, like the one between North and South, is in deep trouble. This becomes increasingly apparent to Johnny as he learns more about Susanna's past. When they visit the ruins of a great house, he learns a version of what had happened from her that he later finds to be untrue. She also has to admit to him that she has lied about the pregnancy.

Johnny continues to teach and throws his support behind Abraham Lincoln. The film makes reference to "Free Labor and Free Men," a concept *Gone with the Wind* scrupulously avoids. But, with the announcement that the Confederates have attacked Fort Sumter, "It means war sure as anything."

Johnny is skeptical. "I'm not sure," he explains. "Now say what you will Americans will never fight each other. We'll settle our difficulties peaceably." The teacher initially determines that he will not fight and watches as the war goes on without him.

In the meantime, the film makes reference to fighting associated with Vicksburg and Gettysburg. Johnny decides to join up and participates in the battle of Chickamauga. He is also at Resaca, Kennesaw Mountain, and Atlanta.

Finally, a newspaper headline informs the audience that the war has ended: "Peace! Lee Surrenders to Grant." Once more, the focus remains on Virginia and Appomattox without reference to other Confederate armies that remained in the field, even inexplicably the one that Johnny has faced in battle himself.

Despite this, *Raintree County* makes considerably more accurate references to military operations and political issues in the Civil War than does its popular predecessor and model. A news bulletin tells that General Grant is besieging Vicksburg. There are other references to this critical military campaign for control of the Mississippi River, as well as to Robert E. Lee's invasion of Pennsylvania and the battle of Gettysburg.

The film also introduces audiences to the idea of Copperheads, a term that is thrown around loosely and employed widely in Civil War westerns. However, much as in those films, *Raintree County*'s definition of the term makes no reference to political affiliation: "A Copperhead is someone who lives in the North who sides with the people who live in the South." Copperhead was also the term Republicans assigned to their Democratic opponents in the North.[13]

Raintree County covers a great deal of ground. This scattershot approach and the terrible automobile accident that bedeviled the lead actor, Montgomery Clift, and rendered his performance more wooden than it might ordinarily have been, diminished the epic. Thus it fell short in its attempt to repeat the sweep and popular appeal of *Gone with the Wind*.

A film that preceded *Gone with the Wind* by four years, *So Red the Rose* (1935) features another strong-willed woman and the plantation theme. The movie begins in the waning days of moonlight and magnolias, as a house servant provides the master of Portobello, "the proudest plantation in Mississippi," with his mint julep. He is the contented squire of all he surveys, but the distant rumblings of a storm are approaching his idyllic world.

Word arrives by rider that hostilities have begun and "The whole South is ablaze. The folks in Charleston just captured Fort Sumter from the Yankees." Members of the First Mississippi Volunteers ride up, and the hotheads prepare to go off to war, with one prominent exception, Duncan Bedford (Randolph Scott). "I don't believe Americans should fight Americans. . . . Why we have the same blood and the same traditions. I can't kill another American just because he's wearing a different uniform."

The film uses the device of bulletins on a chalkboard to move the military aspects of the story along, and these references demonstrate at least a glancing homage to history. "Confederates victorious at Bull Run." "General Lee attacks in West Virginia." "Desperate fighting in Kentucky." "Many killed in Mill Springs battle." "Union forces advancing through Tennessee."

Under the press of such headlines, the master decides to go to war. "I want you folks to guard and protect the plantation," he tells the slaves in a scene reminiscent of *The Birth of a Nation*. "I've never been a bad master to you and you've never been bad slaves." As he departs, the slaves express their loyalty to him. Emancipation waits for now, but other changes are already coming to Portobello. Duncan decides to forego planting cotton to plant corn instead. "The men and horses must have corn," he explains. "Don't you know there's a war?"

Finally, after traveling to Shiloh to retrieve a fallen family member, Duncan joins the forces of the Confederacy. A scene follows of him in uniform, leading men forward in a loose formation more appropriate to twentieth-century warfare than the extended shoulder-to-shoulder lines of the Civil War era. War has also come to Portobello's doorstep as word arrives that Grant has reached Vicksburg. "Most disreputable, unkempt man I ever saw," one of the matrons of the plantation pronounces. The family tries to continue with a semblance of normalcy, but their world is falling apart around them. All of the slaves except the loyal house servant William revolt against the continuation of slavery on this plantation, although they express themselves in terms that would have fit comfortably in *The Birth of a Nation*.

Only when the master's daughter, Valette, confronts the rowdy mob does a sense of the old deference return, particularly when she insists that one of the ringleaders recall raising her as a girl. "I don't say that you should be slaves," she tells them, "but I do say you must work to eat. The Yankees won't free you from work. You'll have to work whether you're free or not." For good measure, she reminds them, "This is your home."

As if to confirm that all is once again right in the ordered world that had once existed, the master himself returns from the war. Although clearly in physical distress from the exertions of war, he reclines with a drink and the house servant quietly observes, "Old times is here again, massa." Valette has salvaged the situation for the moment, and in the tradition of the prewar days the slaves once more express themselves in song. "They still sing," the master notes with a smile, and dies. The slaves are now "free to go where you please."

But if the old times are now in the past at Portobello, the war threatens the present. Skirmishing between elements of the opposing forces produce at least one wounded Union soldier who is left to the tender mercies of the Southern household. Perhaps out of a sense of their mutual loss, Valette takes the young man under her protection. But the Confederates who have wounded him are close on his trail, and they include Captain Duncan Bedford.

There is no time for an extended reunion in all of the excitement and confusion. Duncan finds the wounded Union soldier and threatens to see him hanged as a plunderer and house burner. Valette pleads for his life. Duncan the pacifist who had once opposed killing has now returned to Portobello a changed man. "How cruel you've grown," Valette tells him. "It's war, Valette," he responds.

Other Confederates arrive, and Duncan has to respond quickly. Perhaps under her chiding, he decides not to turn the Federal over as a prisoner. But the act of mercy proves to be in vain. The soldier dies, and as Duncan tries to leave the house he falls into Union hands. The Federal commander orders the house burned. "I want you to understand I'm not acting on my own discretion," he explains to the women as justification. "I'm only obeying orders." Portobello goes up in flames and is lost, with the exception only of "the master's chair," which the servant William salvages. A cabin becomes the plantation's big house, a poor reminder of better days. But the war that has wrought such sweeping changes in the genteel plantation world ends, and Duncan returns home from a Union prisoner-of-war camp to reunite with Valette.

Roy Kinnard, author of a compendium of Civil War movies, describes *So Red the Rose* as successful in depicting "the emotional damage wrought on a Southern family by the Civil War." He commends its efforts to address "the political issues of the War" and concludes that the film is "the best sound-era Civil War film made before *Gone with the Wind*."[14] Certainly, if one looks beyond the stock characters, the impact of the conflict on a family caught in the middle of it comes through.

To its credit, *So Red the Rose*, like the later *Raintree County*, works more history into the story line than its prestigious MGM counterpart. References to battles such as the Union victory at Mill Springs on January 19, 1862, and fighting in West Virginia and Kentucky make the viewer aware that not all of the fighting took place in Virginia and Tennessee. The film's evocation of hard war outside of William T. Sherman's "March to the Sea" in Georgia is also important. Likewise, the wartime transition that Southern agricultural producers made from major cash crops such as cotton to the more practical and necessary grain crops, such as corn, mirrors historical realities as well. Such historical references get little elaboration on film, but are significant nonetheless.[15]

Despite these historical allusions, *So Red the Rose* is not cinematically the film that *Gone with the Wind* is. Margaret Sullavan does not dominate the screen as Vivien Leigh does four years later. Nor is Scott's Duncan Bedford comparable to Gable's Rhett Butler, although both share a disdain for war before joining the conflict in the later stages. In the end, neither *So Red the Rose* before it nor *Raintree County* after capture *Gone with the Wind*'s scope and power on-screen.

Consistently rated as one of the best films ever made, *Gone with the Wind* will doubtless continue to influence audiences for generations to come. It will also surely serve as the inspiration for other films that try to recapture its glory and stature. But the producers of those future efforts will certainly come to understand that the mighty wind that blew into movie theaters in 1939 can never return in the same way again.

CHAPTER 4

The House Divided

Copyright © 1965, Universal International. All rights reserved. Permission granted for Newspaper and Magazine reproduction. (Made in the U.S.A.)

JAMES STEWART
"SHENANDOAH"
TECHNICOLOR®
Co-starring Doug McClure
A Universal Picture

"Property of National Screen Service Corp. Licensed for display in connection with the exhibition of this picture at your theatre. Must be returned immediately thereafter."

65/194

Papa Charlie Anderson (James Stewart) listens as his son (Glenn Corbett) asks when the family will take part in the war that is raging around them in *Shenandoah*.

A house divided against itself cannot stand.

—Abraham Lincoln

THE SENSE OF divided houses is pervasive throughout Civil War cinema. Numerous films touch upon the prewar connections that the sectional conflict severs. Movies such as *Drums in the Deep South* (1951) represent the effects of war upon close friends. *Shenandoah* (1965) and *Friendly Persuasion* (1956) depict the same phenomenon in the individual family unit. *Tap Roots* (1948) explores divisions within a broader community at war with itself between those who support and those who resist governmental authority. The most obvious explorations of the theme seem to be associated with Abraham Lincoln, the man who uttered the famous words before the Republican state convention in Illinois in 1858: "A house divided against itself cannot stand."[1]

As a candidate for the U.S Senate seat in Illinois held by incumbent Stephen Douglas, a lanky lawyer named Lincoln expressed the dilemma that the institution of slavery posed for America. Lincoln employed the same image of divided houses in his debates with Douglas as a means of attacking the senator's position on "popular sovereignty," the notion that people in a territory could decide for themselves whether or not to embrace slavery. In several of the debates, Lincoln called upon history to force Douglas's hand on slavery.[2] Lincoln did not win election to the Senate in 1858, yet in large part because of such rhetorical flourishes, he would succeed when he tried his hand at challenging the "Little Giant" for national office. No figure stands taller in American history or American Civil War cinema than the man who became the sixteenth president of the United States.

Hailing originally from Kentucky, Lincoln settled in Springfield, Illinois, and became an opponent of the South's "peculiar institution." Even so, he took the more politically acceptable moderate position of supporting "gradual, compensated emancipation" rather than the extremism of abolition. Lincoln even embraced the positions of the American Colonization Society, which attempted to encourage and facilitate the repatriation of freed men and women to Africa.

Gore Vidal, whose novel *Lincoln* became the basis for a film on the sixteenth president, laments the efforts of Hollywood to capture him. "In our time," he assesses, "the screening of Lincoln has been every bit as inadequate as the prosing of Lincoln."[3] Film portrayals of Abraham Lincoln abound, with numerous actors trying their hands at the distinguished politician. Earlier cinematic efforts by Raymond Massey and Henry Fonda have been followed more recently on the smaller screen by those of Gregory Peck, Jason Robards, and Sam Waterston. Yet, without a doubt, the most prolific of these performers was Frank McGlynn Sr., who established himself as the Abraham Lincoln of the 1930s, with no less than nine films during that decade in that role.[4]

Famed director D. W. Griffith demonstrated an interest in the president in *The Birth of a Nation*, making him and his assassination a component of the film. But many of the Lincoln appearances on celluloid are limited in scope. Frank McGlynn's Lincoln saves Shirley Temple's captured Confederate father in *The Littlest Rebel* (1935), while John Carradine's portrayal in *Of Human Hearts* (1938) has the president taking time out from the demands of war to chide a young army lieutenant and surgeon (James Stewart) for neglecting his mother by failing to write her.

Santa Fe (1951) opens with a shot of the Lincoln Memorial in the nation's capital and a narration stating, "'With malice toward none and charity for all,' this the great man said at Gettysburg." In actuality, President Lincoln spoke these words in his second inaugural address and not as part of the Gettysburg Address, although the sentiment is certainly appropriate to the unifying message of the movie.

Other films focus on the prewar Lincoln, struggling with his law practice and honing his skills for the future that awaits him. Henry Fonda captures this early Lincoln superbly in John Ford's *Young Mr. Lincoln* (1939), and Raymond Massey ably carries the same figure to the steps of the White House in *Abe Lincoln in Illinois* the following year.

Perhaps it should not be surprising that producers often choose to focus on moments of highest drama or rhetoric when featuring the sixteenth president. The threat of assassination before Lincoln can assume the presidency forms the dramatic basis for *The Tall Target* (1951). In the heated atmosphere following the 1860 election, agent John Kennedy (Dick Powell) prevents the tragedy and makes it possible for the president-elect (Leslie Kimmell) to assume his post as the nation's commander-in-chief.

The assassination of the president while attending a play at Ford's Theater, with all of its dramatic elements, appears in various films. In a speculation worthy of Oliver Stone and the death of another popular president, *The Lincoln Conspiracy* (1977) suggests that Secretary of State Edwin Stanton (Robert Middleton) lay behind John Wilkes Booth's (Bradford Dillman's) assault on Lincoln. Thus, the figure of Abraham Lincoln becomes a frequent feature of Civil War film.

Those wishing to learn more about the president from Illinois would do well to consult historical works rather than the portrayals of Lincoln they can find on film. Biographer David Donald authored what many scholars have termed the best single-volume treatment of Lincoln in 1995. Limited as any one-volume work on a complex subject, Donald succeeded in covering Lincoln without overglamorizing him.[5]

Historian Mark Neely examined what many might feel would be President Lincoln's most vulnerable position, in relation to civil liberties in the United States during the war. Neely's findings do not confirm the image of a benevolent "Father Abraham," as frequently seen in film, but indicate that he was

40

hardly the arbitrary constitutional tyrant portrayed in pro-Southern or anti-Lincoln propaganda, either.[6] As was so typical, the character of this presidential icon was as complex off-screen as it was often simplistic on it. Even so, the attempt to capture a historically accurate Lincoln on celluloid, particularly in his role as a wartime president, has so far proven elusive.

The same can be said concerning the two most recognizable military architects of Union victory, Ulysses S. Grant and William T. Sherman. Both make brief appearances in Civil War cinema. In *How the West Was Won* (1962), Grant has his ever-present and stereotypical cigar clenched in Harry Morgan's teeth. John Wayne's Sherman is awkward and ill fitting. The men share their thoughts in connection with the battle of Shiloh, while two witnesses, soldiers from each side, watch the proceedings. When the Confederate (Russ Tamblyn) decides to try to kill one or the other of the two Union commanders, the Federal soldier (George Peppard) steps in to prevent him from doing so.

Lee appears equally sparingly in Civil War cinema. Martin Sheen tries his hand at the role in *Gettysburg*, while director Ron Maxwell turns to veteran actor Robert Duvall to portray the Confederate general in *Gods and Generals*. But neither of the roles dominates the screen nor offers the actors opportunities for portrayals that could remotely be considered fully developed.

Another colorful character that emerges in Civil War cinema is George Armstrong Custer. Ronald Reagan portrays Custer in the historically suspect *Santa Fe Trail* (1940), riding alongside Errol Flynn's James Ewell Brown "Jeb" Stuart as they confront the rabid abolitionist, John Brown (Raymond Massey). However, the most well-known of the Custer films that depicts the flamboyant officer's service in that conflict is *They Died with Their Boots On* (1941). This version of Custer is portrayed by the equally ostentatious Errol Flynn, carrying Custer the Michigander through West Point to the battlefields of the Civil War before sending him to his fate, albeit highly stylized and romanticized, at Little Big Horn. With regard to its coverage of the conflict itself, author Bruce Chadwick perhaps summarizes it best, "In the world of *They Died with Their Boots On*, no one seems to have started the war and no one seems to have won it."[7]

Historically, the Raoul Walsh product left much to be desired. At West Point, Custer finds himself under a commandant named Philip Sheridan, who takes a liking to the headstrong cadet. All of this would be well and good, for Sheridan himself was suspended for fighting with a cadet whose tone he did not appreciate, except for the fact that Sheridan never acted as superintendent of the Academy.[8] Likewise, Flynn's Custer ingratiates himself to Winfield Scott (Sydney Greenstreet), the Mexican War veteran and general-in-chief of the Union armies, over a dish of onions, then depends upon the old hero for salvation when he acts on his own at Gettysburg. By the time he could have done so, Scott was retired from the army, not supervising the Gettysburg campaign or fretting over an independent-minded brigadier general, as he does in the film.[9]

Of far less use to film students of the Civil War for any purpose is the 1968 motion picture *Custer of the West*, with Robert Shaw in the title role. Precious little is done with the boy general's Civil War career as the people responsible for the film's development clearly wanted to hasten his appearance against the Indians, where the viewing public would expect to see him.[10]

Despite the limited roles for these significant figures in cinema, they represent the most popular archetype of a civil war: the "brother's war."[11] This was particularly true of the general officers on both sides, many of whom came from the same background, from education at the U.S. Military Academy at West Point or the Virginia Military Institute and military service in the Mexican War or against the Indians.[12] Certainly not atypical of this phenomenon are the subjects of John Waugh's *The Class of 1846*. In it, Waugh examines thirty-four members that included future Confederate generals Thomas Jonathan Jackson, Ambrose Powell Hill, George Edward Pickett, and Dabney Herndon Maury and future Union generals George Brinton McClellan, John Gibbon, George Stoneman, and Samuel Davis Sturgis.[13] James M. McPherson observes, "Officers who fought shoulder to shoulder against a common enemy in Mexico from 1846 to 1848 fought against each other in the war of 1861 to 1865. . . . Most of the commanders of the Union and Confederate armies that slaughtered each other to the tune of 620,000 war dead from 1861 to 1865 had fought together as brothers in arms in Mexico—and in the Indian wars of the 1850s."[14]

West Point colleagues figure prominently in *Drums in the Deep South*. The three friends will cast their lots with opposing sides. Northerner Will Denning (Guy Madison) chooses the Union, while Southerners Clay Clayborne (James Craig) and Braxton Summers (Craig Stevens) enlist with the Confederacy.

The tone of the film is set early, with references to "a storm coming up." In a scene almost certainly designed to be reminiscent of *Gone with the Wind*, the slaves in the field return to the quarters as a thunderstorm breaks around them.

"It's happened!" the elderly uncle interrupts the reunion. "We're at war! Fort Sumter has been fired on." The friends take their leave of each other. Clay announces, "I'll report directly to Richmond," despite the fact that Virginia has yet to secede and Richmond is not yet the Confederate capital.

Still, the friends are off to war, which the film hastens through in a series of silhouetted images, smoke, and explosions with the years superimposed. The scroll stops at 1864, where the bulk of the action to be depicted will take place.

Several officers await the arrival of an unusually bold and courageous major who is to be given a difficult, if not impossible, task. As a sentinel ushers

Clay Clayborne into the presence of a general, identified only by his title in the dialogue and the insignia of his uniform, we learn that it will be his task to disrupt the Union supply lines. "Sherman's whole army poured out of Chattanooga three weeks ago," the commander explains, without reference to any military action around Dalton, Georgia. As the invading force moves toward Georgia, the plan is to cut the single supply line supporting the advance and allow the Confederates the chance to turn on Sherman's isolated army.

The place designated for this blockading effort is Devil's Mountain, a sheer precipice that commands the railroad as it passes through Snake Gap. Although the railroad in question is the Western and Atlantic, no reference is ever made to it. Snake Gap also seems to have come from Snake Creek Gap, near the opening defensive positions of the Confederates under Joseph E. Johnston. Several times throughout the film, characters refer to Johnston's name as well as Sherman's.

The general orders Major Clayborne to take twenty handpicked men and four cannon, place them atop Devil's Mountain, and use them to shut down the Union rail line. The cannons are to be twelve-pound Brooke guns. Clayborne confidently asserts, "General, if I can get cannon on top of Devil's Mountain, I could fight there 'til doomsday."

The major selects his men and sets out with four pieces pulled by four-horse teams, as was common in Confederate artillery. The men wear a variety of uniform styles, although most carry the red piping of artillery meant to designate their branch of service.

The Confederates find that the Federals have hanged a local sympathizer who was supposed to aid them. Major Clayborne goes to Monrovia to seek a guide there and finds that his friend Kathy Summers is still there. Yet supporting the Confederate cause will undoubtedly come at a cost. "You know Sherman gave orders to burn down every house from here to Atlanta," a Union sergeant tells her, before she slips out to help her old friend.

With Summers as a guide, Clayborne locates a route through the caverns on the interior of the mountain. Even so, by the time the Confederate major has his men and guns atop Devil's Mountain, he has already lost several men to accidents. The soldiers hasten to reassemble the artillery pieces before Union work crews can repair damage to the rail line from earlier raids and allow the Federals to continue to pass supplies on to Sherman's command.

Back at Monrovia, Summers learns that the tracks are repaired and Union supply trains are about to roll. She signals the Confederates on Devil's Mountain with a mirror, but is caught by the sergeant. Her uncle shoots the soldier and is shot, in turn, by the wounded man. But the men have received the message and are prepared when two supply trains steam into their sights.

Another historical anomaly occurs here in the film when a Union sergeant informs the mistress of the plantation he is guarding in 1864: "First thing I knew I was drafted. When I left home I figured it would be for three months, that was three years ago." The fact that conscription in the North actually occurred less than three years earlier did not trouble him in the least.

In the meantime, artillery fire from the mountain disables both trains, but identifies the location of the Confederates to their opponents. Union reinforcements arrive, as does former friend Will Denning. Declaring that Sherman cannot move without his supplies, the Federals determine to drive the Confederates from their formidable position.

When preliminary attacks fail, Major Denning turns to a heavier artillery piece with greater range. As the large caliber naval gun arrives, Kathy slips away from Monrovia, witnesses the gun's appearance, and manages to find enough time to return to the mountain, climb it, and warn the Confederates of the impending barrage. Clayborne determines that only with double-charged and reinforced weapons will he be able to respond to the big gun's fire.

But time is running out for the Confederates. Major Denning decides to gather barrels of gunpowder in the chambers below the summit and silence the guns in one dramatic blast. Although informed that, given the slope of the peak, any blast will fill the gorge of Snake Gap and close the line, he pushes forward with his scheme.

In the meantime, Kathy Summers learns of the plan and begs to be taken to Major Denning to ask him to allow the Confederates to surrender. He reluctantly agrees. She climbs the interior passageway, but is shot as she reaches the top. Summers manages to convey her message as Clayborne orders the survivors off the summit and prepares to carry her down. When she dies in his arms, he determines to stay. Denning, who has finally ordered the fuses lit, watches as the rest of the Confederates scamper out. The explosion silences the threat, but also seals the mountain pass, for a time at least.

As the film closes, a unifying message declares, "Out of the chaos of brother against brother, came a new realization of one common destiny. From the smoke and debris and the sacrifice, a new meaning of unity was forged for the United States of America, one nation indivisible, now and forever."

While *Drums in the Deep South* deals with the strains of war on preexisting friendships, *Shenandoah* examines similar stresses on a tight-knit Virginia family. Charlie Anderson (James Stewart) is a widower with a large clan over which he presides with a benevolent authority. Sons Jacob (Glenn Corbett), Nathan (Charles Robinson), John (James McMullan), Henry (Tim McIntire), and the "Boy" (Philip Alford) perform their chores as if nothing more than a passing storm stands off the distant horizon. Charlie Anderson is a proud man who insists, even at the dinner table prayers, that the family has earned everything it has gotten with the sweat of its brow. In regard to the conflict that surrounds them, he consistently maintains that it does not concern the Anderson family.

Then the war comes to the Anderson household as elements of it invade the isolated farm property. First, a Confederate patrol arrives with the intent of enlisting the sons in the service, only to leave the property empty-handed before riding into a Union ambush. Subsequently, Federal agents appear demanding that the Andersons sell their horse stock for cavalry mounts. A brawl ensues, as the males fight to retain the family's autonomy. Finally, the boy finds a Confederate kepi drifting in the river and is innocently wearing it when Union soldiers appear. They determine that although he is young he must be a soldier, and they make him their prisoner.

Anderson learns what has happened from Gabriel (Eugene Jackson Jr.), the boy's black companion. The patriarch realizes that he can no longer be isolationist. "Now it concerns us," he observes. He gathers his sons and acquiesces to a daughter when she declares that since she can outride and outshoot any of them she will accompany them. They set out to find the boy, determined to bring him back home. The remainder of the film depicts the attempts of the father to locate and retrieve his lost son, while simultaneously trying to hold together what he can of the increasingly fractured family unit.

Shenandoah does not deal directly with military events in the Shenandoah Valley and thus is not associated with either Stonewall Jackson's brilliant 1862 campaign or the 1864 fighting that ended with Philip Sheridan's smashing defeat of Confederates under Jubal Early. The references to specific landmarks are vague and general. For instance, the Anderson farm is located at Shenandoah Gap. The group goes to the depot at Ivy Glen in its search. After several Confederates escape from a prison stockade prior to being shipped to Union prisons on steamboats, the soldiers manage to avoid an encounter with a Union patrol that includes cavalrymen as well as an artillery piece (pulled by a four-horse team rather than the six horses the Federals normally employed).

When the escaping Confederates, including the Anderson youth, reach a Southern camp, there is no designation of units, but the men sense immediately that they have returned to friendly company. One of them observes that he smells wood smoke. "That's a Confederate camp," another declares exuberantly. "Wood smoke ain't all you smelt. You smelled country boys." With that the six refugees race toward their comrades. Later, as the men locate weapons and something to eat, a soldier explains, "Down in Vicksburg I hear they're eating rats."

A subsequent skirmish between unnamed opposing forces, which includes artillery and cavalry charges, as well as infantry combat, has no apparent or specific connection to any historical engagement. But the unnamed battle will bring the boy closer to home. In the fighting, his newly acquired friend Carter (James Best) dies. The boy also suffers a wound but is saved from further harm when Gabriel, now a Union soldier, happens upon him. Gabriel moves his friend into some brush and rushes back into the fighting.

The Anderson party, now exhausted and worn from what has seemed to them a fruitless search, turns for home. As they approach a bridge, they startle a Southern sentry, who fires into them, killing Jacob. Anderson has now lost another child. When he and his party make their way home, they find that stragglers have murdered the son and daughter-in-law left behind to tend the farm in their absence.

After visiting the gravesite of his departed wife, Martha, for strength, Anderson gathers his remaining flock and goes to church. The pews are not as full as they used to be, but during the service the boy returns, hobbling back into the arms of his loving father.

Shenandoah is a Civil War film, with a strong performance by James Stewart, but its place in Civil War cinema is less clear. The units and historical references are vague. The fighting is generic, with spectacular charges designed more for screen presentation than military prudence. The strongest element is the desire by Charlie Anderson to remain aloof of the conflict, a sentiment the fictional father surely shared with many real ones.

In this regard, *Friendly Persuasion* (1956) has a great deal in common with *Shenandoah*. Set in "Southern Indiana 1862," the film features Gary Cooper as the leader of a Quaker family who also wants to avoid involvement in the war, even when it arrives at his doorstep. Like the Virginian, Jess Birdwell (Cooper) will find the conflict impossible to ignore indefinitely.

But as the film opens, the war is but a distant entity. The biggest threat, to the smallest member of the family at least, is a pet goose. The farm is idyllic, untouched by the troubles that plague the country to the south. Only the youth's pantomime of shooting Jefferson Davis and Stonewall Jackson betrays the existence of the conflict. "What would thee do if thee met old Stonewall?" he asks his older brother innocently. "Momma told thee not to talk about the war," the elder sibling, Josh (Anthony Perkins), responds.

The family may try to keep the war at arms length, but Confederates under John Hunt Morgan are headed their way. A convalescing officer interrupts the church service to call on the able-bodied men to abandon their neutrality and join the Northern cause. "Ma'am, the Union has endured two years of bloody Civil War," he tells Mrs. Birdwell, one of the congregation's leaders. "Thousands have given their lives in battle to free our country from slavery," he adds, explaining the key motivation for waging the war. "We are opposed to slavery," she rejoins, "but we do not believe it right to kill one man to free another."

The Union officer shifts tactics. "Are you afraid to fight?" Still failing to incite any of the Quakers to volunteer their services, he intensifies the point. "Do you think it's right to let others do the fighting for you to protect your lives and your property?" Finally, the officer leaves, his recruiting mission unfulfilled.

The closest that the Birdwell family comes to experiencing war firsthand is in the person of Gard, suitor to the Birdwell daughter. "Did thee shoot any Rebs?" the youngest Birdwell inquires of the furloughed soldier. "What are they like?" "They're just people like us," he responds. When Gard next appears, he has been wounded in action and assigned to the duty of organizing the home guard against Morgan's Confederate raiders.

The moment of truth is approaching as Josh rides up. "Papa, the Rebs are coming. Morgan's raiders crossed the Ohio day before yesterday. Fifteen hundred horsemen burning and pillaging all the way from Mockport." Gard advises Jess to take his family to the safety of the woods until the danger passes. Yet the Quaker refuses. "This is our home," he replies. "This is where we'll stay." Gard insists, warning of the hazards. "Mr. Birdwell, the raiders don't draw a line between soldiers and civilians. They're the toughest troops in the Confederacy and there's no telling what they'll do when they get here." "They're going to come, they're going to come, like fire or flood," Mrs. Birdwell explains stoically. "If it's the Lord's will, there's nothing we can do."

Josh volunteers to join the militia in challenging the Southern raiders. "Mother, I hate fighting. I don't want to die. I don't know if I could kill anyone if I tried. But I have to try so long as other people have to." In the battle to come, he will have to confront his own fears as much as the Confederates.

But the Southerners are having an effect, even on the Quaker community, that no patriotic rhetoric could have produced. "Some of Morgan's thieving men [have] burnt my barn, stolen my horses, and cleaned out my smokehouse," one neighbor laments.

In the meantime, the militia takes up a critical position at a ford in the river that the Southern cavalrymen must cross. Two riders approach to reconnoiter and the citizen-soldiers maintain perfect fire discipline. When the riders return, they are part of the main column, Confederate rectangular battle flag prominently displayed at the front. As the Southerners start across the river, the militia unleashes a volley that empties saddles and halts the advance in midstream. The veteran Confederates return fire, and the first of the militia fall. The Southerners bring up artillery to clear the crossing, lighting the rounds with torches at the breech, the limber chest resting beside the artillery piece. More Confederates fall as the militia holds its ground.

In the meantime, Josh's riderless horse returns. The wood is now all cut and stacked, and the fight has hit home for Jess. He grabs his gun and heads out. "Kill a Johnny Reb for me, Papa," the youngest calls out. "Son, never talk that way about a man's life," his father replies. But he knows that the circumstances of war may call upon him to do so.

As he rides out to find his son, Jess leaves the family farm behind. The remaining members will face Confederates, too, as riders soon appear on the horizon and descend upon the farm to look for food and plunder. Mrs. Birdwell disarms the Southerners by inviting them to eat. But when one of the more rambunctious of the raiders chases her beloved goose, the normally placid woman hits the culprit with a broom. Amused by the drama, the raider Rebels do not retaliate. "Thanks for the chickens, Ma'am," one of them calls back in a tone especially friendly for a scavenging marauder, and the storm of war passes.

Like his son, Jess has his opportunity to face the dilemmas of pacifism. He finds a friend lying mortally wounded by an unseen gunman. The Southern sharpshooter draws a bead on Birdwell, too, but only slightly wounds him. As the Confederate comes forward to check the condition of his victim, Jess surprises the bushwhacker and takes his weapon from him. All of the reasons for pulling the trigger cross the troubled man's face, but he chooses to adhere to his beliefs and refuses to take the Confederate's life. "I'll not harm thee," he tells him as he lets his antagonist escape.

At the ford, Jess finds his son lying amid the detritus of war. "He's not very old," Josh tells his father of the young Confederate lying next to him. "I killed him." The boy has confronted his demons and, although physically unharmed, must face the psychological demands war has made of him as he goes home. Yet the extent of any transformation caused by these traumatic events for either father or son remains largely unexamined in the film.

Much of the tranquillity that has characterized life before the appearance of Morgan's raiders returns when the Southern raiders have departed. Once again the goose holds court, and the family routine is restored. Only the indiscretion of the youngest Birdwell concerning his mother's impromptu battle with a Confederate reminds the viewer of any lasting effects of the war on the family. "Momma whacked a Reb?" Jess asks incredulously. "Well, by sugar, that's news." But the lapse in his wife is endearing. "Well, come on veterans," he jests as he leads the family back into the home. Unlike the Andersons, the Birdwells have survived their brush with the Civil War and returned rapidly to what on the surface at least looks like the prewar status quo. Unfortunately, it is outside the scope of the film to explore the lasting psychological impact of the killing that Josh has experienced or the violence that Jess and his wife have confronted.

The film's setting and circumstances are those of the raid of Confederate cavalryman John Hunt Morgan into Kentucky, Indiana, and Ohio in the summer of 1863. Aside from posing a moral dilemma on the fictional Birdwell family, the historical Morgan accomplished little in the spectacular raid and ended up in the Ohio State Penitentiary, from which he subsequently and famously escaped.[15]

Both films, *Friendly Persuasion* and *Shenandoah*, suggest the ways in which war affected even those who determined to do everything they could to avoid or ignore it and thus paid a price for their indifference. In the former, the family unit emerges with its faith tested, while in the latter the family is torn and battered, but both are closer for their shared hardships.

Of course, if families could be divided, so could whole communities. *Tap Roots* (1948) attempts to tap into this phenomenon with Van Heflin, Susan Hayward, and Ward Bond determining to stand for the Union in the heart of the Confederacy. Southern officials try unsuccessfully to exact loyalty out of a Mississippi community that prefers neutrality at a minimum. The circumstances are right for a confrontation that will settle the issue with blood.

The debate continues to rage as to the extent to which Jones County, Mississippi, the undoubted basis for the novel, and thus the film, *Tap Roots*, became a "free state" within the Confederacy. The author, a journalist named James Stewart, lived near Jones County and, according to one historian, "was inspired by tales he had heard as a boy." However, the novelist disdained the notion that the principal figure in his fictional work, Hoab Dabney of Lebanon County, had any specific historical inspiration.[16]

Wartime events in the Mississippi community suggest that Stewart's assertion was disingenuous. As in many areas of the South, division characterized Jones County throughout the conflict as Unionists battled with Confederate authorities for the upper hand. The leader of the Knight Company, Newton Knight, clearly provided at least a part of the historic foundation for *Tap Root's* nonconformist hero. The one-time Confederate became disillusioned with the government, particularly over exemptions from the draft on the basis of slave ownership: the "Twenty Negro Law."

Knight and other leaders in the region won widespread support in flouting Confederate rule, often among the poorest members of society, who had suffered the most from the war and its effects. Author Victoria Bynum explains, "Families with the widest networks of nonslaveholding kinfolk exhibited the most consistent opposition." Such kinship groups served as the core of the Knight Company.[17] Many of these were also motivated by a sense of Unionism, although resistance in this part of Mississippi did not automatically equate to loyalty to the Union cause.[18]

Alternately considered heroes or desperadoes, depending on the position of the viewer, the Unionists in Jones County were reasonably well armed and certainly well organized by the last year of the war.[19]

In early 1864, the Confederacy took steps to combat the opposition growing in Jones County and the surrounding region. Lieutenant General Leonidas Polk informed Dabney Maury, "My orders are that as these men have become a lawless banditti . . . they be dealt with in the most summary manner. . . . No time should be lost."[20] A month later, the Episcopal-bishop-turned-soldier informed the War Department that the number of "conscripts and deserters [that] have banded together in Jones County, and others contiguous" had reached "several hundred." "They are increasing in numbers and boldness," the general exasperatingly noted. The remedy, as he saw it, was to dispatch a force sufficient to "put down this combination, which is fast attaining formidable proportions."[21]

In March, General Polk reported that Colonel Henry Maury had led a force against the "traitors and murderers of Jones and other counties in Southern Mississippi," resulting in "killing and capturing a number of their ringleaders and breaking up their band." Although this claim proved to be a bit premature, Polk felt comfortable enough with the outcome to proclaim that the operation had produced a "salutary effect" on that "infected district." He felt that the expedition had achieved tangible results, noting that "many of the deserters are now coming in."[22]

Subsequently, Colonel Robert Lowry brought troops into the region to bring it under Confederate control. The "Lowry Raids" ravaged the resistance in Jones County, predominantly through hangings and capture, with a number of the guerrillas fleeing or forced to reenlist in the Southern forces. As successful as the operations proved, they failed to eradicate Unionism in the region altogether. "Despite the havoc wreaked by Colonel Lowry and his men, including their decimation of the Knight Company, core members Newt Knight, Jasper Collins, William Wesley Sumerall, and James Morgan Valentine were among approximately twenty deserters who remained uncaptured, unrepentant, and a potent force in Jones County."[23]

Historically, Southern officials had problems enforcing taxation on communities for any number of reasons, from disaffection to the disruptions of the war and the proximity of opposing troops.[24] That any community, in Mississippi or anywhere throughout the South, had difficulty with the centralistic and nationalistic demands of the Confederate government was certainly nothing out of the ordinary.[25]

Indeed, at the height of the war, the Confederacy experienced a range of reactions and resistance to its policies. President Jefferson Davis had to assist in quelling a "bread riot" in the capital city in the spring of 1863.[26] Shortages so plagued the people that communities often had to raise funds to help the poor and indigent in their midst subsist.[27]

None of these films really deals with these phenomena in any substantive manner. They are left as window dressing or background motivation for the reaction of some of the characters to their difficult wartime circumstances. The historic examinations of these deeper issues is left to the monographs that explore them in greater depth than the screen would allow.

Thus, given the properties of Civil War cinema, each of these films demonstrates once more that the content projected on the big screen is meant to serve the interests of entertainment rather than history. None of these motion pictures will be confused with documentaries on Georgia, the Shenandoah Valley, or Mississippi during the war. Wartime issues take second place to the development of characters and their personal conflicts. The main effort is the telling of a good story and not the advancement of historical understanding or analysis. But in each of these motion pictures, the audience sees the peculiar impact of a civil war in reflecting and creating divisions in every segment of society.

CHAPTER 5

The Personal War

A pensive Henry Fleming, played by World War II hero Audie Murphy, awaits his trial by combat in John Huston's film version of the Stephen Crane novel, *The Red Badge of Courage*.

That war was a widow-maker.

—Narrator, *Pharaoh's Army*

We all died a little bit in that damn war.

—Josey Wales

A S ONE WOULD EXPECT of any warfare, the American Civil War was an intensely personal conflict for the individuals who found themselves engulfed in it, particularly if judged through several films. The classic Civil War soldier motion picture, John Huston's *The Red Badge of Courage* (1951), assesses the psychology of war through a young man's personal journey from novice to combat veteran. *Of Human Hearts* (1938) explores the travails of a fellow who becomes a surgeon in the war only to neglect those at home who should have been more important to him than his career. *The Man from Colorado* (1948) depicts a man at war with himself, as well as with his former wartime associates. Likewise, *The Proud Rebel* (1958) explores the psychological impact of war on a young man who shock has rendered mute. *The Beguiled* (1970) pits a wounded Union soldier against the occupants of a small Southern girl's school who have taken him in to nurse him back to health. *Pharaoh's Army* (1995) brings the war into the home of a Southern widow and her son when a Federal patrol appears with orders to gather supplies from local residents. *Cold Mountain* (2003) features the struggles of a Confederate soldier who deserts to return to the woman he loves and of the civilians left behind on the home front. Indeed, the personal struggles and varied outcomes that result from the influences of the conflict on the people who become involved in it mark the characters of a wide range of films.

The personal nature of the war is as near as any Civil War correspondence, any journal or diary, Union or Confederate, Northern or Southern. Examples abound of individuals, families, and whole communities who found war suddenly thrust upon them. Writing on the Appalachian region of the South in the war has become particularly popular.[1]

The best film depiction of the common soldier is John Huston's *The Red Badge of Courage*. Based on Stephen Crane's powerful novel, the movie features highly decorated World War II veteran Audie Murphy as the soldier who faces combat for the first time. Murphy plays Henry Fleming, an introspective Union soldier who will have to confront his anxieties as much as the Confederates on the battlefield. In his first taste of fighting, Fleming remains steadfast, controlling the fear he has worried would make him turn and run when he "saw the elephant," as the popular phrase of the time labeled the initial combat experience.[2] Unfortunately, the youth finds that he must summon the courage again when the Southerners attack once more after their earlier repulse. This time, the chaos of battle is too much for him, and he breaks for the rear.

Henry remains plagued with guilt as he collects his wits and reexamines his actions. The soldier will return to his unit and to the battlefield, and will find the courage that he thought had forsaken him. In the counterattack that follows, he carries the flag to the enemy's works, triumphant over his battlefield opponents and his fears.

All of the action in *The Red Badge of Courage* occurs in the midst of the Civil War, but much of the film *Of Human Hearts* focuses on relationships in a family prior to the war. The most significant dynamic through the first half of the motion picture is that established between the strong-willed preacher/father (Walter Huston) and his son, Jason Wilkins (Gene Reynolds/James Stewart). Each struggles to relate to the other, and neither can find the means to express his feelings. The chasm becomes irreparable with the death of the father. The boy aspires to attend medical school and when he reaches sufficient age travels to Baltimore for that purpose.

In the meantime, it is the widowed mother who makes sacrifices to see that her son has whatever he needs. These sacrifices continue as hostilities open between the sections and the doctor announces his intention to enlist. In a rare letter home, he tells his mother that he has "joined the army as a *Surgeon*," but now needs to purchase an appropriate uniform at a cost of "about seventy dollars." He encourages her to sell the only remaining companion she has, a horse named Pilgrim, suggesting, "The government is paying good prices for horses."

The widow takes the prized animal to an army corral and learns that "$80.00 is our limit lady." She bids the animal goodbye and accepts the fee. The camera work is powerful and poignant as she receives the money and the son then pays it out for the coveted uniform. With the change, he purchases a pair of gauntlets to accessorize. Soon, he is marching off to war, immaculately dressed.

As the war progresses, the letters from the front grow scarce. When the widow finds no letter waiting for her in town, she quietly observes, "Next week." One of the community members watching the tableau notes, "She's been saying that for two years."

To be sure, Jason is busy working in a field hospital as the casualties from a recent, and unnamed, battle pour into the makeshift facility. Suddenly, a message arrives that the surgeon is expected in Washington. "The President wants to see you at once." "The President?" he replies. "Well what on earth does he want to see me for?" When no answer is forthcoming, he observes rather reasonably for his circumstances, "How can I leave now? They're bringing in the wounded by the hundreds." But the summons is too important to ignore. Soon, Lieutenant Wilkins is on his way to see President Lincoln.

In Washington, Wilkins has his audience with the commander-in-chief. The conversation begins cordially. "I want to congratulate you, Wilkins," the president tells him. "You've been doing great things in the field." When the surgeon responds modestly, Lincoln continues. "I have a request from General Grant that you be transferred to his medical corps."

But just as Wilkins accepts accolades from the president, Lincoln reveals his ulterior motive for calling the young man into his presence. He has received tremendous assistance from home, but has failed to appreciate it. More grievously, he has "neglected to write" the mother who has sacrificed so much on his behalf. Lincoln employs the homespun style for which he is famous, but orders the surgeon to write home every week. "If you fail, I'll have you court-martialed," he vows sternly.

Thus, reprimanded for his omission, Lieutenant Wilkins returns to the hospital. One of the individuals he attends to is a badly wounded officer who now owns the horse Pilgrim. "Save my arm and you can have the horse," he tells the doctor.

The horse's name is apparently symbolic of the personal journey that the officer must undertake. Wilkins soon makes his way home on the beloved animal, reunites with his mother, and begs her forgiveness. He has learned, thanks to the president of the United States, that there are no more cherished connections than those at home. The soldiers themselves understand this, as evidenced by the classic ballad heard in the camps of both sides, "Home, Sweet Home."

The war clearly has had an impact on the hearts and minds of these very human soldiers. Yet few films capture the posttraumatic stress that must also have been present. *The Man from Colorado* is the closest film in the Civil War repertoire to the Korean War–based psychological thriller, *The Manchurian Candidate* (1962). *The Red Badge of Courage* examines the immediate confrontation of the soldier with combat, but other than *The Man from Colorado*, no other feature film attempts to explore the longer-term effects of the war on one of its participants in this fashion. Nor does any other movie employ a bona fide World War II hero (Glenn Ford) to take on such a role.

In the motion picture, Ford plays a Union colonel who has suffered a severe psychological shock from his experiences in the Civil War. He grapples with his sanity and his humanity early on in the film when the Confederates he faces in battle attempt to surrender. He refuses to allow them to do so, despite the protestations of his trusted lieutenant and friend, Captain Del Stewart (William Holden). Unlike the political treachery seen in *The Outlaw Josey Wales* (1976), when Union soldiers and their sympathizing political patrons connive to slaughter Southern guerrillas by pretending to allow them to surrender, this action is part of the Union officer's internal struggle.

In an engagement that purports to take place "Toward the close of the Civil War—in the year 1865—in Colorado," a well armed Union command encounters the "remnants" of a Confederate unit at "Jacob's Gorge." The unnamed Southern commander watches as the Federals deploy an overwhelming force, buttressed by artillery pieces, and hands a subordinate a white flag to display his intention to surrender rather than resist. "We ain't licked yet Major," the man protests, "they'll never lick us." But the odds are clearly too great, and the token of surrender gets displayed on the end of a bayonet.

From his vantage point, Union Colonel Owen Devereaux (Glenn Ford) spots the gesture and confirms it through his binoculars. But he has determined to smash his opponents and will not be denied that opportunity at this stage. Cold-bloodedly, he orders the Union artillery to open a devastating fire on the Southerners.

Captain Del Stewart (William Holden) rides ahead to inspect the effectiveness of the bombardment. Around him lie the bodies of the Confederate defenders, and he calls for burial teams to come forward to do their grim work. In the meantime, Stewart notices the white flag. He ponders briefly what options he might have before sliding the symbol into a hole and hastily covering it with his foot.

Stewart is Devereaux's close friend and subordinate. He has witnessed his commander's murderous excesses but chosen to remain silent and find some way to justify what he has seen. Devereaux has been a dedicated soldier and a good friend, but the war has clearly transformed him into a psychopathic killer.

Despite Stewart's doubts about his commander, the two men continue their association after the war. Devereaux becomes a federal judge while Stewart serves as his marshal. However, the relationship between the men, who also share a love for the same woman, becomes strained. Devereaux begins to exhibit signs of jealousy and rage toward his lieutenant, and ultimately convinces himself of Stewart's betrayal. The friendship further deteriorates as the judge becomes increasingly affiliated with a rich mining baron who is out to carve a personal empire for himself.

This time, the victims of the judge's excesses are not Confederate opponents in wartime, but former Union troopers who served with him in the war. When some of them fall prey to the mining magnate's manipulations, they strike back and run afoul of the judge. Coldly and clinically, Devereaux hunts some of these former comrades down and metes out justice with a disturbing zeal. Stewart becomes increasingly aware of his old friend and commander's irrationality and seeks to have him removed from the bench.

Stewart also tries to warn Caroline Devereaux (Ellen Drew) of her husband's instability, drawing his ire upon her as well. When Stewart finally joins forces with his comrades against the judge, the stage is set for a confrontation between them. With Stewart now a "rebel" himself in the eyes of his old commander, there is nothing for the judge to do but to root the criminal out and kill him. This Devereaux attempts to do in a fiery conclusion to his mental breakdown as he battles his old friend to his own death.

Although the psychological toll of later wars would become much better known than that taken on soldiers and civilians in the Civil War, the hardships and human devastation undoubtedly affected people on both sides in that conflict as well. Eric Dean, who has studied the effects of war on Vietnam and Civil War veterans, noted, "In reading the memoirs or letters of these soldiers, one often sees a progression in each life from an initial carefree optimism about 'soldiering' to a growing weariness and sense of vulnerability."[3]

Alan Ladd is John Chandler, the title character of *The Proud Rebel*, who is determined to find an answer to the silence that has plagued his child (Ladd's real-life son David) since the boy witnessed the death of his mother and the destruction of their home during the war. "Had a big house just outside of Atlanta," he explains. "They shelled it. There was a big fire. His mother was killed. Well David saw it. That's how it happened. When I came back everything was burned to the ground." The boy had ended up in an orphanage in Pennsylvania with his dog, Lance, as his sole companion. "Since then we've seen a lot of doctors and a lot of country." Despite his devotion to finding a cure for his son, the efforts continue to prove unsuccessful.

In the meantime, tension brews between the local sheep baron, Harry Burleigh (Dean Jagger), and the woman farmer, Linnett Moore (Olivia de Havilland), who stands in his way by refusing to sell her land to him. Moore befriends the pair and Chandler reciprocates by helping to improve her ranch. Burleigh and his sons escalate their intimidation by burning the woman's barn and threatening other violence against them, but the "proud rebel" remains determined to resist. His overriding concern continues to be with his son's inability to speak.

Finally, the opportunity comes for experimental surgery that might help the boy to regain his voice. To secure enough money to allow his son to travel, the father sells the boy's beloved dog. The effort fails, and the guilt-ridden father informs his son that Lance no longer belongs to them. Chandler tries to buy the animal back, only to find that it has been sold again and now belongs to Burleigh. He rides to the Burleigh ranch determined to retrieve the dog and obtains permission to do so. But the sheep baron has no intention of honoring his word and plans instead to kill Chandler as he collects Lance, under the pretense that he believes Chandler is stealing the animal. A final confrontation nearly leads to Chandler's death, when the son finds his voice in time to warn his father that he is in danger. Burleigh and one of his boys die in the shootout, freeing Chandler and David to bring Lance home and pick up their lives, with the war and its effects squarely behind them.

The war has had a traumatic effect on the boy in *The Proud Rebel*. It will have a devastating effect on the principal character in *The Beguiled* as well. *The Beguiled* is an unusual Clint Eastwood motion picture. Set in Mississippi at the time of the Vicksburg campaign—there is a brief reference to Champion Hill—the film depicts an incident that occurs on the fringe of warfare. Corporal John McBurny (Eastwood) is a wounded Union soldier of dubious integrity. Flashbacks serve to illustrate that he is not the man of character that he represents himself to be. When one of the members of the Farnsworth Seminary for Young Ladies stumbles on him, the headmistress, Martha Farnsworth (Geraldine Page) makes the Christian decision to tend to his injuries, although he wears the uniform of their enemies.

McBurny responds to the kindness with manipulation and guile, luring one after the other of the young women to serve his needs. Although the wounded soldier is on his way to recovery, his lascivious actions cause a setback when he tumbles down the steps and reinjures his leg.

Farnsworth decides to remove the damaged limb in a harrowing amputation scene. When McBurny awakens, he attributes the act to jealousy and retribution, as he gives way to the ruthless nature he has previously tried to conceal. The situation reaches a climax when the soldier lashes out at the youngest of the girls. She joins the others in turning upon their tormentor and picks the poisoned mushrooms that will kill him.

Just as Corporal John McBurny experiences the caprices of war outside of the battlefield, *Pharaoh's Army* depicts the arbitrariness of life in the backcountry during the conflict. Here death strikes swiftly, often through treachery. The film opens ominously, with the sound of digging as a family buries a young daughter. The tale, "inspired by a true story," takes place in the area of Meshack Creek, Kentucky, in 1862. The narrator informs us, "All of the able-bodied men had gone off to fight the Civil War." He adds that in the evening after they buried his sister, "some Yankee bastards dug her up, tossed her out like a rag doll on account of Pap siding with the South." He concludes, "In these Cumberland Mountains down near the Tennessee line, half the folks sided with the South and the other half sided with the North. The neighbors turned against their neighbors and it was rough through here."

With the backdrop thus established, the boy and his mother return to their isolated cabin to rebury the lost sibling and go on with their lives. But the war, in the form of a small Union patrol, intervenes once more. "Yankees," the mother gasps when her son points out the strangers splashing through the creek and heading for the cabin. She and the boy scramble to hide their provisions and scatter their livestock. "They'll steal everything we got," she tells him.

The captain of the squad of Federals rides up to confront the mistress of the house. "Sarah Anders," he calls out, "your husband's fighting against his country," undoubtedly as justification for what he and his men are about to do. He quickly adds the purpose for the visit: "We have orders to resupply with contraband from the enemy. That means we'll take forage provisions from you."

What follows is a general free-for-all as the Union troopers gleefully round up supplies, shooting hens and scrounging through the cabin with abandon. The captain, John Hull Abston (Chris Cooper) is clearly awkward about the role he has been called upon to play in this patrol and is sensitive and apologetic toward Anders (Patricia Clarkson) and her young son. He tries to engage her in conversation to assuage her fears. "I got a piece of bottom land across the river, Ohio River," he observes, to show that he is not so very different from her and her family. "Why didn't you stay there?" she inquires sharply in reply.

One of the Federal troopers speaks with a foreign accent, and we learn later that he has come to America from Poland. He and a comrade find the tintype of Anders's husband she has buried in her flour barrel. "What do you think he's fighting for?" he asks. "To keep us from stealing his chickens," the other replies. "That's a good reason," he adds, an indication that their mission is less about being punitive toward these people whose lives they have interrupted than it is about securing something to eat from the only place that is available.

Then the fateful visit turns on an accident, as one of the foraging soldiers falls on a farm implement and injures himself severely. What might have been a stay of short duration has been extended indefinitely, and the Union farmer-turned-soldier decides that he and his men must remain at the farm. "We can't move him till the fever breaks."

Torn between her desire to have the intruders gone and a benevolence that prompts her to tend the hurt soldier, Anders tells her son that if the soldier gets well, "he might be the one shooting at your Pap." She admonishes the boy that until his father returns, "you're the man around here," and he takes the wounded Federal's pistol and hides it.

In the meantime, Captain Abston continues to try to win over the Southern woman with kindness and consideration. He takes up the plowing, perhaps as much to feel the reins in his hands once more as to help her with a difficult chore, and seeks to learn more about her circumstances. "Where's your husband fighting?" he asks. "The Army of Tennessee," she responds without reference to where that army might be at the time. "Was he at Shiloh?" Abston wants to know, and when she answers that he was, he adds, "That was a bad mess." But then the Union officer reveals that neither he nor his men were actually at the battle; indeed, they have yet to see "a big scrape. Meet the elephant, boys call it." Other references to military action at Camp Wildcat and Mill Springs give the film a ring of authenticity, particularly with regard to battles in Kentucky in 1861–1862.

In one of the more revealing scenes, Abston and Anders discuss the burning of a local homestead. "Some old man and his wife was killed. You know whose place it is?" he wants to know." "Yankees," she replies matter-of-factly. "They sent two boys into the Union army." "Ma'am they weren't Yankees," Abston responds. "Just some old farmer and his wife. They were just farmers." The voice of the narrator reminds us, "Like I said, the war was rough through here."

Nor is the reason for the killing particularly clear. One of the soldiers has lost a brother to "a Rebel sniper." But when he notes that his sacrifice has been to save the Union and to free the slaves, the rejoinder comes quickly: "Nobody that I know wants to get killed to free a bunch of nigs."

Under the pressure of the forced period of introspection, the unit cohesion in the small patrol begins to break down. The Federals start to fight among themselves. One of the men, Rodie (Richard Tyson), prepares to leave, forcing Captain Abston to face the necessity of shooting him for desertion. Suddenly, the matter is settled for them as a shot rings out from an unknown assailant and the soldier falls. "It's time to meet the elephant," the Union officer calls out, using the phrase common in the war for the experience of soldiers coming under hostile fire for the first time. He directs the others to fire in the direction of the sniper and circles around the cabin to try to locate him. As with so much else Abston has had to confront on this mission, the outcome is not as he had expected. The shooter is no ordinary bushwhacker from the neighborhood, but a black man who has been working with the local preacher (Kris Kristofferson), apparently sent by the minister to frighten the Federals into leaving. The Union captain knows only that someone has shot one of his men and sets out to locate the sniper and stop him before he does further damage. Coming up behind the man, Abston flushes him from his cover and kills him.

There is nothing left for Abston to do now but gather the injured man, bury the dead one, and take the remnant of his force out by wagon. To do so he has to renege on his promise not to take the mule Anders and the boy use for plowing. As the Federals depart, the boy scrambles to get the pistol and follows. He makes headway against the slow-moving team and shoots the wounded Federal, a boy-soldier named Newt.

The lad races back to the cabin. The Union captain also returns, bringing Newt's lifeless body with him. "Your mother might tell you that it's alright to kill Yankees," he shouts in agonized frustration, "but I just want you to know that that boy he had a brother just like you. And he had a family just like you. And he never hurt a fly in his life." But Anders is just as quick with her reply, "And he wouldn't be dead if you hadn't come down here stealing from us. We were doing fine until you showed up."

The Union captain draws his weapon, but in the end cannot bring himself to exact revenge for the death of his men. "What'd you do to 'em?" one of his men asks as he rejoins them. "You heard the shots," he explains, without admitting that he had fired the rounds harmlessly into the air before leaving.

Yet, for this act of kindness toward her and her son, Anders shows no inclination for forgiveness. "Get that damn Yankee out of our yard," she orders the boy, before helping him drag Newt's body to a sinkhole and float Rodie's corpse down the creek. "The Captain asked us to do the decent thing," the narrator, Anders's son, explains. "I don't guess the Civil War was about being decent." But he has suffered at its hands, too. "Pap never made it back," he adds somberly. "That war was a widow-maker."

Pharaoh's Army is an outstanding case study of the warfare that took place in the Southern backcountry. No major battles erupt on-screen, but the depiction of war on the small scale likely represents the type of conflict most individuals experienced out of the mainstream of combat. The uniforms and accoutrements of the soldiers are authentically rendered. The film ends with a clarification of its adherence to history: "In 1941, a Kentucky mountaineer returned to a remote sinkhole, the place where during the Civil War he had killed and buried a Union soldier. This film was inspired by his story as told to the folklorist Henry Caudill." Certainly, it tapped successfully into the psychology of the war on the individual level.

Pharaoh's Army examines the impact of war on a family and the men whom that conflict had caused to intrude into their lives. Intrusions of a different kind plague characters in *Cold Mountain*. Jude Law plays a North Carolina craftsman-turned-soldier named Inman. The film opens "near the end of the Civil War," in July 1864 at the siege of Petersburg. The Federals are busy stocking a tunnel with gunpowder as they prepare to blast a hole in the Confederate lines and force open a route into the town for the assembled Union troops.

For the Confederate defenders it is another ordinary day, except for the appearance of a jackrabbit that starts a race between soldiers to be the one to capture it and put it into a stew pot. Suddenly, the ground rises beneath the feet of one of the pursuers. An explosion hurls him and many of his comrades skyward as a plume of dirt and debris mushrooms into the air, carving out an enormous crater in the midst of the obliterated Southern position.

Inman digs himself out of the dirt and surveys the damage all around him. Others are barely able to stumble from the places where the blast has tossed them. After a stunned moment or two, the advancing Union troops appear through the receding pall of dust, closing rapidly upon them.

The Federal troops move forward with confidence, but fail to realize that they are funneling into the enormous crater they have created. As they jam together, the Union soldiers come under increasing fire as their opponents regroup. The Northerners recognize too late that they have entered a death trap. One Southerner exuberantly calls out that it is like shooting fish in a barrel. Another repeatedly tosses bayoneted muskets like spears into the huddled mass of blue-coated soldiers. As some of the opponents engage in hand-to-hand combat, the first African American Union troops appear.

Once the fighting at the crater subsides, the Confederates begin to gather their dead and wounded colleagues. The Union dead lie in great mounds. Inman tends to a wounded friend from his North Carolina home of Cold Mountain and remains with him until he dies.

Later, Inman receives orders to clear out a wooded area in which Union troops have taken refuge following the debacle at the crater. The men engage the Federals, but suffer casualties in the process, including a severe neck wound to Inman himself. He remains in a Confederate hospital for a time as he recovers.

In flashback, the film introduces the budding relationship between Inman and the daughter of a preacher recently arrived from Charleston, South Carolina. War comes to the tiny mountain community, which embraces the Confederate cause with enthusiasm: "We got our war," one of the local young men shouts triumphantly.

When Inman has recovered sufficiently from his wound, he determines to return to Cold Mountain, even if his actions make him a deserter. During his journey, Inman surprisingly ends up on the Carolina coast and at one point asks if he is "near the Cape Fear River," which runs inland from Wilmington.

In the meantime, Ada Monroe (Nicole Kidman) struggles to keep herself, her father (Donald Sutherland), and their farm afloat. The task becomes immeasurably harder when the preacher dies. Ada survives with assistance from neighbors until rough-hewn Ruby Thewes (Renee Zellweger) arrives to help her. Ruby encourages her to develop more practical skills than any she learned in Charleston society before coming to her new home.

At the same time, members of the home guard scour the area around Cold Mountain for deserters. The commander is a captain who had lost most of the land his family formerly owned on Cold Mountain and sees the war as an opportunity to reclaim his birthright. In the process, he and his troops ferret out deserters from among the families whose land he covets. He justifies his actions by accusing them of aiding the deserters in avoiding detection.

The stage is set for a final denouement as Inman makes his way back to the North Carolina mountains, while Ada and Ruby work their farm and harbor deserters that include the latter's estranged musician father, and the home guards display additional cruelty and menace the people of the community they are supposed to protect.

Following a romantic reconnection with Ada, Inman helps the two women in a confrontation with the guards. The captain and his bloodthirsty lieutenant die in the ensuing firefight, but Inman is also hit. He and Ada reunite a final time, but Inman's sacrifice allows Ada and Ruby to raise their families in peace on Cold Mountain in the aftermath of the war.

Cold Mountain depicts the battle of the Crater at Petersburg. The basic elements of the engagement are present. Men of the Forty-Eighth Pennsylvania constructed a tunnel beneath the Confederate lines at Elloitt's Salient, a strong point in the Southern line that held a battery of artillery and supporting troops. The Federals filled chambers in the tunnel with black powder. The film does not exploit the drama of the fuse going out after it had been lit, which required men to reenter the tunnel to relight it. Finally, at approximately 4:45 a.m., on July 30, 1864, the detonation wrenched the ground.

The explosion that obliterated Pegram's South Carolina battery in Elliott's Salient is well done. Four tons of powder smashed the Southern works and sent men and debris hurling through the air. The Confederates were thought to have lost 278 men in the explosion itself.[4] The blast ripped a gaping hole 170 feet long, 60 feet wide, and 30 feet deep.[5]

However, the effort to portray other characteristics of the siege of Petersburg falls short. The Confederate entrenchments have a World War I quality, with a scattering of chevaux-de-frise (logs with sharpened posts projecting from them) to suggest the 1864 conflict. The field between the two lines is much too broad for positions that were less than forty yards apart from skirmish line to skirmish line in the vicinity of Elliott's Salient. Period images suggest that the Southern lines were less sophisticated at this stage of the siege than they appear here, but there are no gabions (baskets of earth), abatis (sharpened tree limbs), or other traditional siege defenses, and a watch tower on the Southern line is painfully out of place here on a battlefield covered by sharpshooters on both sides.

When Union general Ambrose E. Burnside launched the assault that culminated in the battle of the Crater, he had anticipated the use of black troops to lead the operation. At the last minute, fearing a reverse that would give the impression that these troops had been sacrificed deliberately, the Union authorities shifted the order of battle. This rearrangement took the blacks who had been held out of the front lines and prepared especially for this type of operation from the lead, and replaced them with white troops who had no idea what would be required of them or of the circumstances that they would encounter as they reached the scene.

The concern felt at Union headquarters did not lessen with the explosion of the mine. Almost an hour after the blast had taken place, General George G. Meade, commander of the Army of the Potomac, communicated personally to Burnside wanting to know, "What news of your assaulting columns?"[6] Burnside promptly replied that his troops "have the enemy's line and occupy the breach." He promised to exploit the advantage immediately. "I shall endeavor to push forward to the crest as rapidly as possible."[7] Meade still could not rest easily. His chief of staff fired back to Burnside, "The general commanding learns that your troops are halting at the works where the mine exploded." They were not advancing as they were supposed to do, and precious time was elapsing. "He directs that all your troops be pushed forward to the crest at once."[8]

But the assault, begun with such promise, was doomed to fail as its force ebbed against the massive hole torn into the Confederate line. The tone of the communications between generals Meade and Burnside intensified as the morning progressed and each man clearly began to position himself for any formal investigation or explanation that might be required in the wake of the disaster.[9] A subsequent court of inquiry found that one of the causes for the failure of the operation was the inadequate placement of the assaulting troops. The film shows the men lying parallel to their own lines awaiting the explosion of the mine and the order to move forward. Instead, the court findings note, "The troops should have been formed in the open ground in front of the point of attack parallel to the line of the enemy's works."[10] Testimony alluded to the inability of some of the troops to move forward as the attacking columns jammed into narrow covered ways.[11] Of course, given the proximity of the opposing lines and the knowledge of the Confederates that the Federals were constructing tunnels, deployment of troops in the open would have indicated to the Confederates that an attack was imminent and generally where it might be expected to occur.

The attack was supposed to allow the Union soldiers to go around the rim of the crater, exploit the gap they had created with the blast, and break through the Confederate lines.[12] The film accurately reflects the miscalculation of the assaulting troops, many of whom instead plunged directly into the gaping hole. The failure of these men to carry scaling ladders and the suddenness with which the Confederates recovered kept many of the men pinned down, with no real possibility of advance, particularly as reinforcements under Confederate general William Mahone reached the site. Among the men who helped to plug the gap were members of the Twenty-Fifth North Carolina Infantry.[13] Included in their number was Private William P. Inman, listed as present "until hospitalized at Petersburg, Virginia, August 21, 1864, with a gunshot wound to the neck." The report added that this Inman "Deserted from [the] hospital at Raleigh on or about November 2, 1864" and ultimately went "over to the enemy," a considerably different decision than Jude Law's character makes on the screen in *Cold Mountain*.[14]

The fighting turned especially vicious as the slopes of the crater turned slippery with blood and gore. Light field artillery and Coehorn mortars coupled with Confederate musket fire to cover the area over which the Union troops had advanced, making reinforcement or return extremely hazardous, if not virtually impossible. By 9:30, nearly everyone on the Northern side had come to recognize that the assault had failed. Meade instructed Burnside to withdraw his men from their exposed position to the safety of their own lines and reiterated the order fifteen minutes later.[15] When the fighting ceased, the Confederates had inflicted 3,828 casualties and brought the Union plan to shorten the war dramatically to naught.[16] General Ulysses Grant referred to the debacle as, "the miserable failure of Saturday."[17] To Army Chief of Staff Henry Halleck, he termed the fighting at the Crater, "the saddest affair I have witnessed in the war."[18] Well after the war, in his *Memoirs*, the former Union general observed bluntly, "The effort was a stupendous failure."[19]

Apart from the battlefield scenes, *Cold Mountain* falls into the *Gone with the Wind* mode by showing slaves working in cotton fields, when the subsistence farming of the upcountry would not likely have featured this particular cash crop. Aside from this yielding to stereotypical temptation, the film makes numerous references to historical elements. When the home guard announces that deserters will be hunted down, they note that they are doing so under the authority of North Carolina governor Zebulon Vance, the state's chief executive from 1862 to 1865.

The film does shed a popular light on the notion that people on the home front felt for protecting themselves and their property. Interestingly, given the significance of the two female leads in the motion picture, at least one Georgia community depended on the women who remained at home for its defense. In the process, as one of the members of the self-styled "Bascom Home Guards" explained to a friend, the effort proved transformative and empowering. "We have formed a Female Company in Bascom for the purpose of learning to shoot so that if all of the men go to war we can protect our homes and selves," Bess Bell wrote from Bascom, Georgia, on May 10, 1861, "We have only 9 in the Company and we drill every Wednesday and Saturday evenings," she added to her friend Kate Enecks. A couple of the members of the unit were married women, but for each of them the experience was life changing. "You know how nervous and timid Mollie was," she explained by way of one example, "well now she can load a gun and fire and hit a spot at a good distance." What was more, Bess observed triumphantly in a way that would have made Ruby Thewes proud, "We are all delighted with the idea of learning to shoot."[20]

One of the most visually disturbing scenes in *Cold Mountain* has a firm foundation in historical fact. As Teague (Ray Winstone) and his band of self-anointed enforcers combs the area for deserters, they target the farm of Sally and Esco Swanger (Kathy Bates and James Gammon). The men surround and kill Esco, and then a sadistic Junior (Giovanni Ribisi) stomps heavily on a rail in which the men have placed Sally's hands. Hearing the screams of their mother, the boys rush out of the barn to confront their family's attackers, only to be gunned down.

The scene is reminiscent of what happened in the case of a North Carolina Unionist and his wife, although the torture occurred in that instance because the assailants thought she was hiding her husband from them. To get Cornelia Henry to tell them where her husband could be found, the men "dragged her out of her house, placed her fingers between two fence rails, and walked along the top one." When those tactics failed, in no small measure because her husband was not actually at home, the men turned on the son by threatening and finally killing his dog before they tired of the whole sordid activity."[21]

Certainly *Cold Mountain* conveys the sense that some communities must have felt when those designated to provide protection became as dangerous, if not more so, than any outside intruders. In hamlets and villages throughout the Appalachian mountain regions in particular, people quickly learned that, as one author puts it, there was "war at every door."[22] Indeed, various authors have noted the proliferation of "home guard" units of both unionist and secessionist derivations as local residents sought to steel themselves against the depredations of "bushwhackers," "outliers," and "deserters."[23] One observer captured the ambiguities of life in the backcountry for so many: "These mountain soldiers were mostly of two classes, both opposed to the war, but doing home-guard duty in lieu of sterner service in the field. Numbers were of the outlier class, who wearied of continual hiding in the laurel brakes, had embraced this service as a compromise."[24]

Indeed, the well-acted but dramatically dismal 1971 film, *No Drums, No Bugles*, starring Martin Sheen, may have depicted one element of the "outlier class" best, in telling the story of a man who spent the bulk of the war living in a cave rather than allow himself to be caught up in a conflict he disdained. Ashley Gatrell (Sheen) sacrifices all, including very nearly his humanity, to escape the war.

The negative effects of the war come across for many characters throughout Civil War cinema. Some of these eventually reconcile themselves to elements of their own personalities that allow them to put the conflict behind them. In John Ford's *The Searchers* (1956), Ethan Edwards (John Wayne) is an ex-Confederate who becomes as obsessed with locating his kidnapped niece Debbie (Natalie Wood) as he is filled with hatred for Indians and bitter about the outcome of the war. The sense of the hostility simmering just beneath the surface appears only in small but powerful glimpses such as when a Texas ranger and preacher (Ward Bond) tries to swear him to an oath and Edwards asserts, "a man's only good for one oath at a time. I took mine to the Confederate States of America." Ultimately, the tortured veteran will locate his niece, now assimilated into the Indian world he despises, but he cannot bring himself to harm her and shoves aside his own bigotry to embrace her instead.

In much the same way, the Reconstruction drama *Sommersby* (1993) demonstrates that even under the worst of conditions, the war can impact lives in a positive manner, as Jack Sommersby (Richard Gere) illustrates when he returns from the conflict a better man than when he left to fight in it. Whether he is an imposter who has assumed another man's identity to obtain a new start in life is less relevant than the goodness and tenderness he now expresses, particularly toward his long-suffering wife, Laurel (Jodie Foster), as well as his neighbors.

There is an additional way in which several of these motion pictures, as well as others, represent the most personal elements of war. In *The Beguiled*, Corporal McBurny suffers wounds and endures amputation. *Cold Mountain* takes Inman through the ordeal of wartime hospitals before he recovers sufficiently to begin his trek for home. In *Dances with Wolves* (1990), Kevin Costner's Major John Dunbar nearly loses his leg before leaving a field hospital to attempt to commit suicide by riding his horse across the face of the opposing lines, only to find himself a Union hero for inspiring the troops. In *Wicked Spring* (2002), two Federal soldiers caught up in the carnage of the Wilderness attempt to nurse a wounded comrade while fraternizing with several of their Confederate counterparts. The specter of terrible wounds and amputations appears frequently in films, ranging from *Gone with the Wind* and its powerful scenes in Atlanta to the fields of *Gettysburg* and the ordeal of Stonewall Jackson in *Gods and Generals*. Nothing seems to grip the audience quite like the physical impact of combat on those who engage in it.

In each of these instances, the American Civil War as presented on film is an intensely personal experience for those individuals who find their lives swept up by it. This fact certainly mirrors the reality that the people those characters represented experienced in their own lives. Some were soldiers who chose to put themselves into harm's way; many were conscripts or civilians who could not exercise such a choice. For the men in arms, the price was at least quantifiable. The number of Federals killed or mortally wounded exceeded 110,000, and the number of Confederates surely approached that total.[25] Many more on both sides perished of disease or exposure. The ultimate butcher's bill reached at least 620,000 Americans.[26] The number becomes even more staggering when incorporating the individuals who endured physical and psychological wounds from the conflict. That so many could endure so much staggers the imagination and ensures that those who lived through this great conflagration can be measured among the greatest of any generation. Furthermore, the compelling nature of these personal sagas and the sacrifices they represent suggest that such stories will continue to find a place in Civil War cinema.

A War without Boundaries

PAGE 4 TOP: (Left to right) JONATHAN RHYS MEYERS and JIM CAVIEZEL star in the Ang Lee film RIDE WITH THE DEVIL, a Universal Pictures presentation and a USA Films release.
BOTTOM: (Left to right) SKEET ULRICH, SIMON BAKER and TOBEY MAGUIRE star in the Ang Lee film RIDE WITH THE DEVIL, a Universal Pictures presentation and a USA Films release.
Photos: John Clifford

UNIVERSAL

USA FILMS

© 1999 Universal Studios, Inc. All rights reserved.

The young cast of *Ride with the Devil* included (bottom, l. to r.) Skeet Ulrich, Simon Baker, and Tobey Maguire in a gripping screen depiction of the war on the Kansas–Missouri border.

There is no border. Not anymore. Not anywhere.

—Major Charles Wolcott, *A Time for Killing*

For those who struggled along the border, the paths of glory petered out.

—author Alvin Josephy

I N THE 1967 FILM *A Time for Killing*, Union Major Charles Wolcott (Glenn Ford) has finally reached his breaking point in his dogged pursuit of Captain Dorritt Bentley (George Hamilton) and his band of escaped Confederate prisoners of war when he and his men corner the Southerners in a church just across the Mexican border. Wolcott's sergeant advises him that they have crossed the international border, but the officer's obsession for vengeance has taken him over. "There is no border," he snarls at the sergeant. "Not anymore. Not anywhere."

Such a conclusion might have proved true for a wide range of individuals, male and female, Unionist and secessionist, soldier and civilian, had it been possible to poll sentiment in the American Civil War. This was particularly the case in areas where boundaries quickly became blurred along the Kentucky/Tennessee/Virginia lines or the long-heated border regions of Missouri and Kansas. With the inauguration of the conflict and the haste with which Union forces overran other portions of the South, additional areas fell into a no-man's land marked by harassment and bushwhacking, assassination and depredation. Out of these regions came some of the Civil War's most notorious killers and outlaws: Champ Ferguson, William "Bloody Bill" Anderson, Frank and Jesse James, and others on both sides of the war. A few of these tried to cloak their activities in military necessity, if not legitimacy; others simply seemed to enjoy killing, robbing, and terrorizing their victims.[1]

However, in terms of the cinema, one man has risen above all others in his appearances on the big screen as epitomizing the war on the border. William Clarke Quantrill, a guerrilla, partisan, or bushwhacker, associated with the Southern, Confederate, or proslavery cause in the Trans-Mississippi Theater has been the subject of numerous Civil War films. Some of these treat the brutal border warfare in Missouri and Kansas, and Quantrill's role in it, more generally; others veil the historical players with a thin veneer of fictionalized names and place references. In either case, the character of the one-time teacher and his bloodthirsty band of followers have drawn moviemakers and audiences alike by suggesting the Civil War in microcosm.

The effort to capture William Quantrill's war on celluloid has taken many forms. *Dark Command* (1940) stars Walter Pidgeon as a Confederate guerrilla chieftain named William Cantrell. Jack Palance plays the role of a Quantrill-like character in *The Desperados* (1969). *Kansas Raiders* (1950) brings Jesse James

(Audie Murphy) to Quantrill's side. *Red Mountain* (1951) casts John Ireland as "Quantrell." *Quantrill's Raiders* (1958) puts Leo Gordon in the guerrilla leader's role.

Other films that touch upon the subject include a little-known film entitled *Woman They Almost Lynched* (1953), which centers on the sacking of Lawrence. In *The Tall Men* (1955), Clark Gable is a former soldier who fought in the war, as he puts it, in a "left-handed way," as one of Quantrill's men.[2] In 1965, history takes a back seat when *Arizona Raiders* has Audie Murphy's good guys battle Quantrill's bad guys in a state to which the Confederate raiders never actually ventured.

Not all of the figures on the fringes of the war are directly associated with Quantrill. *Belle Starr* (1941) features Gene Tierney as the fiery Southern belle in Missouri who cannot accept the verdict of the war and the defeat of the South. Some of the men riding with her and husband Sam "was with Quantrill," but her war is an intensely personal one.

Likewise, Josey Wales (Clint Eastwood) is an embittered outcast from the war in *The Outlaw Josey Wales* (1976), forced into the conflict by the killing of his family and the destruction of his farm, then compelled to continue the fight when Unionists slaughter the members of his command in a rigged surrender ceremony.

Most recently, *Ride with the Devil* (1999) attempts a sympathetic update of the young men and women caught in the fighting in Kansas. Utilizing fresh faces to draw a young audience, the film features actors Skeet Ulrich and Tobey Maguire as well as pop music artist Jewel.

Thus a number of these Quantrill/Kansas-and-Missouri films—*Dark Command, Red Mountain, Belle Starr, The Outlaw Josey Wales,* and *Ride with the Devil*—provide suitable contrasts for the ways in which the movies have handled this controversial subject matter.

Dark Command contains a disclaimer: "Some portions of this photoplay are based upon actual incidents in the lives of the principal characters. All other events and characters are fictitious and any similarity to actual events or persons is coincidental." Even so, there is no question of the historical inspiration for the story. An opening scroll establishes the context for the film: "In those years, 1859 and on, in the dusk before the nation plunged into the red night of civil warfare, the plains of Kansas were an earlier battleground. Down from the north, down to Kansas: up from the south, up to Kansas, came hordes—each bent on voting the territory into the Union as its own. The battle cry of the day was—'On to Kansas.'"

Signs establish the divisive facts visually: "Georgia Emigration League," "Kansas Belongs to the South" for one side, and "Boston Emigration League," "Kansas for the North" for the other. Speakers harangue for their respective causes: "The South needs your vote" and "We want to people Kansas with good, hard-working Northern farmers."

Lawrence, Kansas, becomes the focal point of these opposing camps. Will Cantrell (Walter Pidgeon) is the local school teacher. Bob Seaton (John Wayne) is a recent arrival who has decided to settle down in the community. They vie with each other to become marshal, and Cantrell vows that if he is beaten "by that cowhand I'm through with books and teaching." When Seaton wins, Cantrell becomes embittered. "I'm sick of doing what's right." He had been teaching Seaton to read and cannot understand why the people would select a man of such limited education over him for the office. "I can write my name," Cantrell burns with a growing fury, "and I'm going to write it across this territory in letters of fire and blood if I have to. I'm going to be somebody in this country, somebody big." His ambition is now fueled with an intense desire for revenge at the rejection by the voters. "I'll be running Kansas yet. I'm going clear up to the top, but I'm not going for the climb or the view."

Cantrell raids slave owners under the guise of abolitionism, but then sells the slaves himself across the border in Missouri. Ironically, it is in this context that Cantrell refers to the abolitionist John Brown, and then only to suggest that his fate has made this avocation too hazardous for him to undertake. Seeking a safer scheme, Cantrell graduates to gunrunning. Finally, the opportunity for establishing himself comes on a grander scale as the bleeding in Kansas threatens to engulf the entire nation. "Looks like this fellow Lincoln's liable to win with the Democrats dividing up between Douglas and Breckinridge," one man predicts.

Events begin to favor Cantrell in his rise. When hotheaded Southerner Fletcher McCloud (Roy Rogers) shoots a man for disparaging the South, Cantrell uses his terrorist tactics to ensure that the jury will not find him guilty. The acquittal wins Cantrell the affections of Fletch's sister Mary (Claire Trevor), but it is the announcement, "The South has seceded from the Union and war has begun," that offers Cantrell the greatest chance for advancement.

The film audience learns that Kansas will be a battleground in this conflict. "While armies drew their battle lines in the east, like a swarm of locusts over Kansas came hordes of Guerrillas, loyal to no flag . . . following but one line—the promise of pillage. In Kansas these men found an empire to loot . . . and few to defend it." Chief among them is Will Cantrell, who tells his men that the war will be a long one and promises to reward their loyalty to him. "You're not fighting for the North and you're not fighting for the South," he explains to them. Cantrell robs, burns, and loots his way through Kansas, without regard for politics. "Guerrillas Pillage and Loot Southern Border Towns," one headline screams, while another asserts, "Southern Raiders Looting and Burning Northern Towns." Then the outlaws capture a Confederate supply train and obtain uniforms. Cantrell sees the opportunity and seizes it. Rather than burn the clothes, he has his men appropriate them for their use. "From now on we'll be Confederate soldiers."

Cloaked in the veneer of legitimacy, Cantrell convinces Mary to marry him. But he has not forsaken his path and leaves the wedding hurriedly to set an ambush for Seaton and the local militia. In the meantime, Cantrell writes letters to his wife asking that she not believe the untrue things being written and said about him. She has her doubts, but when compelled to leave town she goes to Cantrell with Seaton's assistance. Mary quickly realizes that war has transformed her husband. "It took a grubbing schoolteacher and made a major out of him and gave him all this," he retorts. Cantrell interviews Seaton, assuring him in front of Mary that he is a "guest" who will receive "every courtesy," although he clearly has no intention of letting his "guest" leave the encampment alive.

By this point, Mary has seen enough to convince her that what she has heard is true—Cantrell is using the war to accumulate wealth for himself. She and Seaton escape, with help from Fletch, who has also discovered Cantrell's darker side. Cantrell and his men follow, finally launching a raid on Lawrence. Yet this is not the type of surprise assault on a largely defenseless community that made William Quantrill infamous. Seaton has the town ready to defend itself, and although the raiders succeed in burning the larger portion of it, they suffer heavy losses. Before it is over, Cantrell dies in a gun battle with Seaton.

A similar attempt to win the war on the border attributed to Quantrill and his men is the basis for *Red Mountain*. "1865. In the South the Confederacy lay dying of the wounds Sherman slashed in the Valley of the Shenandoah. Northern armies pressed toward the inevitable victory. . . . But in the vast no-man's land of the West, fate still hung in the balance. There a last incredibly daring dream of Southern victory was attempted in the Battle of Red Mountain, by General Quantrell, Confederate hero, fanatical soldier and master of guerilla warfare."

As in many Civil War films, facts inserted in the dialogue to produce authenticity actually strain the intended historical veracity. For instance, when a Northern sympathetic woman confronts Brett Sherwood (Alan Ladd) the statements are a historical hodgepodge. "That's the way war is ma'am. My home was Columbia. Saw it after the Federals got through with it. A town a burned out shell, not a building standing. It was after they had destroyed Atlanta. If anyone wants peace," he adds emphatically, "they should listen to General Sherman's boast, 'If a crow should fly over the Shenandoah Valley it would have to carry its own rations.'" Philip Sheridan might have been amused to know that his actions in the Shenandoah Valley would be attributed to William T. Sherman. But then Sherman was the man movie audiences expected to say such words and commit such dire acts in the name of Union victory. Of course, all of this came from "a Captain on Pickett's staff," detached from the Third Georgia Cavalry, now serving the Confederate cause beyond the Mississippi River.

Adding to the historical free-for-all, *Red Mountain* places William Quantrill in the West as the war winds to a close. "You're supposed to be in Kansas general," Captain Sherwood understandably notes. Quantrill plans to continue his war in the West, even as it is ending in the East. "When I took my commission, sir, I didn't know my loyalties changed with the fortunes of war," he explains self-righteously. But the soldier and former school teacher is actually a ruthless bushwhacker, and not a man who Captain Sherwood can support or defend. "The South is dead," Sherwood explains, "I'm not going to help a vulture like Quantrill feed on its corpse." Thus, with his course chosen, Sherwood confronts and kills Quantrill. "The war is over. Brett, Lee surrendered at Appomattox." "Lee surrendered?" "Two days ago. We're one country again, Brett. All the bitterness will pass." To which the wounded man answered simply, "'A house divided against itself cannot stand.' Your president said that. Our president."

Yet William Quantrill, or some other screen incarnation of him, is not the only notorious figure Hollywood filmmakers found appealing. *Belle Starr* is the typical production of the period. Featuring Gene Tierney in the title role, the film reflects the stereotypical attitudes film audiences of the time would expect. The black figures are stock characters, as reflected in their demeanor. "Miss Belle ain't never going to die," an elderly man tells his granddaughter as they survey the wreckage of the plantation that once belonged to her, "'cause round here in old Missouri Miss Belle is what the white folks call a legend."

In the midst of war and the absence of able-bodied men, Belle and Mammy Lou run the plantation. Belle illustrates her gumption by getting the better of a horse trade, buying the animal for $500 Confederate, which is quite sufficient for a horse that she tells the man has been stolen anyway. "I don't want no Confederate money," the trader calls out, "I got a whole trunk load of that stuff. You know it ain't worth two cents on the dollar." But Belle ignores him and dashes off on her new acquisition.

As she rides along, Belle meets her brother Edward coming home. "The war's over," he tells her. "We're licked. Lee surrendered." "But he couldn't," she gasps. "Joe Johnston surrendered, too," he adds. "Even old Bedford Forrest." But Belle cannot accept the news. "Alright, supposing they have," she retorts. "They're not the whole South. Missouri hasn't surrendered." Her brother is resigned to the outcome, but she remains adamant. "It hasn't ended for me."

In the Missouri that emerges following the close of the conventional war, much has changed. A speaker cradling a carpetbag under his arm harangues a mob, largely composed of former slaves, with the promise to "run every one of these Confederate traitors out of the country." Another man stops in a carriage to enjoy the scene of dancing and frivolity that fills the streets, patting his carpetbag with evident satisfaction. Belle and Edward sift their way through the throngs, considerably less pleased with the changes the war has wrought in the carefully constructed social order they once enjoyed.

When Edward meets a prewar acquaintance, Major Thomas Grail (Dana Andrews), he learns that the Union officer is on the trail of an ex-Confederate desperado named Sam Starr (Randolph Scott). Belle seems as determined as ever to resist the outcome of the war. "Belle is one of those Southerners who are neither resigned nor repentant," Edward explains to Grail. She has also become intrigued with what she has heard about Sam Starr, particularly when the Southerner rides some forty miles to meet her and confront the Union commander. As the evening unfolds, Grail hopes to capture the rebel, but finds himself Starr's prisoner instead. Only the timely arrival of Union cavalry, spurred by the trader who sighted the Southerners when he came to steal his horse back, allows the Federal officer to escape. With the tables turned, Captain Starr and his band scatter; he suffers a wound in the process, and a subordinate brings him back to the plantation house to have his wound treated.

When the Union patrol returns, Major Grail finds evidence of Starr's presence on the property. Despite denials from Belle and Edward, Starr emerges and tries to deflect blame from them while giving himself up. The gesture proves futile when the Union major orders Edward arrested and the house burned for harboring a criminal. Belle is inconsolable as soldiers and the horse trader set torches to curtains and furniture, her hostility toward the Federals and their sympathizers intensified.

She rides to Starr's camp, sealing her fate by connecting it to him. The Southerners contrive to break their leader and Belle's brother from jail, and she convinces Starr to let her join his band. The raiding continues, Sam and Belle collaborating in running the carpetbaggers out of the region and harassing Union targets. Posted rewards illustrate the success the band of raiders is having, although that success becomes a magnet for unsavory elements who ride to join Starr's forces. Among these are the "Cole brothers," who supposedly have ridden with Quantrill and are clearly meant to represent the historical Confederate guerrillas and outlaws Cole and Jim Younger.

Belle protests that such men as these are not fighting for the same legitimate reasons that motivate Sam and herself. "Sam's fighting for the South," she explains at one point, "and everything it stands for." Despite her misgivings, Belle agrees to marry Sam, but as the situation deteriorates for them, they decide to conduct only one more raid before heading to Texas. Unfortunately for Sam and his men, the last ride will be into an ambush unless they can be warned in time. Belle learns of the trap and tries to give the warning when the same man who tried to sell her a stolen horse, waiting along the road, shoots her from her horse. Even sympathetic townspeople ostracize him for the murder, but it convinces Sam that the fight is over. He comes into town to surrender himself and goes to see the body. He and Mammy Lou refuse to identify the corpse for the Federals, with the acquiescence of Major Grail, denying the killer of his reward, but the days of resisting the outcome of the war, even for such diehards, are over.

The historical liberties in *Belle Starr* come fast and furious. Biographer Glenn Shirley dispels a number of the Belle Starr myths in his 1982 study of her life and times. The "bandit queen" of his pages bears little resemblance to the screen portrayal of Gene Tierney. Shirley's examination reveals that the depiction on the big screen suffers from a number of other notable historical digressions as well.

Unlike her brother Edward in the motion picture, Belle's brother Bud did not survive the war to reconcile with his enemies, but died at their hands during it. Her other brother, Edwin, died in Texas either in a wild shootout or, more consistently with the film, from ambush while riding his horse. Similarly, Myra Maybelle Shirley did not marry Sam Starr first, but a guerrilla fighter known as James C. Reed. It was not until 1880 that Belle Reed would become Belle Starr, marrying the dark-haired fellow some twelve years her junior in the Indian territory of Cherokee Nation. Her own death would come as a result of an ambush as in the motion picture, but in 1889, and Starr would not be present to identify her corpse, having perished himself in a gunfight three years earlier.[3]

Biographer Glenn Shirley notes that another war, World War II, caught up with the 20th Century–Fox version of the Missouri "bandit queen," limiting its box office appeal.[4] But *Belle Starr* has become established as one of the popular interpretations of the war without boundaries that the Civil War represented.

The Outlaw Josey Wales provides another variation on the same theme. In the 1976 motion picture, Josey Wales (Clint Eastwood) is a family man with a farm to tend when war arrives at his doorstep. Kansas Jayhawkers attack and burn his homestead, kill his wife and son (played by Eastwood's son Kyle, as David Ladd played his real-life father's son in *The Proud Rebel*). The Jayhawkers leave the homesteader for dead, bearing the scars of their sabers and vowing to seek revenge as a way of assuaging his loss as he sifts through the wreckage and buries his dead.[5]

A resurrected Wales joins Confederate guerrillas as he seeks vengeance for the murders of his loved ones. As the war reaches its conventional conclusion, his compatriots reluctantly agree to surrender to the Federal authorities. But the Federals use the opportunity to turn the surrender into a trap and slaughter most of the Confederates. Only Wales and a young comrade succeed in escaping. The hunt for the outlaws begins.

Perhaps the most entertaining element of the film comes at a river crossing. Josey and his companion have the Federals in hot pursuit. He induces the ferryman to carry them across the river, but then rests calmly as the Union troops arrive. The ferryman demonstrates a willingness to support the cause of whomever he fears the most at the moment, singing "Dixie" and the "Battle Hymn of the Republic" with equal vigor.

The blue-coated pursuers board the conveyance and start across the river. Only Captain Fletcher (John Vernon), the ex-Confederate who earlier betrayed his men to curry Union favor, seems to be aware that Wales has a plan for them. His Union counterpart is willing to sacrifice a few of his men if the Southerner tries to pick them off and gloats that Wales cannot possibly get them all before they can get him.

But Wales has no intention of trying to shoot the men, however vulnerable they might be on the open flatboat. He has noticed that the craft depends upon a rope extended from one bank to the next to cross against the swift current. Josey lets the loaded ferry reach the middle of the stream before introducing the occupants to "the Missouri Boat Ride" by shooting the rope that tethers the ferry. Men and horses frantically begin to plunge into the water as the boat floats out of their control down the river, the threat of pursuit dispelled for the time being.

Wales will have to confront his antagonists again, but he exacts his revenge upon the "Red Leg" leader by killing him with his own sword.[6] The Confederate also confronts his old commander, who betrayed him and the other guerrillas at the surrender, but the antagonists make a peace of a sort among themselves, and the blood feud between them ends.

One of the best film depictions of the war on the borderland of the upper Trans-Mississippi region is *Ride with the Devil*. Ang Lee's film is a modern version of the unconventional warfare that marked the fighting there. Vicious combat scenes contrast with scenic landscapes in a vehicle that showcases a host of performers at the early stages of their careers. Their youth is a stark reminder that the individuals who battled in the 1860s on the border of Missouri and Kansas were often quite young themselves.

The movie opens with an overview of the volatile situation in the region to establish context for the viewer: "On the western frontier of Missouri, the American Civil War was fought not by armies but by neighbors. Informal groups of local Southern bushwhackers fought a bloody and desperate guerrilla war against the occupying Union army and pro-Union Jayhawkers. Allegiance to either side was dangerous, but it was more dangerous still to find oneself caught in the middle."

The scene is a wedding where there are immediate references to current political events. "It will soon be war between us and the Yankee aggressors with that Black Republican Abe Lincoln in the White House," one fellow explains to one of the guests. "Missouri is no longer safe from the depredations of Jennison and his Kansas Jayhawkers," he observes. "Lawrence, Kansas, and its abolitionists are a long way from here," the other man replies. But the first will not be ameliorated. "There are Union men even here among us."

The main character, Jake "Dutchy" Roedel (Tobey Maguire), is German-born and thus under some initial suspicion from the proslavery, Southern faction. His father insists that he go to St. Louis, where he can be safe among the large number of German settlers there. "I'm not going to huddle with all the Lincoln-loving Germans in St. Louis," he insists. "I was reared here. These are my people." His father attempts to explain that he is likely to be disappointed by these friends. But when Kansas raiders attack the home of Jake's friend, Jack Bull Chiles (Skeet Ulrich), killing Chiles's father in the process, Roedel's mind becomes set. He joins with the men who will fight in the cause of the South.

A year later, Jake has hardened into a guerrilla fighter, sporting long locks of hair that he has vowed not to cut until the war is over. He is part of a squad, dressed in Union uniforms, who ride up to a country store. A small Federal detachment is availing themselves of goods, "Rooting out Rebels and conscripting chickens," as one of them explains. A sharp gunfight erupts as the Southern guerrillas shoot the genuine Union troopers and the storekeeper who has done business with them.

Roedel sends a letter to the Chiles household explaining that the men who committed the depredations against them have been killed. He admits that they have used unconventional methods, but concludes, "Where we find true Missouri men we make our own army." These "true" men include at least one African American, a man named Daniel Holt (Jeffrey Wright). When Jake meets him for the first time, one of their companions describes Holt as a "damn fine scout. When George tosses him a gun, a good Yankee-killer, too." Roedel is unimpressed. "A nigger with a gun is a nervous thing to me." But he will soon have plenty of opportunities to reassess the man he has so easily dismissed and will develop a genuine friendship and affection for him.

Because of his German heritage, some of the Southerners still doubt Roedel's fidelity to the cause, but Jack Bull observes without hesitation that his friend is "Southern to the core." The men will soon find that loyalty tested when the house they seek refuge in comes under attack. In an example of the worst nightmare for guerrilla fighters, they have been pinned down by a force of undetermined size and with ample firepower. They decide to make a dash for safety, which some succeed in doing while others fail, and their numbers are whittled down.

In camp, the Southerners hold three Union soldiers. The commander decides to offer an exchange of these men for two of his who the Federals are threatening to hang. Roedel notices that one of the men is a friend, Alf Bowden (Mark Ruffalo). He suggests that one of the Union troopers be used to send the message and offers the chance to Bowden. Word later reaches him that instead of delivering the message as he has promised, Alf has gone to Roedel's home and murdered his father out of retribution. Such are the uncertainties in this borderless war, where a staunch Unionist dies at the hands of a Federal soldier who has been a friend of his son's.

The guerrillas disperse for the winter, seeking safe haven with sympathetic citizens who will feed and hide them. During a quiet period, the local resident who has been helping the boys invites them to the house. He has lost his own son in the war, and in the course of the conversation asks, "Have you ever been to Lawrence?" He offers that he has and has seen the reason they will lose. It is the schoolhouse in the town that represents opportunities for advancement for all.

Jack Bull replies, "Are you saying sir that we fight for nothing?"

The man resignedly answers, "Far from it Mr. Childs. You fight for everything that we ever had, as did my son. It's just we don't have it anymore."

The peace is only temporary. Union raiders hit the farm and kill the man who has befriended them. In the ensuing firefight, Jack Bull is wounded. With the help of a local young woman, Sue Lee Evans (Jewel), Dutchy tries to nurse his friend back to health. Infection sets in with its consequent fever and Dutchy has to amputate the damaged arm. Jack Bull dies from the effects of the makeshift operation.

When the men return to the main guerrilla camp in the spring, George Clyde (Simon Baker) greets them with an ominous, "Welcome back to Hell, boys." But the situation has changed. There is a great energy in the air, for the guerrilla leader, Black John (Jim Caviezel), has called for assistance from William Clarke Quantrill.

Quantrill has big plans, which he slowly reveals as he addresses the assemblage of irregulars:

> My boys: Today I'm a sad man. I am sad because I mourn for our sisters and mothers who slept in that Kansas City jail, who slept until the walls fell down around them and they died.
>
> I am sad boys, and I am tired. The best of us are dead. And now we're just dogs chased into the woods.
>
> I am sad boys, but I am vengeful. And I shall not sleep. I shall not sleep again until I . . . look down upon the abolitionists of Lawrence.

In the background are cries of, "Yeah, kill those thieving Jayhawkers. Kill those redlegs."

Quantrill: "I shall ride through Kansas to get those boys and meet any Yankee army put in my way because I will fight them myself if I have to. But I shall reach Lawrence. That's right, I will. Fight them all myself unless there be any man among you who would ride with me. So I'm asking: Are there any men here who will ride with me?"

The men respond enthusiastically. Quantrill: "Then, Hell boys, ride with me to Lawrence. Let's ride to Lawrence."

The guerrillas set their sights on Kansas, picking up reinforcements along the way. They reach the town of Lawrence and begin the raid by shooting down a man as he milks his cow. The town contains an insignificant number of Union soldiers who the raiders easily overwhelm, shooting many of them as they emerge from their tents startled by the early morning firefight.

What follows is an uncontrolled exhibition of burning, looting, and murder. "They ought not to murder the young ones," a raider mumbles in quiet protest, but the arbitrary shootings continue. Roedel risks his life to save two from slaughter, but news of Union troops riding to intercept them causes the raiders to mount up and leave behind the destruction of Lawrence.

The Federals pursue, forcing Quantrill to engage in several firefights. In one, a disgruntled Southerner, Pitt Mackeson (Jonathan Rhys Myers), taking the opportunity in the chaos, shoots at Dutchy. Holt sees and turns to fire at Pitt, but takes a round in the side. As George races toward him, he is hit in the throat and killed. The fight, like the unit of guerrillas, is disintegrating. Dutchy and Holt escape, but the news from the war continues to be dismal. "They're all busted up," a rider tells them. "Quantrill?" "Headed to Kentucky." "Anderson?" "Dead, I've heard tell."

Roedel and Holt spend the time recovering physically and psychologically from their recent experiences in combat. "You know, Holt, I probably got one more fight left in me," Dutchy tells his friend, referring to the confrontation he plans to have with Pitt. When he asks Holt what he plans to do, the black man replies, "What cause you think I got, Roedel?" He had "stood with George Clyde" but now, for George and Jack Bull, the circumstances were different. "They're both good and dead now Roedel. Just as dead as they can be. Where does that leave you and me? Where does that leave me?"

Finally Holt manages to put into words what he felt with the death of the man who had bought him, only to set him free, and with whom he had become friends. "That day George Clyde died, it changed me. I felt something that day I ain't never felt." But, this was not because of the sadness of the loss as Roedel surmised, but because, "I felt I was 'free.'"

Roedel cuts his hair, recalling that he said he would not do it until the war was over. Holt reminds him that for them, it is. Roedel marries Sue Lee and accepts Jack Bull's baby as his own, finally free of the bitterness of the border warfare that has characterized so much of his young life. In a final opportunity to confront Pitt, he lets go of the need for revenge. The film ends as the two friends and former Southern guerrillas, German-born Jacob Roedel and African American Daniel Holt, part and go their own ways.

The real William Clarke Quantrill was born in Ohio on July 31, 1837, the oldest of twelve children. He taught school in Ohio, Illinois, and Indiana before venturing west to Kansas. Quantrill quickly learned that farming did not suit his personality. Just as quickly, he found himself expelled from the community into which he had settled in Kansas as a thief.

With this taint upon his reputation, Quantrill joined a band heading to Pike's Peak for gold. Whatever redemption he sought from the adventure, nature and the circumstances of the journey taught him the larger importance of survival. Out of the nineteen men who went with him, twelve perished from exposure. Quantrill would return from the aborted treasure hunt, wiser in the ways of survival and endurance and convinced that he lived something of a charmed existence.

By mid-1859, Quantrill was back in Kansas. He ran a small school in Osawatomie for approximately a year. When he gave it up in March 1860, the restless teacher sought entertainment and enrichment through gambling and theft. Ironically, in the process, he became associated with free-soilers who plotted a raid into Missouri to liberate the slaves of at least one wealthy Missouri planter.

As Quantrill rode with five antislavery companions on their mission, he feigned the desire to scout the area to set up the raid. Instead, Quantrill had decided to set up his friends by riding to the farmhouse and informing the occupants that they were about to be hit.

Now the hunted became the hunters. The planter's son called in help from nearby farms and with Quantrill's assistance laid a trap for the unsuspecting free-soilers. With the Missourians lying in wait, Quantrill went back to lure his companions into the ambush. As they approached the house to make their demand, he stepped inside as if to negotiate, but actually allowed the Missourians to spring from their hiding places and rake the Kansans with their fire. One of the Kansans fell dead outright. Two others were wounded, although one managed to escape. One of the Kansans returned for his wounded companion, only to be pursued and slaughtered by the Missourians.

For proslavery Missourians, William Quantrill was a man to be admired. He had thwarted the lawbreakers from Kansas who had descended upon their neighboring state to steal rightful property, as the slaveholders saw it. Quantrill fabricated an elaborate story to seal his newfound reputation. William Clarke Quantrill had become the nemesis of the free-soil people of Kansas.[7]

With the outbreak of the Civil War, Quantrill sided with the Confederate cause and raided Union settlements with impunity. He received a formal commission as a captain in the Confederate States Army, although he remained on the fringes of the law and the usages of war. His most famous, or more correctly infamous, exploit was the August 21, 1863, sack of Lawrence, Kansas. This attack quickly broke down into a binge of looting and pillaging that ended with more than 150 civilians dead.[8]

The Union reaction to this raid was immediate. Kansas Governor Thomas Carney sent word to Secretary of War Edwin M. Stanton on August 22: "Kansas is again invaded; Lawrence burned and plundered."[9] Two days later, he was able to supply more precise information regarding the attack: "Just returned from Lawrence. City in ashes. One-hundred and twenty-eight peaceable citizens now known to be murdered."[10] To Stanton, Governor Carney had been especially measured and temperate in tone. Major General John M. Schofield expressed his wrath in no uncertain terms. "Disaster has again fallen on our State," he began.

> Lawrence is in ashes. Millions [of dollars] of property have been destroyed, and, worse yet, nearly 200 lives of our best citizens have been sacrificed. No fiends in human shape could have acted with more savage barbarity than did Quantrill and his band in their last successful raid. I must hold Missouri responsible for this fearful, fiendish raid. No body of men large as that commanded by Quantrill could have been gathered together without the people residing in Western Missouri knowing everything about it. Such people cannot be considered loyal, and should not be treated as loyal citizens; for while they conceal the movements of the desperadoes like Quantrill and his followers, they are in the worse sense of the word their aiders and abettors, and should be held equally guilty. There is no way of reaching these armed ruffians while the civilian is permitted to cloak him. There can be no peace in Missouri—there will be utter desolation in Kansas—unless both are made to feel promptly the rigor of military law. The peace of both States and the safety of the republic demand alike this resolute course of action.[11]

Prompted by such pressures, the military reaction was also swift and merciless. From his headquarters in St. Louis, General Schofield instructed Brigadier General Thomas Ewing Jr. concerning Quantrill, "Spare no means by which he may be destroyed."[12] On the next day, Schofield sent his subordinate an order that he planned to implement regarding "the notorious Quantrill" and the men who "made a descent upon the town of Lawrence, Kansas, and in the most inhuman manner sacked and burned the town, and murdered in cold blood a large number of loyal and unoffending citizens." Schofield proposed removing disloyal people from the bordering counties to prevent them from assisting the Southerners.[13] Ewing simultaneously issued "General Orders, No. 11," essentially executing the order that his superior had propagated.[14]

To be sure, progress was being made. "No prisoners have been taken," General Ewing assured his commanding officer on the 27th, "and none will be."[15] In the same dispatch, Ewing reported, "Quantrill's men are scattered in their fastnesses throughout the border counties, and are still being hunted by all available troops from all parts of the district. Many of them have abandoned their worn-out horses and gone to the brush afoot."[16]

But Quantrill was not yet finished. The Confederate followed this success with an attack on Union troops at Baxter Springs, Kansas, in which ninety bluecoats fell. Quantrill lost six of his raiders.[17]

The Federals labeled Quantrill and his men "outlaws" for this activity. Soon their efforts to run him down led to his movement out of the territory. In subsequent fighting in Kentucky, Quantrill suffered a fatal wound, abruptly ending the career of the man who had terrorized Unionists in Kansas so effectively.[18]

William Clarke Quantrill's death ended the controversial life and career of a ruthless figure in the Civil War. But the motion picture Quantrill has continued to roam the wide screen in search of his borderland enemies. For an audience that can be unsettled through the labeling as evil of one side or the other in this, our American war, he remains an accessible figure for common reproach, and thus also for reconciliation.

CHAPTER 7

The West's Civil War

MAJOR DUNDEE®

Copyright 1965
COLUMBIA PICTURES, INC.
Printed in U.S.A.

Permission is hereby granted to newspapers and other periodicals to reproduce this photograph for other than advertising or pin-up poster purposes. Must not be sold, leased or given away. Also may not be used to create the appearance of a specially licensed or authorized supplement or publication.

Jaw set with determination, Major Amos Dundee (Charlton Heston) prepares to lead a varied lot of Union troopers, Confederate prisoners, and civilians in an independent operation against marauding Apaches.

The West, in truth, was a very stormy part of the nation during the Civil War.

—historian Alvin Josephy

The "war" of the West was the Civil War.

—author Jay Hyams

CASUAL STUDENTS of the American Civil War might be somewhat confused by the nomenclature of the conflict, and nowhere is this more evident than in the labels applied to the military theaters of operation. The best known of these has been the Eastern Theater, with its battles in Virginia, Maryland, and Pennsylvania and its star-studded cast of generals: Robert E. Lee, "Stonewall" Jackson, and eventually, Ulysses S. Grant. With territory clearly defined by Virginians and the critical battle of Gettysburg as its centerpiece, the East has long held its status as the major theater of the conflict.[1]

However, historians have increasingly observed that the most decisive arena of the war was the Western Theater, located across the Appalachians and bounded on the west by the Mississippi River. This theater also boasted important battles, such as Shiloh, Vicksburg, and Chickamauga, and saw Ulysses S. Grant, William T. Sherman, and George H. Thomas rise to fame. One British observer noted that the East has received "a disproportionate" amount of attention, before concluding, "It was in the west that the decisive blows were struck."[2] With Union armies ranging victorious throughout the West while Robert E. Lee held conditions relatively stable in Virginia, the identification of the West as the most significant theater of military action in the war was certainly logical.[3]

The third theater, in geographic extension from the Atlantic seaboard and in military importance, was the Trans-Mississippi. It lay beyond the great river and included Texas, Arkansas, and Missouri. This theater of operations covered the vast area of the American West and included diverse activities from set piece battles such as Wilson's Creek and Pea Ridge and a major campaign in New Mexico and Arizona, to raids and skirmishes with the Indians in locations as diverse as Minnesota and Colorado.

Alvin Josephy has lamented that the "West" has not received its due, leaving the impression that little of importance occurred there while the inhabitants awaited the outcome of the conflict in more settled regions. "The West, in truth," he argues, "was a very stormy part of the nation during the Civil War, a tumultuous area in constant motion and conflict."[4] Referring also to the Trans-Mississippi, Jay Hyams explains, "The 'war' of the West was the Civil War."[5]

Several cinematic plot lines have emerged related to the Civil War in the "West." These include the extraction of precious metals, attempts to wrest portions of the region from Union control, and operations against Native Americans. A common theme early in Civil War cinema is to have Confederates, or at least Southern sympathizers, attempt to heist Union gold shipments originating in the region.

Such films included *Virginia City* (1940), with Errol Flynn and Randolph Scott, and continued in the 1950s with *The Redhead and the Cowboy* (1950), starring Glenn Ford and Rhonda Fleming; *The Last Outpost* (1951), featuring Ronald Reagan and Bruce Bennett; *Hangman's Knot* (1952), with Randolph Scott and Donna Reed; *The Black Dakotas* (1954), starring Gary Merrill; and *Five Guns West* (1955), with John Lund and Dorothy Malone.

Although screen Confederates usually schemed for Union gold, they could set their sights on other assets as well. Southern sympathizers targeted Western horses in *Springfield Rifle* (1952). In *Rocky Mountain* (1950), agents of the Confederacy hoped to establish control over California in the waning days of the war. Perhaps most creatively, *Stage to Tucson* (1950) speculated that Confederate agents could cripple the Union war effort, or at least disrupt it severely, by seizing stagecoaches and shipping them into the South via Mexico.

For those who might feel uncomfortable with the notion of Americans fighting among themselves, there was the more acceptable prospect of Northerners uniting with Southerners to fight together against a common foe. Native Americans provided the necessary unifying element for these embattled whites, and Hollywood was not shy about portraying them in this light.

The Civil War in the West was an odd mixture of clashes with the Indians, frontier garrison duty, and the occasional skirmish between forces representing the North and the South. Civil War westerns covered all of these bases, often simultaneously. In the 1950s, in particular, Hollywood seemed to appreciate this blend with a series of Civil War westerns such as *Two Flags West* (1950), starring Jeff Chandler and Joseph Cotten; *The Last Outpost* (1951), with Ronald Reagan; *Jack McCall Desperado* (1953), starring George Montgomery; *Escape from Fort Bravo* (1953), with William Holden and John Forsythe; and *Revolt at Fort Laramie* (1957), with John Dehner.

Many of the 1950s films that employed the device of uniting North and South against a common foe featured "Galvanized Yankees."[6] These were Confederates who, rather than remain in Union prisons, chose to take the oath of loyalty to the United States, on the provision that they would serve in the U.S. Army in the West and not against their former comrades. In each case, the history was dubious, but the intent was to bring the sides together despite their differences and mutual suspicions. In the end, even Southerners who were torn by their desires to desert their Northern colleagues and return to their homeland chose to sacrifice those interests and, frequently, their lives to remain.

On occasion, Civil War westerns have served as extensions of the tremendous bloodletting that characterized the battlefields east of the Mississippi, but often in inexplicable and ahistorical ways. For instance, *The Good, the Bad and the Ugly* (1966) features a bloody battle for a key bridge that prevents Clint Eastwood and Eli Wallach from reaching the gold that they are seeking, until they help to destroy it and the armies that are fighting over it mysteriously disappear. Writer Richard Schickel explains that among the factors that complicate the simple goal of securing hidden gold coins are "the chance, megahistorical intrusions of the war."[7] While in *A Time for Killing* (1967), that is all that George Hamilton, Glenn Ford, and Max Baer Jr. seem to have the time or desire to do to each other, even when there is no reason to do so except for revenge and the pure joy of destruction. Finally, and perhaps most absurdly, two films prominently feature machine guns. In *A Reason to Live, A Reason to Die* (1974), alternately and much more appropriately entitled *Massacre at Fort Holman*, Union raiders wipe out an entire Confederate garrison led by the notorious Major Ward (Telly Savalas), mostly by shooting them down with Gatling guns. Confederate guards use machine guns of a different type to hold prisoners in check in *Macho Callahan* (1970). When the prisoners stage a rebellion following the execution of one of their number, many of them fall victim to these weapons.

Regardless of the subject or its historical validity, it never seemed enough that Civil War westerns had the beautiful vistas of the West as a backdrop or the established performers to draw upon. To ensure box office success, movie moguls often turned to the stars of other stages. Casting big names outside of traditional Hollywood circles might offer the opportunity to expand the audience for their films. Thus music legend Elvis Presley tried his hand at acting, as well as singing, in *Love Me Tender* (1956). Michael Landon took the title role of a film based on the Kingston Trio's hit of a tragic figure in *The Legend of Tom Dooley* (1959). Singer Jimmie Rodgers took the lead in the 1961 remake of *The Little Shepherd of Kingdom Come. The Fastest Guitar Alive* (1967) featured singer Roy Orbison. More recently, and much more successfully, the popular singing artist Jewel took a prominent role in *Ride with the Devil* (1999).

Regardless of the type of performers called upon to breathe life into them, author Bruce Chadwick has defined "Hollywood's Civil War western characters" as fitting into several distinct categories: "the embittered reb," "the hard-fighting [and happy] Union veteran," and "the cavalryman."[8] The first two are really as much states of mind as representatives of an occupation. To be sure, Union and Confederate infantrymen (and presumably artillerymen, too) traveled to the West, but the emphasis seems less on what these soldiers did than the attitudes they engendered. The Reb has sought to reject the outcome of the war. "In frustration, and with nowhere else to go," Chadwick explains, "he has sought a new life on the plains, carrying all the old animosities with him." In contrast, the Yankee seeks new opportunities, trying to exhibit harmony and understanding in relation to his former enemies.[9]

But Civil War westerns frequently have included a fourth group—individuals outside of the mainstream—who bring the former antagonists together, usually in the name of their common survival. Indians represent these outsiders in most early westerns. Ronald Reagan and Bruce Bennett are brothers warring on opposite sides in *The Last Outpost* (1951) when the threat of rampaging Apache Indians brings them together to save a town from destruction, reunite the siblings, and rekindle their brotherly affection. In *Major Dundee* (1965), Southerners and Northerners who clearly despise and distrust each other are thrown together to save kidnapped white children from renegade Apaches. In the *Undefeated* (1969), the outsiders are Mexican, while in more recent films such as *Dances with Wolves* (1990), the outsiders are the racist elements of the society the hero is supposed to be defending.

Whatever the device employed to move the story along or give it meaning, some of these Civil War westerns take great pains to suggest that their stories reflect fact as much as fiction. For instance, *Rocky Mountain* uses an opening designed to persuade its audience of its historical validity. A modern car pulls up to a historical roadside marker. "Rocky Mountain Also known as Ghost Mountain 2 miles" it begins. "On March 26, 1865, a detachment of Confederate cavalry crossed the state line into California under secret orders from Gen. Robert E. Lee." These soldiers were to join with Southern agents for the purpose of planting the Confederate flag in the far West.

Captain Lake Barstow (Errol Flynn) provides further narration for the bold scheme as he leads his small troop westward for the rendezvous. "Two thousand miles behind us, Lee was fighting for the life of the Southern Confederacy. We were some of Lee's men," he explains. "He had sent us here, eight of us, in a last desperate effort to save the war." Barstow recognizes the futility of the mission, "but we had to succeed. For we knew now that we were living the last days of our cause, unless we ourselves could turn the tide."

The plan seems not so much to have been to pry California from the Union as to force the Federals to divert vital men and resources to defeat the underground movement. At one point, one Confederate observes, "What if an army had to be brought out West here to stop 'em. That could change the whole course of the war." But nothing is destined to go as planned. The Confederates rescue travelers on a stage under attack from the Indians only to discover that one of the passengers is the fiancée of a Union lieutenant stationed at nearby Fort Churchill. When he comes at the head of a small patrol to locate the stage, the lieutenant and his men become prisoners of war of the Mississippi Mounted Rifles under Barstow.

Another clash with the Indians is inevitable, threatening the already tenuous mission. "General Lee dealt the hand," Barstow notes stoically as he decides to use the detachment to draw the Indians away from the civilians in his custody. "All I can do is play the cards he gave me."

With the Confederate flag aloft, the Southerners turn to charge the Indians in a maneuver that would have made Nathan Bedford Forrest proud. But the command is hopelessly outnumbered, and although the lieutenant escapes and manages to get back to Union lines, the help arrives too late. Barstow and his Confederates have been wiped out.

But even then, the film offers the message of reconciliation that movie audiences must have come to expect. The Union lieutenant arrives amid the carnage and orders a sergeant to take the Southern banner and place it on the mountain as Barstow intended to do. Instead of symbolizing the rebellion, it now becomes a tribute to fallen soldiers who receive a saber salute from their former enemies as "Dixie" plays and the flag waves.

Interestingly, despite the creation of what is billed as a "historical" event, *Rocky Mountain* is credible on some of the other details. In a conversation with the fiancée, Barstow learns that she has suffered a heavy personal price in the war. "I had a brother in it, too," she tells him. "He was killed at the Antietam." "I was there," Barstow answers. "We called that the Battle of Sharpsburg." "You were at the Sunken Road?" she inquires. "We called it Bloody Lane," he replies. The dialogue demonstrates that Northerners and Southerners often had different names for the same engagements and correctly gives the river (Antietam) and the town (Sharpsburg) for the respective sides.

Unlike many of its counterparts, at least one film, *Stage to Tucson*, chooses an unusual premise on which to base its story line. Yet despite the awkward notion of stealing stagecoaches for the Southern cause, the subject of the film has a basis in historical fact. The owner of the line, John Butterfield, depicted as meeting with President-elect Abraham Lincoln in Illinois, was a New Yorker who formed "the first transcontinental state line" in 1858. Later one of the founders of the American Express Company, Butterfield had a Southern route for his stage line forced upon him by President James Buchanan's postmaster general.[10] Thus it is perfectly reasonable that the film's Butterfield, in responding to Lincoln's comment that only Buchanan "can order out Federal troops to protect your stages," asserts, "He's not making a move to save one of the biggest weapons that can be turned against the South if war comes."

For the purposes of the film, Butterfield tells Lincoln that he has lost ten stagecoaches in the previous five weeks. "If fighting breaks out," he notes for effect, "an operating stage line will be worth two divisions of foot soldiers. We must have California's gold to buy guns and food and uniforms. The Butterfield Stages are the only way we can bring that gold East."

To be sure, California's approximately $185 million in gold would prove vital in helping to finance the Union war effort, but it would hardly depend on a commercial stage line, particularly one designed for carrying light cargo, for transportation to the North. Nevertheless, the Butterfield line, with its convoluted route, played a significant role in linking the country together as the conflict settled on a nation dividing. "For three years, 1858 to 1861," a student of the war in the West notes, "John Butterfield's stagecoaches, plying twice monthly between St. Louis and San Francisco, provided the nation with its first transcontinental mail and passenger service."[11]

By one account, the operation grew to include "dozens of stagecoaches, hundreds of employees, and thousands of animals."[12]

Another interesting service of *Stage to Tucson* is that the motion picture offers reasons other than slavery for the conflict itself, a rarity in Civil War westerns. As prosecessionist citizens begin drilling, one of the Southern sympathizers observes, "You think the only slave is from the South? What about the wage slaves in Northern woolen mills and iron foundries? What about the bloodsucking protective tariffs?"

Hostilities open in the East, and Abraham Lincoln, now president, issues the call for seventy-five thousand volunteers to suppress the rebellion. "We're not just working for Butterfield anymore," one of the Unionists asserts, "We're working for the Union." But a "little private war" continues in Tucson. Acting as detective on behalf of the stage line, Grif Holbrook (Gary Cooper) has been working to crack the Southern ring and bring an end to the assaults on the stage line. The secessionists might be "fighting for a cause," but Holbrook figures out and exposes the scheme, ending the Rebel activity. Yet there are no real villains in the drama. As the film ends, Holbrook and his compatriots don Union uniforms to the strains of "Rally Round the Flag, Boys," while the local doctor and Southern espionage chief, Noah Benteen, leads his men off in the opposite direction, wearing his Confederate uniform, to the tune of "Dixie."

In *Springfield Rifle*, the Confederate target is not Northern stage lines or gold, but Union horseflesh. The film opens in Washington at the "War Office." "Our whole spring offensive depends on the strength of our cavalry units and that means horses," General Henry W. Halleck tells a subordinate. "We've known for a long time that the Confederacy has a well-organized spy system, and they know the importance of those horses to us," he continues. But the War Department has failed to respond adequately to the threat. "They won't stand for our men in uniform being secret agents," Halleck explains. "They think spying is beneath the dignity and honor of our fighting men."

However, the Union general-in-chief has reached such a point of desperation that he sanctions a plan to combat the Confederate spy ring. Back at Fort Hedley, Colorado, Major Alexander Kearny (Gary Cooper), Fifth U.S. Cavalry, will allow himself to be dismissed from the service so as to be able to infiltrate the Southern ranks. Kearny is ideal for the charade, being a native Virginian whose loyalties have been suspected previously. "At West Point before the declaration of war he openly sympathized with his home state," a court-martial reveals. "At the outbreak of the war he submitted his resignation from the army giving as his reason his reluctance to fight against the South." Although he rescinded the request, he was transferred to the West when he demonstrated "indecision in the presence of the enemy." Found guilty of "violation of the 52nd Article of War—neglect of duty and cowardice in the face of the enemy. Sacrificing war materiel. Specifically a vitally needed shipment of horses," Kearny is drummed out of the service.

139/56 20th Century-Fox presents "THE UNDEFEATED," produced by Robert L. Jacks and directed by Andrew V. McLaglen in Panavision and DeLuxe Color. Col. James Langdon (left) (ROCK HUDSON) and Col. John Henry Thomas (right) (JOHN WAYNE) have a drink as they watch a wild melee.

Confederate Colonel James Langdon (Rock Hudson) and ex-Union Colonel John Henry Thomas (John Wayne) share a drink as their men begin to fight with each other during a Fourth of July celebration in *The Undefeated*.

Through a series of actions, Kearny wins the confidence of the Southerners and joins their ranks. A South Carolina sergeant (Fess Parker) tells him, "You know sir, I had you in my sights once. I used to ride with Stand Watie. Now, I'm right glad I missed you." Sergeant Randolph is one of a number of uniformed Confederates who works with the horse rustlers to transfer the animals into Southern hands.

Kearny meets secretly with his Union contacts and reports that "about a third of them are Confederate soldiers on assignment for this work." The Union agent knows that the Southerners have an inside contact, but cannot figure out who it is. Kearny determines to eliminate and replace the leader of the civilians so that the agent will have to reveal himself.

When the moment of truth arrives, the double agent proves to be the Union post commander, Colonel Hudson. By using the last two numbers in the price Hudson gives for each lot of horses, the raiders can pinpoint the coordinates on a map and intercept the herds. "Remember when I bought your horses the price never came out round numbers," he tells Kearny. "That was because the last two digits had to indicate the route of the drive. Simple, but effective." He adds, "Lex, I can't tell you how glad I am to have you with us. I wasn't sure of you at the court-martial."

Now, with Kearny supposedly in his confidence, the colonel offers an even more significant prize. "We'll work well together, Lex," he assures. "Oh by the way, there's a shipment coming in. A new kind of rifle. The South could make good use of them. When the time comes I want you to organize a little raid of our supply wagons."

The Southern sympathizing colonel has underestimated his friend and former subordinate. As the final confrontation plays out, Kearny uses the new weapons to rout the Southerners, killing and capturing large numbers of them. When Colonel Hudson makes a break for it, Kearny pursues and captures him as well. General Halleck travels to the distant post to commend the formerly disgraced officer personally. "Major Kearny, you have been returned to duty with the commendation of the commanding general of the Army of the Republic," he begins. "And I'm recommending that you be transferred to head the newly formed Department of Military Intelligence in Washington." But the major's greatest contribution lies elsewhere. "However, the most important accomplishment that came out of this entire operation was your successful demonstration of an experimental weapon. You proved on the field of action its superior effectiveness over our older firearms. As a result, the Springfield rifle has been made standard equipment of the United States Army." Then, in a final reflection of the theme, lest the audience be allowed to forget it, Halleck concludes, "I'm sure it will play a large place in ending this war and bringing peace and unity back to our country."

Unity of a very different sort is the central feature of *Major Dundee*. The film is set in the latter part of the Civil War, in the remote New Mexico Territory. Amos Charles Dundee (Charlton Heston) is the reluctant warden of Confederate prisoners at Fort Benlin. He has been friends before the war with a Southerner now in his custody. Captain Benjamin Tyreen (Richard Harris), along with several of his comrades, is destined for a rendezvous with the hangman for killing a guard. His opportunity for a reprieve, if not redemption, comes when Chiricahua Apaches raid an isolated ranch, killing a detachment of soldiers and a number of noncombatants, as well as kidnapping two children. Searching for volunteers from the garrison and a handful of hardscrabble civilians to make up an independent expeditionary force, Dundee has to turn to the Confederates. They agree to serve, "until the Apache is taken or destroyed."

The distrust in this group is palpable from the beginning and builds as the campaign continues. Disaffection among the Confederates threatens the cohesion of the band, although Tyreen, who has given his word, holds them in place. When they have entered Mexico, Dundee and his troop encounter examples of the civil war that plagues that country, too. Before their task is complete, the troopers will have to engage French troops as well as the Indians they are after.

In the end, it is not Dundee or Tyreen who kill the Apache leader, Sierra Charriba. That honor belongs to Trooper Tim Ryan (Michael Anderson Jr.), the young trumpeter whose diary entries have provided the basis for the story. Yet one last clash with the French remains before the force can return safely to American soil. In this final confrontation, Tyreen sacrifices himself to save those who remain, and the remnants leave the last battlefield to return to Fort Benlin.

Inspiration for Major Amos Dundee seems to have been taken from Colonel James H. Carleton. Historian Alvin Josephy describes Carleton as "a vigorous and demanding professional soldier," which is certainly true of Dundee, too. Other descriptors fit as well: "Hard and flinty as the southwestern plains and deserts," a "stern perfectionist and disciplinarian," "autocratic and righteous." Josephy observes that Carleton's "tyrannical, unbending conduct often landed him in controversy."[13]

Carleton, like his fictional counterpart Amos Dundee, had a prewar career in the old army. He served in the West and in Mexico, earning a promotion to brevet (or temporary) major for his gallant conduct at the battle of Buena Vista. However, unlike Dundee, James Carleton did not participate in the fighting in the Eastern Theater, in particular at the battle of Gettysburg.[14]

In the operations he conducted against the Indians, Carleton commanded primarily California volunteers and certainly not paroled Confederate prisoners. The units consisted in whole or in part of the First and Fifth California Infantry, the First and Second California Cavalry, and the Third U.S. Artillery.[15]

After occupying Tucson from a small force of Confederates who abandoned it, Colonel Carleton declared himself military governor of the territory and proceeded to arrest persons he deemed unsavory, including individuals known to be sympathetic to the Confederate cause. One of the men with Southern leanings that Carleton put under arrest and placed in chains at Fort Yuma was Sylvester Mowry.[16] He may well have been the figure upon whom Captain Benjamin Tyreen, Dundee's Southern antagonist and one-time friend and compatriot in the old army, was based. Again, any resemblance to the historical Mowry is very loose, given that he had been a civilian, not a soldier, and the men had been neither friends nor comrades in the U.S. Army before the war.

The scout who assists Major Dundee in his expedition, Potts, was undoubtedly based upon the famed Westerner, Christopher "Kit" Carson, who commanded the First New Mexico Cavalry and served with Carleton in a similar capacity earlier. Carson differed with his friend and commander on the issue of what to do with the renegade Apaches, many of whom had conducted raids and committed depredations to obtain food supplies. Carson made his argument, but failing to persuade Carleton to adopt a more flexible approach toward the Indians, joined the expedition against them.[17]

Fort Davis, to which the diarist in the film refers, was a historical fort in western Texas. Apaches caught Captain Albert H. Pfeiffer bathing with his family near one of the forts, killed his wife, and chased him, naked, back to the fort.[18]

On November 25, 1864, Carson attacked an Indian camp that he quickly overwhelmed, but during the pursuit he ran into others who had come to the aid of their beleaguered brethren. Now significantly outnumbered, Carson's men dismounted and formed a skirmish line to repel any attack that might be made against them. Several hardier souls obliged, but the troopers had little difficulty driving them off.

In the meantime, Kit Carson reached the scene with some light artillery pieces. The howitzers scattered the Indians briefly, but they regrouped and returned. Although successful in repelling these attacks, Carson determined that the safest course would be to retreat. Both sides used fires in the high prairie grass to mask their movements and intentions. Ultimately, Carson reached his wagon train and withdrew his command with the loss of two killed and twenty-one wounded, despite the odds against him. This expedition represented the end of the collaboration between the famed scout and the perfectionist professional soldier.[19]

As for the Confederate prisoners who accompanied Amos Dundee and Benjamin Tyreen in pursuit of the Apaches, there is at least a historic foundation from which the movie drew. "Galvanized Yankees" did exist, recruited from Southern volunteers who preferred service to military prison. Historian Dee Brown notes, "Between September 1864 and November 1866 they soldiered across the West"; he sets the number of recruits at six thousand from prisons such as Point Lookout, Maryland; Rock Island, Illinois; Camp Chase,

Ohio; Camp Douglas, Illinois; and Camp Morton, Indiana.[20] The First U.S. Volunteers helped to garrison posts in the Northwest, in Minnesota and the Dakotas.[21] Alvin Josephy explains, "Altogether, six regiments of the former Confederates saw duty in the West, escorting supply trains, rebuilding telegraph lines, fighting off Indian raids, and manning posts as far west as Camp Douglas at Salt Lake City until the last of them were mustered out of service late in 1866."[22]

Richard Slotkin has linked *Major Dundee* to the "paradoxes of Vietnam" and found in the principal character a distortion of the original ideals of the mission through his own obsessions.[23] Amos Dundee clearly has his demons, but it is impossible to know, given the limitations of the film, whether he learns from his experiences, including the death of his friend Tyreen. The movie ends with that outcome unresolved.

Like Tyreen and his compatriots, Confederate prisoners of war play prominent roles in other films, such as *Escape from Fort Bravo* and *A Time for Killing*. In the former, when Confederate Captain John Marsh (John Forsythe) contrives to escape from his confinement at Fort Bravo, Union Captain Roper (William Holden) follows. But it is the breakout from prison by Captain Dorrit Bentley (George Hamilton) and some of his men in *A Time for Killing* that triggers a manhunt by Major Walcott (Glenn Ford), whose obsession to catch the Confederates mirrors Dundee's pursuit of the Apaches. The obsession lies with Bentley as fully as with his adversary, to the extent that he hides the fact that the war is over from his men after reading a dispatch from a dead Union courier. Killing becomes the key feature as the two forces play cat and mouse. Even when the Confederates reach the Mexican border, they receive no respite.

Just as escaping prisoners serve as a motif for Civil War westerns, so does the sense of divided loyalties. Such divisions among the garrison are at the center of two films: *Two Flags West* and *Revolt at Fort Laramie*. In the first, Colonel Clay Tucker (Joseph Cotten) is a "galvanized Yankee" who joins the cavalry in the West. His nemesis is his post commander, Major Henry Kenniston (Jeff Chandler). Although befriended by another Union officer, Captain Mark Bradford (Cornel Wilde), Tucker remains under Kenniston's closest scrutiny.

In the second film, Major Seth Bradner (John Dehner) is the commander of a bitterly divided Fort Laramie. Beset on the outside by a hostile Chief Red Cloud and on the inside by a building hatred between advocates of the North and the South, Bradner does his best to hold his post together. His Virginia birth makes him suspect, but he remains true to his commission until released by the army.

The motion picture adequately captures the dilemma that many individuals faced as they made, in the words of Major Bradner, "The bitterest choice of all: to break your oath or your heart." Bradner was planning to announce the engagement of his daughter to a trusted lieutenant, but events elsewhere have now overtaken the moment and forced the major as "the commandant of Fort Laramie," to break different news to the garrison instead. "Fort Sumter has been fired on," he begins. "President Lincoln has called for immediate military intervention against the Southern states."

The new developments in the East create additional tension inside the distant outpost. As feelings intensify, the Southern-born commander promises his daughter, "I'll try to do my duty, whatever that might be." In the meantime, Bradner separates the two factions into different barracks, but when a verbal exchange escalates, he assembles the troops and reminds them of their duty. "Each of you has chosen his own loyalty," he explains. Then, with his own inner turmoil undoubtedly in mind, he adds, "Perhaps there are some of you who have yet to make that decision." Whatever emotions might boil beneath the surface, the post commandant instructs them that "within the fort you will remain a company of soldiers."

Bradner faces more than dissension in the ranks and the threat of mutiny by the Southern cohort of cavalry troopers. His junior officers remain loyal to the Union and deeply suspicious of their superior. Captain James Tenslip (Gregg Palmer), who has sought to marry Bradner's daughter, is particularly torn by doubts of the major's loyalty. "The Mason–Dixon line runs right down the middle of that square," he explains to his would-be bride. "The only neutrals are out in the graveyard." But, even with word reaching the post, through a newspaper, of a Confederate victory at Bull Run, Bradner remains committed to his duty. Only when explicit orders arrive that he is to release any man from the garrison whose loyalty is in doubt does the major make his own fateful decision. He calls in Captain Tenslip and turns over command, and control of a quantity of gold being held at the post, to that officer before making plans to set out for Texas.

But the Southerners quickly learn that they will not be allowed to leave the territory unmolested, although the difficulty will not come from within the cavalry ranks. The two sides will unite for a final time against the Indians, before the surviving Southerners continue their trek toward Texas and the Union cavalrymen return to Fort Laramie, the flag at the post lowering to half mast symbolically as the credits roll.

The story is somewhat different in *The Undefeated*. Set in the closing days of the Civil War, the movie makes use of the Mexican Revolution of Benito Juarez against the French-backed puppet regime of Emperor Maximillian. With regard to the Civil War, the film is thin historically. Presumably, the battle action that opens the movie takes place in Virginia, although no specific reference is made beyond a geographic point known as "Dottie's Crossroads."

As the Union commander of a successful charge, John Wayne reprimands a courier for his undisciplined behavior, referring to "General Masters." The credits give the full name of the character as "General Joe Masters." It is to this officer that Colonel John Henry Thomas (Wayne) submits his resignation from the Union army at the close of the war.

Masters is almost certainly a stock character, meant to suggest no historical figure. There is no obvious attempt to have this character represent any specific person, and there is no record of the existence of a Union general officer by that name. Masters's function is to serve briefly as a foil for Colonel Thomas as the latter makes the transition from soldier to civilian and the film from Civil War to western.

References to the Mexican Revolution abound as the action moves south of the border. Yet the film makes no effort to explain for the viewer the issues at work on either side, or the involvement of the French in Mexico. The representatives of Maximillian are portrayed favorably in comparison to the U.S. Army agents, only to become obscure when they turn against the Americans. The audience first sees the Juarista general who detains the Southerners as sinister, then pleasant, when the deal to exchange the Confederates for horses is consummated.

As for the film itself, from the battle-scarred Confederate flag that opens the film to the closing sequence showing "Yankee Doodle"–singing repatriates returning home, *The Undefeated* boasts stereotype after stereotype from the era. The film's only Civil War sequence puts Federal cavalry under Colonel Thomas against ragtag Rebel remnants under a one-armed Confederate major (Royal Dano). Not surprisingly, the Union attack smashes the Southern line and sends the survivors scurrying in retreat.

Yet, in his moment of triumph, the Union colonel is compassionate and respectful. No sooner is the charge complete than a rider races into the lines to tell Thomas that the war is over. It ended three days before at Appomattox Court House, where General Robert E. Lee surrendered to Ulysses S. Grant.

Thomas surveys the scene of unnecessary carnage surrounding him and rides forward to convey the news to the Confederates under a flag of truce. When he arrives, he finds the Southerners beaten, but unbroken, as represented by an interchange between himself and the Confederate commander.

This interchange between the antagonists is everything a 1969 audience, still living the real-life struggle of Vietnam, would want. Enemies, yes, but still Americans, first and foremost:

Colonel: Major, I've just received word that Lee surrendered to Grant three days ago.

Major: Yes, sir.

Colonel: You knew it?

Major: We received news yesterday.

Colonel: I don't think you understand, major. The war is over.

Major: No, sir.

Colonel: Are you telling me that you intend to keep fighting?

Major: Haven't we just proven it, sir?

Colonel: But, why?

Major: Cause this is our land, and you're on it.

Colonel: We're all Americans.

Major: Yes, sir. That's always been the saddest part of it.

Colonel: Good day, sir.

Major: Colonel (extending his good hand), thank you for your courtesy.

Then, as the opening credits roll, the viewer is treated to a microcosm of the end of the war as Hollywood sees it. The weary Union troopers ride amid the debris and destruction of war. Freed slaves walk quietly along, carrying all of their worldly possessions in bundles or a few meager carts. Then victorious Federal infantry burst out in hearty strains of the "Battle Cry of Freedom" as they meet homebound Confederates, who strike up a weak, but defiant "Dixie" in response.

In addition to these expected images of the Civil War, the film has the requisite villains. There are the carpetbaggers who attempt to wrest the 1,500-acre Langdon Hall Plantation from Colonel James Langdon (Rock Hudson) before it can be collected for taxes that Langdon no longer has the money to pay. "You went busted outfitting that Rebel regiment of yours," Thad Benedict (Henry Beckman), "late of Pittsburgh but now of Natchez," explains. Indeed, the scene with the white opportunist and his black compatriot might well have been taken from stock footage based on stereotypical depictions of such characters.

Likewise, Thomas, now a civilian, confronts two corrupt Federal government agents as he attempts to sell horses to the army. Then, both Langdon and Thomas fend off an attack by Mexican bandits upon the Southern caravan. The action in each of these incidents is heroic and decisive, with the protagonists driving away the agents of corruption and greed in rough and satisfying fashion.

Yet fate has more in store for these two new allies than the rude dismissal of moral inferiors. The two men are bound to each other as they find themselves swept up in the Mexican Revolution. When the Juarista general Rojas captures the Southern party, Langdon must appeal to Thomas and his men for help. In the meantime, the emperor's representatives alert a French command, which mobilizes to keep the horses out of the Mexican rebels' hands. Thomas and his men, with Langdon assisting, must battle the French troops before they can bring the horses to General Rojas and free the Southerners from execution.

Once the rescue is effected, the men and their parties proceed back to the Rio Grande, where they will begin life again, as Americans. Thomas flirts with the widowed Langdon sister, while the former Confederate colonel ventures the notion of running for the House of Representatives. As the credits roll, the now-united countrymen disdain their sectional music for a song they can all agree to sing, "Yankee Doodle."

Hollywood could not resist the opportunity to take box office stars such as Wayne and Hudson and pair them with National Football League standouts Roman Gabriel and Merlin Olsen. Still, spicing the rest of the cast with solid character actors such as Ben Johnson, Bruce Cabot, and Dub Taylor, as well as heartthrob Jan-Michael Vincent, ensured that the film would have a sufficient mix to draw a wide audience. In the final analysis, the movie is less a Civil War piece than a Western, and more entertaining than educational.

The Civil War often found itself mistaken for the West in films, as producers sought to exploit both worlds in a fashion that would not offend supporters (and ticket-paying moviegoers) of either North or South. What they produced tended to do Hollywood's typical injustice to Native Americans, and precious little justice to history. The writing frequently weighed the acting down with stereotypical characterizations. Often, the films were excuses to offer the standard western fare without the baggage of historical veracity.

CHAPTER 8

Shiloh's Bloody Harvest

Journey to Shiloh takes the Concho County Comanches, under their leader Buck Burnett (James Caan), from Texas to Mississippi to experience the war. (l. to r.) Don Stroud, Michael Sarrazin, Jan-Michael Vincent, Caan, Paul Petersen, Michael Burns, Harrison Ford.

Sure ain't nothing like I thought it'd be.

—Miller Nalls to his friend
Buck Burnett in *Journey to Shiloh*

To an unsuspecting nation the news of Shiloh was like a thunderbolt.

—historian Wiley Sword

THE BATTLE OF SHILOH, or Pittsburg Landing, was the first great land battle of the Civil War in the Western Theater. In the two-day engagement, April 6–7, 1862, some 62,000 Federals in the Armies of the Tennessee and the Ohio clashed with approximately 40,000 Southerners. The result was a bloodbath that cost the Union 13,047 casualties and the Confederates 10,694. These staggering losses served as an indication that the war remained far from over in what would prove to be the most decisive theater of action in the conflict.[1]

Several Civil War films use the battle of Shiloh in one form or another to advance their stories. The battle may appear as only a small portion of a larger whole, as in the monumental *How the West Was Won* (1962), act as a plot device and symbol as in *So Red the Rose* (1935), provide a key element of a biographical story as seen in *Johnny Shiloh* (1963), or serve as the central feature in studying the effects of war on a band of soldiers, such as in *Journey to Shiloh* (1968). But, whatever the use of Shiloh on celluloid, no film to date has offered a comprehensive examination of this pivotal western theater engagement.

How the West Was Won is a sweeping epic that takes its viewers across vast distances of space and time through the stories. A scene involving the fighting at Shiloh shows a meeting between prominent Union generals Ulysses S. Grant and William T. Sherman to discuss the battle. A lone Confederate, wandering behind the lines, stumbles on a fellow straggler in blue, and both happen upon the discussion. The Southerner decides that he can change the course of the conflict with one shot. The Northerner reluctantly cuts down the Rebel to prevent him from killing either Grant or Sherman. Aside from the commonly expected view of a cigar-smoking Grant, played by Henry Morgan, and the astounding casting of John Wayne as his gruff subordinate and friend, Sherman, the scene offers little of material value to anyone who might want to study the battle itself, although it provides a glimpse at the relationship the two Union commanders enjoyed.

Director John Ford also hoped to capture something of the state of mind that characterized Grant under the weight of the great engagement. The Union commander had been at his headquarters in nearby Savannah, Tennessee, when the Confederates struck unexpectedly, and he hastened by river to the landing, where he began to organize and supervise a defense. At the end of the long and bloody day, Grant was exhausted, still nursing an injury to his ankle he had suffered in the days preceding the assault. Undoubtedly, he was nursing a bruised ego, too. "Well, Grant, we've had the devil's own day, haven't we?" Sherman observed to his friend that night. "Yes," Grant rejoined through the smoke of his cigar and the splash of rainwater that fell from the brow of his hat, "Lick 'em tomorrow, though."[2]

Roundly criticized for allowing his army to be caught by surprise, the general who would ultimately forge victory for the Union in the war, just as he had done on the banks of the Tennessee River in 1862, remained consumed with self-doubt. Undoubtedly, such a reevaluation would have been less possible in the busy and chaotic night that followed that first bloody day of Union setbacks at Shiloh than the film depicts. But historian Wiley Sword records that shortly after the battle, "Sherman found Grant, visibly shaken, packing his belongings to leave the army." As in the Shiloh scene in *How the West Was Won*, the red-headed Ohioan tried to console his friend and convince him that his services were indispensable to the army. "It was with difficulty that Sherman persuaded him to stay," Sword concluded.[3]

Doubts about Grant's, and to a lesser extent Sherman's, capabilities for command crept up the chain of command to Washington, D.C., where they reached the ear of the president. Yet when Abraham Lincoln considered the alternatives, he was less certain that the Union cause could be served with Grant relegated to some distant or subordinate post. "I can't spare the man," the lanky commander-in-chief noted plainly, "he fights." Ulysses Grant would remain.[4]

William T. Sherman avoided being killed or wounded in *How the West Was Won*, but he was nearly not so fortunate at Shiloh. Disdaining the notion of a Southern attack as absurd, he had exploded at the worried colonel of the Fifty-Third Ohio, "Take your damned regiment to Ohio. There is no enemy nearer than Corinth!"[5] Then Sherman learned firsthand that he had been wrong. The lesson came when soldiers emerged from the woods at Rhea Field. As the Union commander turned to observe them, he suddenly realized his mistake. "My God, we are attacked!" he exclaimed, throwing his hand in the direction of the Southerners. It was almost certainly here that he sustained a wound to that hand from Confederate buckshot.[6]

Sherman's brush with mortality did not prove fatal to him in either *How the West was Won* or on the undulating ground near Shiloh Church and Pittsburg Landing. But the battle became a powerful symbol of the realities of war in both the civilian populations of North and South, and in cinematic productions such as *So Red the Rose*. In the 1935 Paramount Studios motion picture, Shiloh is the battle chosen to symbolize the killing associated with the war. The Bedford family matriarch has a terrible premonition and becomes convinced that her son has perished in that battle. She insists upon determining his fate for herself. Assisted by a relative and a servant, she sets out for the scene of the fighting to locate the young man's body and bring it home.

When they arrive at the shattered battlefield, still bearing the carnage of the combat that swept over it for two days, the mother remains stoically in the wagon while the men move from figure to figure in their grim search. Just as she has feared, they locate her son Edward, a Confederate corporal. The young Southerner's death becomes the catalyst that propels a previously pacifistic Duncan Bedford (Randolph Scott) into joining the war, and the casualties associated with Shiloh become the symbol of the sacrifices in blood so many families will be called upon to make in the conflict.

While *So Red the Rose* only touches briefly on the significance of the battle of Shiloh, *Journey to Shiloh* brings a group of young men from Texas in the Trans-Mississippi Theater to Tennessee, where the bulk of them become unwitting participants in the battle. Buck Burnett (James Caan) leads the six would-be soldiers, Miller Nalls (Michael Sarrazin), Todo McLean (Don Stroud), Little Bit Lucket (Jan-Michael Vincent), Willie Bill Rearden (Harrison Ford), J. C. Sutton (Paul Petersen), and Eubie Bell (Michael Burns), in their quest to join the Southern forces fighting in Virginia.

The young men constitute themselves into a quasimilitary unit they dub the "Concho County Comanches." They are anxious to make their way to the war, and as promotional material for the film proclaimed, are "spoiling for a fight." The opening scene introduces the audience to each of the would-be soldiers, and it becomes instantly clear that they have no idea what they are due to encounter on their journey to war. Eubie Bell, the happy-go-lucky member of the troop, symbolizes the naïveté of all of these young warriors as a voiceover explains: "War the way he heard it, was just another game." All of them seem most preoccupied by the fear that the war will be over before they can reach it.

Along the way, the riders experience difficulties that begin to test their resolve and thin their ranks even before they can reach the battlefield. The first challenge comes while they are still in Texas, from the owner of a large plantation on whose land they have camped temporarily. Two of the planter's sons appear to investigate the strangers, but quickly learn much to their delight that the men are soldiers, not squatters. "We're on our way to Richmond, Virginia," one of the Concho Comanches explains. "We're going to join up with General Hood's Texas Brigade." The young men express an interest to align themselves with the command, and they invite the travelers to attend a ball as honored guests.

On the way to the cotillion, the Texans encounter slavery for the first time. The figure of the elderly slave is not much different from the images of the "faithful soul" of much earlier films. "We're going to fight Yankees," one of the travelers tells him. The slave replies, "I hear tell the Yankees is fighting us. I hear tell they're mighty mean. Oh, I reckon we'll whip 'em though."

"We?"

"Yes sir. Us Southerners."

"I've never seen a slave before," one of the Texans observes.

"Well we just folks sir," he explains, "The only difference is we belong to Colonel Claiborne. He's a mighty fine gentleman." Then as the men ride on, the slave calls out cheerily, "And good luck with them Yankees."

"Did you hear what he said? Us Southerners. What do you suppose he meant by that?"

"Well he lives here don't he?" Eubie observes. "Sure ain't a Northerner."

"Buck, something don't make sense," Nalls adds.

"Yep. Damn if I know what it is," Buck replies.

When the Texans arrive at the mansion, the scale of the operation is over-awing to them. "All these darkies yours?" Burnett asks innocently. "We own a couple hundred of them," one the planter's sons explains "The way the Yan-kees talk about slaves you'd think we keep 'em in chains and beat 'em twice a day. It isn't like that." "Well, we got a lot to learn," Buck concludes.

This is not the world the Texans had left behind them. Social distinctions between the classes here will not be so easy to overcome. Whatever respect they might feel is their due based on their martial intentions they fail to receive when they attempt to attend the party. Instead of welcoming them and saluting them as heroes, the owner immediately issues orders for them to be removed from the premises. This is not the class of person with which he wishes to associate.

Happily, a farewell from an Alabama cousin of the planter's family salvages the situation for the turned-out warriors and smoothes their ruffled feathers as they continue on their journey to war. "Folks here in Texas just don't feel the war the way we do in Alabama," she explains. "Well, you're soldiers of the Confederacy. You're going off to fight their war." Finally, Buck accepts her display of graciousness and patriotism: "Ma'am, we don't know much about this here war. But as long as there are ladies like you supporting it the way you do I'm sure the South can't help but win." He takes his leave with the assur-ance, "We'll remember what you said when we get to the war; it'll help us from getting tired. Yes, Ma'am."

But the lesson of class differences is not entirely lost in the passion of be-ing sent off with the blessing of a beautiful Southern belle. "I figure you're rich enough you don't feel so much like fighting a war," Buck notes to his compatriots, reflecting the popular notion that many will take that this con-flict is a "rich man's war, but a poor man's fight." "Well they're Southerners aren't they?" another retorts. "Maybe that ain't enough, just being Southern."

The Comanches suffer their first loss when the hotheaded J. C. Sutton, chafing under Burnett's leadership, decides to leave the band so that he can ride into Shreveport, Louisiana, for a bit of adventure. While involved in a crooked card game, he finds more than he bargains for and is shot and killed. Interestingly, one of the historical anomalies in the film occurs in the card game. Apparently, the person responsible for the deck of playing cards does not realize that since most individuals were illiterate in this period, the cards should not contain numbers. These do.

Later, as the Texans go by stagecoach to Vicksburg, Mississippi, they meet a distinguished fellow traveler, Colonel Mirabeau Cooney (Clark Gordon), who declares their intention to fight a "noble thing." "We are a united nation engaged in a holy crusade," he adds. They encounter a slave patrol, with hounds searching for the scent of an escaped slave. "Why do you suppose he run away?" one of the Texans asks. "Oh you run into a bad one every now and then," the elder passenger replies. When the Texans seem perplexed, he goes on, "We'll you don't run a hundred field hands by being friendly, sonny."

Suddenly, the slave appears, calling for the stagecoach to stop. Buck forces the driver to pull the horses up, and the slave climbs aboard. They debate what to do with him: "Why he's just scared out of what little wits he's got, that's all," the Colonel explains. "Course the sheriff's gonna make an example out of him, give him a lick or two. Got to. Otherwise they'd all run away." In an effort to ease their concerns, he adds, "But the sheriff will see he gets back to his rightful owner. Now that's the law boys. This here buck, he's worth over a thousand dollars. You don't think we're going to let anything happen to that amount of money do you?"

The argument wins the day, but the boys are uneasy: "I've never seen the likes, running down a man with dogs," Miller observes. The slave's fate is sealed. Then, as the stage and its passengers leave the little hamlet of Munroe Station where they have paused briefly, they pass the sight of the man's lynching. Miller catches the first glimpse. "He said they'd do it and they did," he tells Buck. "We done the right thing according to the law," Burnett replies half-heartedly. Nothing is as clear as it has seemed, but this is the closest that *Journey to Shiloh* comes to a critique of the "peculiar institution."

The Texans experience further adventures when they reach Vicksburg. Buck gets into a bar brawl, but eludes the provost guard with the help of a young lady as soldiers arrive to break the fight up. He falls in love and is tempted to let the war fend for itself. "You gotta go to this awful war?" she asks. "I'll tell you I ain't so anxious to get there as I was yesterday," the soldier responds honestly.

But Buck and his fellow Texans have a mission to complete, and they are soon on their way eastward. At one of the stops on the rail line, they watch as Confederate troops struggle with horses in a corral. It is clear that even under the watchful eye of Confederate general Braxton Bragg, these Southerners cannot handle the mounts. The Texans prove that they are equal to the task, but in doing so get corralled themselves by Sergeant Mercer Barnes (Noah Beery), Corporal Tellis Yeager (James Gammon) and the Pensacola Light Blues. In a matter of course, the Texans take an oath and join the "Army of the Confederacy," but well short of their intended destination of Richmond, Virginia.

As Sergeant Barnes speaks to the new recruits, he displays an extraordinary knowledge concerning Southern strategy. He tells them that traveling on to the Confederate capital is out of the question now that a major offensive campaign is underway. "First off you're going to Corinth, Mississippi. Then you're going to Tennessee and on up to Shiloh with 20,000 infantry, cause we're fixin' to shove that there General Grant and them blue-belly soldiers of his plumb into Lake Erie." "We're not infantry, we're cavalry," the Texans explain in vain. In any event, they have found the war they had been seeking.

In the meantime, the Texans attempt to deal with their new circumstances. Barnes points to General Bragg. "He is your commanding officer. And he is the meanest, the nastiest, the shortest-tempered human being that you are ever going to meet up with." Eubie Bell tries to explain that with them on hand Bragg's worries are now over. "Us Concho County Comanches are the damnedest bunch of Yankee killers you ever did see. I bet there ain't a whole troop in the Confederate Army better than us. And you can tie that hard and fast to your saddlehorn general. We came here to fight." An unimpressed Braxton Bragg demonstrates the accuracy of the sergeant's description of him when he responds to Eubie's declaration by ordering him to be arrested.

None of the glamour the Texans expected to encounter greets them in the service. The mundane duties and the drudgery of soldier life are matched only by the dismal weather. The realities of soldiering begin to create doubts in the minds of some of the men. "You know I've been thinking," Miller tells Buck. "I ain't got a damn thing against a Yankee. I ain't never seen one." But the leader of the band remains steadfast. "Well this is war. We're Southerners. We've got to fight. It's a matter of freedom." Once again, Miller expresses the growing frustration felt by all of them. "A lot of things just don't make no more sense. Now getting ready to go to a battle we don't know anything about, not even why."

In the meantime, life in camp proves to have dangers that are every bit as deadly as those of the battlefield. Rainy conditions exacerbate the disease already rampant among the Confederate troops. Convulsed by chills and a raspy cough, Little Bit (Jan-Michael Vincent) dies in his tent, the second Texan to fall before the group has fired its first wartime shots.

When the remainder of the Texans reach Shiloh, they experience the war firsthand. Buck serves as a courier for General Bragg. "You tell General Johnston word for word that I have hit Sherman and I am driving him back toward the river, but that there's an opening on my right flank and I want it closed." Buck rides off to deliver the message and stumbles on a mortally wounded Todo (Stroud). After a few moments with his dying friend, Buck tries to complete his assignment, but a shell kills his mount. On foot and still looking for General Johnston, Buck reunites with his friend Miller, Sergeant Barnes, and Corporal Yeager. "You've not heard?" Barnes tells him. "Johnston's dead. He caught a Yankee minie ball. That's a fact. I heard Beauregard's taken over command."

The Confederate high command is not the only part of the Southern forces to suffer loss, as the Texans continue to be decimated. "Willie Bill, he got a minie ball right between the eyes," Miller tells Buck. "One of them mortars from the big gunboat blew up right on us and Eubie just wasn't there no more." Nalls concludes of the battle that has decimated their ranks, "Sure ain't nothing like I thought it'd be." He continues, "I don't understand it. We're fighting for the South. They invaded us. What they got to fight about?" The always stoic Burnett replies simply, "Whatever it is they're sold on it."

Buck now joins Miller, Sergeant Barnes, and Corporal Yeager as they prepare for an assault on the Union forces. As the attack begins, Buck falls wounded in a trench. That evening, Barnes finds Buck and helps him and a wounded Federal soldier to a nearby church building. Although it is not identified, the building is clearly meant to represent Shiloh Church, the small one-room Methodist meeting house that would lend its name to the battle being waged around it.

Inside, the refugees find numerous stragglers and wounded who are also seeking haven from the rainy weather and the war. The men take the risk of striking a light so that a Union soldier, whose father is a preacher in Boston, can read for a dying Confederate. When one objects, another calls out, "Let the Yankee read. Reckon it's the same Bible."

Whatever solace the scripture reading offers is quickly lost as Confederate provost guards break into the building. The men scatter, but as he tries to escape with Barnes, Buck takes a round in the arm. The sergeant helps the badly wounded Barnett away from the scene as the guards round up Miller and the other stragglers. Buck will survive the encounter, but loses his left arm to amputation in the process.

In the meantime, combat has so wrecked the Pensacola Light Blues that the survivors are reduced to pulling guard duty themselves in Corinth, Mississippi, to which the Confederates have retreated after their defeat at Shiloh. Buck returns from the hospital and during a brief reunion with Barnes and Yeager learns that Miller has been taken into custody as a deserter. Unfortunately, since then his friend has killed a guard during an escape attempt, but not before suffering a severe wound. Nalls has taken refuge in a local barn, and the sergeant and corporal are about to ride out to track him down. Instead, Buck grabs Barnes's horse and goes off to locate his friend. "Now there's two of 'em I got to get," Mercer notes plaintively.

But Miller is badly wounded and will not likely survive to answer charges for murder and flight. "We didn't make much of a splash now, did we?" he tells Buck. Barnes and a squad of Confederates reach the barn. Bragg arrives himself. Barnes tells him about the deserters and receives the instruction to bring them out. Buck hides as the men find Miller, now dead of his wound. Barnes tells Bragg that there is only one man left of a troop of Texans who had come to fight. "This Burnett, he's the last one of 'em left alive." "In my army we shoot men for that," the commanding general bellows. Then uncharacteristically, Bragg softens. "We've got too much to do to waste time running down one Texas straggler," he tells Barnes, ordering him to leave behind a horse and return with the wagon and Miller's body. Buck slips away to return to his love in Vicksburg, and ostensibly to his home in Texas.

The film ends as it began, with images of the Texans embarking on their journey to war. "There were seven boys from Texas," a chorus starts against the backdrop, "rode off to find the war. They rode as far as Shiloh and never saw no more." Union and Confederate flags flap in the background as the gallant squad that now no longer exists rides past.

Journey to Shiloh does not explore the great battle for which it is named. The combat scenes are largely stock footage that have been used previously. Historical irregularities exist in weapons and characterizations, but the film points out dramatically the heavy price war exacts from those who participate in it. Braxton Bragg was present at the historical engagement, although not in command of the army, a responsibility that fell to Albert Sidney Johnston and P. G. T. Beauregard (who assumed command following Johnston's death on the first day). Bragg was noted for being a strict disciplinarian, prone to execute deserters, a reality that renders the fictional Bragg's compassion out of character.

The same battle serves as a central element for a Disney production, *Johnny Shiloh* (1963). This film features a young boy who serves as much as a mascot for his unit as its drummer. Sergeant Gabe Trotter (Brian Keith) takes the lad, Johnny Lincoln Clem (Kevin Corcoran), under his wing.

John Clem, the boy upon whom the story is based, was a historical figure. The young fellow ran away from home for the first time when he was a mere nine years old. When age prevented his enlistment, he tagged along anyhow with the Twenty-Second Michigan, partly as a drummer and partly as a regimental mascot. Enemy fire destroyed his drum at Shiloh, but won him his sobriquet. Eventually, he traded in his musical instrument for a weapon and participated in the battle of Chickamauga. His promotion to sergeant came as a result of his refusal to comply with a Confederate officer's demand, "Surrender, you damned little Yankee," punctuated by his shooting the colonel out of his saddle. He finished the war as a courier for General George H. Thomas.[7]

The battle that made Johnny Clem famous came about as a result of the plan by Confederate generals Albert Sidney Johnston and Pierre Gustave Toutant Beauregard to tip the scales of war in the Western Theater back in the Confederacy's favor by striking Ulysses S. Grant's army encamped at Pittsburg Landing. Despite delays and indications that the surprise upon which the entire operation rested had been forfeited, Johnston managed to assemble his command for an attack.

In the early morning hours of April 6, figures began to appear at the far end of Fraley's field. Desultory firing turned into volleys. The confusion of smoke and fire, conflicting orders, and the first trickle of casualties signaled that the battle of Shiloh was underway.

The Confederates had planned to assault the positions on the Union left in such a manner as to drive the Federals from the Tennessee River. This maneuver would deprive them of access to their main source of reinforcement and supply and push them into poor ground for defense. That morning, the fog of war insured that the best-laid plans would go awry. The Confederates drove their opponents before them, but back toward the landing and the river instead of away from it. The irony was that as they succeeded, the Union defensive positions consolidated, culminating in a powerful line hastily constructed near the landing and bolstered by a significant ravine to its front.

For the moment at least, the Confederate plan seemed to be working perfectly. The Federals were in disarray, pouring troops piecemeal into the combat. Everett Peabody, whose warnings had been scoffed at by his superiors, raced forward to buy time for a defense to be mounted. As he rode along urging his men to stand firm, the thirty-one year old picked up wound after wound, until the fifth, a fatal round in the head, sent him tumbling from his horse.[8]

Despite the initial success, the ground and the momentum of attack worked against the Confederates. At various points, resistance began to slow the Southern advance, the ravines acted to break the cohesion of the units, and the sheer exhaustion and chaos of battle began to take its toll. Some of the Southerners stopped to gather what spoils they could as Northern camps fell in succession into their hands.

Johnston was elated with the successes he enjoyed thus far and determined to push the fight to a victorious conclusion. Astride his horse, Fire-Eater, and carrying a tin cup he had picked up in one of the Union camps, Johnston exhibited coolness and enthusiasm. At one point during the advance, the general observed, "That checkmates them. Yes, sir, that mates them."[9]

After initial Southern inroads, the Federals managed to delay the Confederate advance, particularly in the area of Sarah Bell's peach orchard and along a farm road at the edge of a thick forest. The Federals under Benjamin Prentiss, Stephen Hurlbut, and William H. L. Wallace had taken up a strong position in this area. Piecemeal Confederate attacks failed to dislodge the Federals from their positions until retreating units left the way open for the Southerners to surround the position. So thick was the firing in the area that it became known as the Hornet's Nest.[10]

That line might still be broken, but Johnston would not know it. Struck in the right leg, most likely by friendly fire, the Confederate general had failed to detect that he had been hit. His aide, Tennessee Governor Isham Harris, saw him ashen and swaying in the saddle, but could not find the wound that caused the Confederate commander to go into shock. Ironically, the general had carried a tourniquet that might have saved his life had the danger been seen in time.[11] Albert Sidney Johnston, the ideal soldier according to his friend Confederate President Jefferson Davis, was dead.[12]

Seriously wounded in the face on the other end of the position, William H. L. Wallace could not be retrieved before the Confederates reached him. Unknown to him, his wife Ann had traveled to nearby Savannah, Tennessee, to be near him. She was nursing wounded aboard a steamer as her husband fell.

Confederate command passed to General Beauregard, and the attacks continued against the Union lines. Despite mounting casualties, the Southerners eventually prevailed at the Hornet's Nest, but the time the Federals bought with their stubborn resistance proved crucial in allowing Grant to cobble together a strong defensive position together near the landing with support from the gunboats *Lexington* and *Tyler* on the Tennessee River.

The Southerners would test Grant's "last line of defense," but find that after experiencing heavy combat their unit cohesion had broken down badly and their losses had mounted severely. In their intermingled and exhausted condition they could not break Grant's line on this day. The Confederates settled into the captured camps of their enemies and awaited a new day to renew the fighting.

In the meantime, the vanguard of Don Carlos Buell's force under General William "Bull" Nelson arrived opposite Pittsburg Landing. Throughout the evening and night, these troops ferried across to join Grant and his demoralized, but not yet defeated army. Their numbers would ensure the Federals would have overwhelming superiority the next day when Grant launched a counterstrike that drove the Confederates from the field and back to Corinth.

With the morning, Grant's reinforced army marched out to engage their Southern opponents and began to roll them back. Hard fighting near White Oaks Pond held the blue tide back temporarily, but the outcome was never really in doubt.

Nightfall came to the Confederates' rescue on the 7th, Nathan Bedford Forrest on the 8th. Indeed, Forrest nearly became the last fatality of Shiloh when he matched his small cavalry command against Sherman's pursuing Federals. The aggressive cavalryman ordered a charge that would force the Union troops into the line of battle and buy the Confederates additional time to withdraw. As he advanced, he failed to realize that his command was no longer following and rode directly into the Union lines alone. The Federals gathered around Forrest, trying to shoot him or pull him from his horse. Instead, the intrepid Southerner turned, and despite being severely wounded in the back, pulled a surprised Union soldier up behind him as a shield, and rode to safety.

Sidney Johnston and Bedford Forrest, Everett Peabody and William Wallace were hardly the only casualties of Shiloh. Altogether, the battle produced 1,723 dead and 8,012 wounded on the Confederate side and 1,754 dead and 6,408 wounded on the Union side.[13] Forrest would recover from his wound, although it would reopen when he tried to come back too fast.[14] Wallace was less fortunate. He lingered under the loving care of his wife for just over a week. Holding her hand, he felt for her wedding ring to be sure she was with him. Then, on April 11, 1862, he lapsed into a coma and died.[15]

For many of the men on both sides, Shiloh marked the first engagement in which they participated, and for many it certainly was the bloodiest. The casualty lists were staggering. A small gathering of water would become known from this point onward as "Bloody Pond." Men and animals in various conditions had attempted to slake their thirst in the water, only to tinge the pond red with their life's blood.

As the Western Theater's first great battle, Shiloh, or Pittsburg Landing, won a reputation for ferocity that few who survived it would ever forget. There would be other great battles in the West. There would be horribly long casualty lists at Stone's River, in the Atlanta campaign, and in Hood's disastrous Tennessee campaign. But Shiloh served as a bloody wake-up call to any who thought the war would end quickly and relatively cost free in lives and treasure.

It is not surprising that several filmmakers sought to use this pivotal battle in the Western Theater as a backdrop. Of these, *Journey to Shiloh* conveys most closely the human devastation of the combat there. The screen fates of Buck Burnett and his Texas compatriots mirrored the real-life experiences of thousands of Union and Confederate troops across the hills, fields, and ravines surrounding Pittsburg Landing. Yet statistics illustrate that, unlike the cinematic Southerners, more men on both sides suffered wounds than death on the battlefield. Clearly, the creators of *Journey to Shiloh* meant for the film to focus on the destruction of war during the time of the Vietnam War. But as the letters, diaries, and reminiscences of participants indicate, it would be hard to exaggerate the price that so many paid on that bloody field amid the blossoms and ravines surrounding little Shiloh Church.

CHAPTER 9

Confederates Raid Vermont

Smoke fills the streets of St. Albans, Vermont, as Confederate officers, Major Neal Benton (Van Heflin, l.) and Captain Frank Dwyer (Peter Graves, r.), coordinate their activities in *The Raid*.

What news from St. Albans?

—Union Major General John A. Dix

It was a most daring adventure.

—Vermont Governor J. Gregory Smith

S T. ALBANS, VERMONT, must have seemed a long way from the seat of war. A quiet community of some 1,600 persons, perched near the U.S.–Canadian border, it was hundreds of miles from the fighting that was occurring in Virginia, Tennessee, and elsewhere.[1] Yet, on October 19, 1864, Lieutenant Bennett H. Young led a band of some twenty-five Confederates on a raid of the town that netted the Southerners over $200,000. They remained in the town for only about a half an hour before fleeing back into Canada.

The Raid (1954) purports to depict the military operation that some thought daring and others little more than an attempt to legitimize bank robbery. The credits roll against the backdrop of images of the St. Alban's Raid in an edition of *Frank Leslie's Illustrated Newspaper* and end with the assurance, "This is a true story." Veteran actor Van Heflin portrays the Confederate leader of the expedition, renamed for the film as Major Neal Barton. Lee Marvin, Peter Graves, Claude Akins, and James Best play his compatriots.

The film establishes at the outset that the story "began on the night of September 26, 1864, in a Union prison stockade at Plattsburg, New York, not many miles from the Canadian border." The Confederates have dug a short tunnel out of which a handpicked group of officers will emerge to subdue the guards, secure weapons, and make for the main gate. Lieutenant Keating (Lee Marvin) cannot resist taking a shot at a sentinel on the wall, and amid a flurry of gunfire seven of the Southern officers scramble for freedom. In the melee, one of the Confederates suffers a serious wound, and although the Canadian border is in close proximity, Major Barton determines to leave the soldier behind.

The wounded comrade holds off the pursuit momentarily before being riddled with bullets, but the delay enables the rest to cross the international border. Major Barton will return again to U.S. soil, but this time dressed in civilian garb. He arrives in the tiny community of St. Albans and immediately scouts the environs, noting the locations of banking establishments and troops. Reminded of his mission by a public display of Confederate war "trophies" in the window of a local business, he spurns the suggestion by a recruiter that he join the Union army by claiming to be Canadian.

The church bell tolls to announce that war news has arrived, and a headline reading "Believe Rebel Officers Reached Canada" is replaced with another that trumpets William T. Sherman's march toward Savannah, Georgia. "They can't stop old Sherman," a citizen calls out. One of the Union recruiters stationed in the town after having lost an arm in the war, Captain

Lionel Foster (Richard Boone) adds defiantly, "Savannah's going to get what Atlanta got. If I were General Sherman, I wouldn't leave a stick standing. They got it coming."

Barton continues his probe under the guise of a Montreal businessman by the name of Neal Swayze, touring potential land purchases with the proprietress of a local boardinghouse. Katie Bishop (Anne Bancroft) is a war widow whose Medal of Honor–winning husband had perished at Gettysburg.[2] Both she and her young son Larry (Tommy Rettig) take an immediate liking to the resolute stranger. The convalescing Captain Foster, also sharing a room at the boardinghouse and clearly affectionate toward the family nevertheless remains suspicious of Barton.

His reconnaissance complete, the Confederate major returns to Montreal, where on October 12, 1864, he rejoins his fellow escapees. Before them rests a model of the Vermont town, and the major lays out his plan. He assigns each of the three banks—the Commercial, the National, and the State—to his most trusted lieutenants and meets with other recruits anxious to join the venture. Among these is Corporal Fred Dean (John Dierkes), of the Fifth Georgia Cavalry, who has had a previous acquaintance with Barton.

Having assembled a final team of raiders, Barton and the men meet with an unnamed government representative who will stamp the operation with the imprimatur of legitimacy. The Confederate official warns, "This is no guerrilla raid." It is an "act of war" designed to "divert troops" to the rear areas and "ease the pressure on General Lee." The men will be permitted to burn the town with liquid fire once the banks have been emptied of their deposits. But the essence of the raid is for obtaining funds, not spreading destruction. "Squeeze every dollar out of those bank vaults," the government representative tells them. "They'll buy a lot of weapons." Barton reminds the assemblage that "St. Albans is just the first of these raids."

By the 14th, Neal Swayze is back in St. Albans. More headlines denote Sherman's progress in Georgia as the Confederate raiders converge on the small town. Keating remains disgruntled. "The only Yankee worth looking at is a dead one," he tells a comrade who has demonstrated a fondness for the fairer sex in the village. The fellow complains, "A man can mix a little biology with war can't he?"

In the meantime, the Southerners convene at a nearby farm Barton has purchased for this purpose following his earlier ride with Katie Bishop. The raiders experiment with bottles of liquid fire and receive their final instructions. When those do not seem to include the complete destruction of the town, Keating challenges the major. "Sherman doesn't make any exceptions." Barton is increasingly reluctant to include the angry Confederate in the plans, but agrees when Keating promises to toe the line.

The raid itself has been planned for Saturday, October 17, but the sudden appearance of a sizable squadron of Union cavalry convinces the major to postpone the operation. Confederate inquiries produce the information that the Federals will leave town on Monday morning. With other troops due to arrive later in the afternoon, the Southerners set noon for putting their plan into effect. But Keating will not accept the delay with equanimity. He goes on a drunken binge that threatens to unravel the Confederate scheme.

Much to Barton's chagrin, Keating resurfaces the next day. As the towns-folk gather in the church for Sunday services, the Confederate bursts into the sanctuary. A sermon on the evils of rebellion provokes him to pull a gun and shoot a Union soldier. The whole affair is coming unglued, and Barton steps out to secure it by shooting the renegade Southerner. The citizens hail the major as a hero, not realizing he has killed his compatriot to keep him from compromising their mission. "You've certainly captured our town," one ad-mirer asserts ironically. The disruption aside, Barton determines to launch the operation on schedule. As anticipated, the Union troopers ride out of the town for Plattsburg, leaving the Confederates free to carry out their assign-ments without any organized resistance.

One last complication arises as Katie and her son discover Major Barton's genuine identity. The boy races to catch the Union cavalry squadron, while the Confederate leader dashes into the street to complete the mission. The church bell summons the populace, but this time St. Albans will be the seat of the latest war news. The other Southerners throw off their overcoats and re-veal themselves in immaculate Confederate uniforms. "This is a raid of the Confederate Army," Barton informs the stunned people as his men fan out to raid the banks and the livery stables. At first, all seems to be going well. Then Captain Foster, who has previously admitted that his injury was the result of a self-inflicted wound and not combat, starts to fight back. The Southerners sustain two deaths before they threaten him with the bottles of liquid fire meant for the town. Running low on ammunition and under fire from several sides, the captain pitches his weapon aside and surrenders. In the chaos and confusion, Katie's son slips out to locate the Union cavalry column and bring it back to the town's rescue.

Barton supervises the final dispositions of Union deposits and sends the bulk of his men out of town ahead of the returning Federal horsemen. He in-structs the citizens to sit in the street to prevent the cavalry from rushing un-inhibited after the Confederates, but refuses to use the liquid fire to stop the troops since the boy is riding alongside. As the Union troopers appear, Barton and Captain Frank Dwyer (Peter Graves) dash for safety. They use the last bottles of the flammable ingredient to set the covered bridge afire and ensure they will cross the border unmolested. The St. Alban's raid has come to an end. The film closes with the bridge consumed in fire, while Barton looks wistfully back toward the town.

The historical basis of the story portrayed on film is sound. Lieutenant Bennett H. Young, upon whom Barton is based, had been part of Confederate cavalry general John Hunt Morgan's Ohio raid in 1863 when the Federals captured him. Initially held in Camp Chase prison in Ohio and then transferred to Camp Douglas in Illinois, Young had managed to escape and make his way into Canada.

It was in Canada that he became acquainted with a former politician now acting as an agent on behalf of the Confederate government, Clement C. Clay Jr. Clay endorsed the young man to the war department and embraced his scheme to conduct raids out of Canada. Subsequently, Young received instructions to act under Clay's authority and "collect together such Confederate soldiers who have escaped from the enemy, not exceeding twenty in number that you may deem suitable for the purpose, and execute such enterprises as may be indicated to you."[3]

Ironically, the actions of the Southerners planning to strike the little Vermont community mirror those of the Union James J. Andrews's raiders in North Georgia. Like the Federal railroad raiders of 1862, the Confederates slipped into place surreptitiously, "two and three in a party," and went by different routes to "arrive all together on the night of the 18th of October, 1864."[4] The new arrivals were amiable enough to avoid arousing suspicion among local residents, hiding their true backgrounds and intentions by claiming to be Canadians in town for "a sporting vacation." No one seemed to think anything was amiss, even as the number of inquisitive strangers grew.[5]

It could not have been a better time for the Confederates to strike the sleepy little town. Horse dealers for the U.S. Army had just been through to procure animals. They had left with seven hundred prized Morgan horses, generating sales that meant that plenty of money would be on hand for the raiders to plunder when they appeared.

Once in St. Albans, the Southerners gathered at 3 p.m., closing time for the local banks. Small bands strolled into the St. Albans, Franklin County, and First National banks, all in close proximity on the town's Main Street. Pulling weapons and identifying themselves as Confederates, the raiders began haphazardly to rummage through those financial institutions. In their haste, the Southerners proved to be poor bandits and in several cases left more money behind than they took with them.[6]

The raiders then "suddenly rallied and formed in the street, with overcoats off and Confederate uniforms on." Armed with "a pair of navy sixes," as soldiers commonly referred to their six-shot .36 caliber Colt "Navy" revolvers, they "proclaimed that they took possession of St. Albans in the name of the Confederate States."[7] One of the Southerners promised that they were going to do to St. Albans "what your Sherman is doing to us."[8] The little Vermont community was momentarily the seat of the war that had until now seemed so very far away.

The Confederates ordered the people to gather in the square. At first, the local citizens seemed not to realize the urgency of the situation, but "when the Confederates began to shoot at men who hesitated to go, and one was wounded," they adhered to the demands.

In the midst of this chaotic action in the streets, other members of the raiding party fanned out to fire the town. The Confederates carried "fifty four-ounce bottles of Greek Fire each" for the purpose of "firing the hotels and other buildings."[9] If it worked as it was meant to do, "Greek Fire" would be a formidable weapon. Unhappily for the Confederates, this supposedly flammable concoction, meant to explode when it made contact with air, failed to do so. One scholar noted that the Confederates employed the substance "liberally, but once again it proved ineffective."[10]

This failure no doubt perplexed the raiders, who most likely hoped to use the flames and confusion to cover their escape as much as for any other purpose. But chaos reigned in any case, even when one of the Confederates targeted a hotel outhouse for destruction.[11]

In the meantime, other raiders gathered horses, saddles, bridles, and blankets. This was done, no doubt, to supply the raiders with fresh mounts and to prevent any pursuers from using them to catch the raiders when they pulled out of the town.

It is difficult to say the extent to which any real resistance from townspeople took place. According to one source, some of the civilians fired weapons from windows overlooking the street, and "three of the Confederates were severely wounded. . . . A skirmish now ensued, and one citizen was killed."[12] Unlike in the film, none of the Southerners died at the hands of either a Union officer seeking personal redemption or anyone else. Nor did Young have the occasion to shoot one of his subordinates, inside or outside of a church.

As the Confederates rode out of town, making for the Canadian border, the aroused citizenry attempted to organize a pursuit. For all of their good intentions, their exertions at following and catching the raiders were as inept as the Southerners' endeavors at bank robbing. The result was a delay that allowed the raiders to enjoy a good head start and at least one instance of mistaken identity when members of the posse chased an innocent farmer. Even with diligence, the effort would probably have proven fruitless, since the border was such a short distance away. Furthermore, attempts to bring in reinforcements proved no better, when a train designed to carry volunteers from Burlington suffered mechanical failure.[13]

Word of the Confederate raid on St. Albans reached the U.S. War Department almost immediately. The ordinarily mild-mannered commander of the Department of the East headquartered in New York, Major General John A. Dix, was particularly perturbed. Long an advocate of a "rosewater" policy toward Southerners, he found this operation against his department especially troublesome. On the 19th, he notified Secretary of War Edwin Stanton that "a party of rebels from Canada had struck St. Albans," robbing banks there and terrorizing local citizens. He expected that the "marauders" would be pursued "if necessary, into Canada," and that the forces pursuing them should "destroy them."[14] Dix employed the same terminology to describe the Confederates and the actions that should be taken against them in virtually all of his communications for the next twenty-four hours.

If the exasperated Union general preferred to "destroy" the Confederates rather than apprehend them, he was not alone in his vehemence regarding the subject. Governor J. Gregory Smith of Vermont was equally adamant as he sounded a similar alarm to Secretary Stanton. "A party of rebels have invaded St. Albans, robbed the banks, killed several citizens, stolen horses, and destroyed property," he explained. Presenting a bill of particulars that ranged from bank robbery to horse thieving and destruction of private property, Smith wanted immediate authorization to receive stocks of weapons for defending his state.[15]

The governor sent his plea to Dix as well, and both the general and the secretary of war responded with assurances that aid was on the way. General Dix reiterated his determination to run down the "marauders" even if the pursuit be carried "into Canada," with the goal to "overtake and destroy them."[16]

From Burlington, more concrete information concerning the raid began to arrive. The Union colonel at that post confirmed to Dix that the chase was underway. "The raiders number about twenty-five," he explained. "Your order to pursue into Canada has been forwarded."[17]

It may have been in the wake of this confirmation that Dix realized the delicacy of ordering U.S. troops to engage in hot pursuit across an international border. Hostilities had nearly occurred between the United States and Great Britain in late 1861 over the seizure of Confederate commissioners James M. Mason and John Slidell aboard the British vessel *Trent*. British forces had mobilized in Canada before the Lincoln administration brought the level of tensions down by releasing the men from their incarceration in Boston and allowing them to proceed unmolested. The envoys had proven to be more effective for the South imprisoned in the North than they ever proved in Europe, and a brash response to the St. Albans raid might produce a similar response.

Dix may have had in mind the possible international ramifications of his orders when he repeatedly called for "a discreet officer" to be put in charge of the pursuit. Such an officer could run the Southerners to ground without creating an incident in the process, even if that officer and his men breached the border between the United States and Canada.[18]

The Confederates had indeed scampered successfully across the border, but not without encountering difficulties of their own. Again, the situation was eerily reminiscent of what had taken place to hamper James J. Andrews and his Union railroad raiders two years earlier. Lieutenant Young and his men had traveled about eight miles from St. Albans and were easily outdistancing their pursuers when they reached the outskirts of Shelburne. As they approached a bridge that could take them to safety, they found their progress blocked by a large wagon loaded with hay. Perhaps thinking that no pursuit was eminent, and likely hoping not to arouse any suspicion, they waited for the conveyance to cross.

Suddenly, shots rang out as pursuers came into contact with them. The Southerners returned the fire, overturned the wagon, lit the hay, and dashed toward the border. The flaming bridge bought the Confederates precious time to reach Canada at about 9 p.m. The Southerners returned to their civilian garb and dispersed, letting the jaded horses they had taken from St. Albans go free. Here all must have seemed satisfactory. The Southerners had outpaced their pursuers and reached the safety of Canadian soil.[19]

In the meantime, additional information was coming to light on the Confederate raid and its effects. Governor Smith issued a statement repeating the basic facts that "twenty-five men rode into Saint Albans this afternoon," but added that they had robbed three banks and absconded with $150,000. In the melee, the raiders had shot five men, "one that is feared fatally." "Having accomplished their object," he noted, "the band left immediately for Canada." By the time the statement could be released, Governor Smith had appended an update: "The man Morrison, who was shot through the body has since died."[20]

With the pursuit in motion, General Dix found himself in the uncomfortable position of awaiting developments. "What news from Saint Albans?" he wired the provost marshal at Burlington plaintively. "I trust the officer understood my orders in regard to pursuing the rebel raiders into Canada. It is only in case they are found on our side of the line, and the pursuit then must be instant and continuous."[21]

Of course, how "instant and continuous" the pursuit could be in the aftermath of the raid would likely be in the interpretation of the participants. Union provost marshal Rollo Gleason responded rapidly to his worried commander, "Your orders were perfectly understood. The pursuing party was close upon the raiders when they crossed the lines and continued the pursuit, and at last accounts had captured eight, who are held by Canadian authorities awaiting requisitions" for extradition. Gleason was also clearly aware of his superior's chief concern and apparently wanted to set Dix's mind at ease. "Canadian authorities are reported to be aiding in the pursuit and capture," he reported.[22]

Lieutenant Young was not part of the tally of prisoners Gleason cited, although by one account, it was midday on October 20 when the Confederate lieutenant learned that a number of his compatriots were under arrest at Phillipsburg (modern Quebec). "He at once decided that this must necessarily compel him to give himself up to the authorities and make the case of his men his own, since he was the commander, and holding a commission and the authority for the raid," the source noted.[23]

However, Young never got the opportunity to turn himself over to Canadian authorities. Instead, while he was resting at a local farm, a party of "twenty-five people from Saint Albans" burst in on him and captured him. Apparently still angry at the brazenness of the attack on their town and homes, the citizens reportedly "proceeded to beat" the Confederate leader with pistols they had taken from him and "with swords."

Bennett Young soon found himself in the rear of a wagon, guarded by three men and headed for an uncertain fate at St. Albans. "The men were excited and carried their pistols cocked, badgering him with threats to shoot, while they denounced him in unmeasured terms." Young responded to the taunts and threats by "insisting that they were in violation of British neutrality, but they said they did not care a d__n for British law or the British nation."[24]

Seeing his predicament, Lieutenant Young attempted to make good an escape. Although he succeeded in freeing himself momentarily from his guards, they managed to subdue him. Only the timely intervention of a British officer prevented further mayhem. Young was able to tell the official his identity, and the fellow spoke to the Americans, assuring them that other raiders were in Canadian custody and would likely be turned over to the United States. The Americans agreed, and the Confederate officer returned to Phillipsburg with his British guardian.[25]

While the leader of the raid found himself in American and then British custody, Union General Dix informed Secretary of State William Seward of the parameters he had set for the operation. At the same time, he explained that he had "dined with Lord [Richard] Lyons [the British minister to Washington] and informed him of what I had done." Since he was convinced that this was only the beginning of such cross-border operations by Confederate agents, Dix wanted to be assured of Canadian cooperation. "There are other raids in contemplation," he warned, "and it is very important that the Canadian authorities should do their duty." The Union general then concluded his message to Seward, perhaps more for his own benefit than the secretary of state's, adding quickly, "I think they will."[26]

The news was good for the North on all fronts.[27] Then Governor Smith added both detail and confirmation of a positive outcome to the pursuit. "Two of our citizens badly wounded at Saint Albans by the rebels, all three of the banks robbed, one hotel fired, and about $150,000 taken, and about twenty horses," the governor tallied for General Dix. "Telegram this morning says that eight of the raiders captured by the pursuing party in Canada, nine horses, and a portion of the money recovered, not able to say how much." The anxious Vermont chief executive noted that the force was "still pursuing the raiders." But even he had to offer the raiders a grudging respect for their audacity. "It was a most daring adventure," Smith admitted to Dix.[28]

By October 23, fourteen of the Confederate raiders were in Canadian hands. In December, a Montreal judge complicated matters by ruling that "the transactions in St. Albans, Vermont, were acts of war."[29] Thus he ordered the men to be released, whereupon General Dix repeated his intentions to round up the Southerners in Canada and return them to justice in the United States, whatever the international reaction might be.

The actions of individuals on both sides exacerbated tensions on the U.S.–Canadian border, but cooler heads managed to prevail. Having made the argument that Canadian actions might adversely affect previous agreements between the two countries, Secretary of State Seward stepped in to defuse the situation. He prevailed upon President Lincoln to revoke General Dix's last order. Young and his men found themselves once more under arrest in what must have looked increasingly like an international chess game with them as pawns.[30] One student of U.S.–Canadian relations in the period has suggested that had the incident occurred earlier in the war, it might have led to more decisive action on the part of the British in response.[31] Another historian asserted that the operation created a backlash among Canadians and "hurt rather than helped the Southern Cause."[32] Confederate commissary general Josiah Gorgas saw a glimmer of hope in the troubles that Young and his band helped to create between the United States and Great Britain.[33] But, by late 1864, the Confederate States of America simply had little left to offer for its own interests in these international matters.

Of course, beyond reaching the bridge and burning it, minus the hay wagon that temporarily blocked the raiders' escape, none of this exciting pursuit made it onto film. *The Raid* centered on the events in St. Albans itself, exaggerating these and creating a fictional love story before allowing the raid to take place.[34] The celluloid pursuit came only as the credits prepared to roll. As fire consumed a bridge, the audience was left to think that the Confederates made their escape unmolested into Canada.

Neal Barton may or may not have ever returned to St. Albans. But Bennett Young did, at least in memory in the latter stage of his life. In 1911, he and his wife traveled to Montreal and hosted a small delegation of representatives from the Vermont town. The former antagonists, one of whom aside from the old Confederate had actually witnessed the raid, received each other graciously and passed an affable evening. The event surely passed better than anything Young could have imagined with the citizens of a town he and his colleagues had robbed and attempted to burn in that distant war so long ago.[35]

CHAPTER 10

The Music Teacher Raids Mississippi

While crossing the length of Mississippi, Colonel John Marlowe (John Wayne) leads his raiders through Confederate defenses meant to prevent the Union cavalrymen from reaching Baton Rouge, Louisiana, in *The Horse Soldiers*.

It was a bold and daring raid. Where were our authorities? Asleep?

—Southern civilian

He has made a most successful raid through the length of the State of Mississippi and a part of Louisiana, one which will exhilarate for a short time the fainting spirits of the Northern war party.

—Confederate Colonel R. V. Richardson

*T*HE HORSE SOLDIERS (1959) is based on the April–May 1863 raid of Union colonel Benjamin H. Grierson across the length of Mississippi and into Louisiana. This bold raid, the brainchild of Union major general Stephen A. Hurlbut, called for a small strike force of 1,700 troopers to penetrate deep behind Confederate lines, thus creating a diversion while Major General Ulysses S. Grant positioned his army for an assault against the Mississippi River city of Vicksburg. By severing communications and supply lines, Hurlbut hoped to provide an annoyance that would force the Southerners to commit most of their cavalry to the pursuit of the raiders, effectively blinding them to Grant's operations. The scheme worked to perfection.

Certainly, Grierson's raid provided an excellent dramatic context for a film. Likewise, the image of John Wayne on horseback, dressed in a U.S. cavalry uniform, was a powerful one as well. Wayne exuded a strong sense of authority on-screen, which must have been the kind of presence director John Ford wanted for his leading role. *The Horse Soldiers* was Ford's only full-length Civil War film. Although the war figured in several of his westerns and his direction of a segment of the epic, *How the West Was Won* (1962), which briefly depicted scenes associated with the battle of Shiloh, no other Ford movie utilized the war as its central element.

Ford brought his earlier work into *The Horse Soldiers*. Perhaps foremost, he assembled a team of veteran actors, many of whom had held supporting roles in earlier Ford pictures. He and Wayne had worked together on several films, including the acclaimed *Stagecoach* (1939), *They Were Expendable* (1945), *Fort Apache* (1948), *She Wore a Yellow Ribbon* (1949), and *The Quiet Man* (1952). In *The Searchers* (1956) Ford even provided Wayne with his only role as a Confederate, a complex former soldier named Ethan Edwards, whom one student of the director's work termed, "Ford's most ambiguous character."[1] In their collective cinematic endeavors the two men formed an impressive collaboration.

Likewise, the director drew upon familiar themes that he had explored in his earlier work. A common Ford device was the placement of his protagonists into isolated situations in which they faced threatening conditions. The collective danger surrounding these diverse individuals would coalesce them into an effective whole that could combat the enemy and allow them to survive the test. Thus, Ford would build a cohesive unit of characters that could learn from the circumstances to function together to accomplish a common mission.

In this film, the unit emerges from the disparate parts it first comprises as the soldiers move deeper into hostile Confederate territory. The shared service and sacrifices binds the individuals together in the quest to fulfill their goal of crippling a major Southern supply line and returning to their own lines unscathed.

Even the existence of the self-serving soldier/politician, Colonel Phil Secord (Willis Bouchey), who at one point in the expedition announces unashamedly that there is "no disgrace in an honorable surrender," does not prevent the command from uniting as it should to achieve its purpose. Indeed, Secord plans to feed off of the raid's success by using it to propel himself, first, into Congress and then, as the effort garners greater victories, into the presidency. Yet, for all of Secord's bluff and willingness to build his career on the lives of his men, he comes across as an essentially harmless blowhard and self-promoter, rather than a manipulative and evil figure.

The most significant internal division exists between the expedition's commander, Colonel Henry Marlowe (John Wayne), and the unit's surgeon, Major Henry Kendall (William Holden). The antagonism between them intensifies as they constantly gibe and joust with each other. Finally, the men strip their blouses in order to solve their differences with their fists, only to have the war intrude on their pugilistic intentions. Such personal hostile displays aside, the unit survives its ordeal, with respect eventually replacing disdain among its members.

This is not to say that Ford succeeds in leaving behind some of the less savory elements of his earlier films. Capable of creating stock characters that reinforce popular stereotypical views of people, the director demonstrates the same tendency here. His Irish sergeants have less to do than in other films, but they, and their love of whiskey, for instance, are just as ubiquitous.

To be sure, *The Horse Soldiers* is a product of its time, like any Hollywood creation. Released in 1959, it reflects, ironically for a Civil War piece, the homogenization moviegoers expected of the America of the 1950s. John Wayne leads troops in a military expedition against their fellow Americans, but in the context of a Cold War as much as a Civil War. Consequently, the Union troopers remain true to their military mission, but their destructiveness comes across as almost playful rather than malicious. Colonel Marlowe, portrayed as a former railroad man himself, deplores the destruction, even pulling one rowdy trooper from his horse when the man exults too openly at the devastation he is witnessing. To the gloating and vainglorious Colonel Secord, Marlowe angrily spouts, "That's how I made my living you know, building railroads." While, in the immediate aftermath of the bloody fight for Newton Station, he tells the doctor, "I tried to avoid a fight."

Similarly, Major Kendall, the regiment's doctor, demonstrates genuine affection for a former colleague, now wearing the gray, by tackling him in the street during the fighting at Newton Station rather than standing by and watching him gunned down. He attends the wounded Confederate and before leaving with the raiders congratulates him on his effort to stop them, unsuccessful though it has been.

The Union officers are uniformly respectful in the presence of the Southern "belle," Miss Hannah Hunter of Greenbriar (Constance Towers), while the enlisted men are gratifyingly awkward around her. Yet, if the troopers do not know exactly how to behave around a "lady," they are essentially harmless, even protective of her. When she loses her servant Lukey to gunfire from Southern bushwhackers, the grizzled Union veterans gather around her to bring such comfort as they can to her in her time of distress.

The film handles the issue of slavery delicately. References to the institution are short and oblique. The servant Lukey is depicted as unfailingly loyal to her mistress, helping her to spy on a Union officers' strategy conference and attending her once she is forced to join the raiders on their way. At one point during the expedition, Dr. Kendall declines to help Miss Hunter, observing, "Fortunately, you Southern people have your own help." The only other reference comes when one of the Confederate deserters the column encounters brags of his comrade's marksmanship in bringing down a runaway slave.

The Southerners in the movie are a mixed lot, yet for the most part, they share the qualities of devotion to the cause and a determination to defend it. Miss Hannah and her servant must accompany the raiders when they are caught listening to the Federals' plans and refuse to promise silence in exchange for their freedom. The one-armed veteran Johnny Miles leads the Confederates in their futile defense of Newton Station, while the men he leads in the attack are shot down in droves.

Even the most reprehensible characters, the two Confederate deserters, have a humorous rather than a repellant or hostile quality. Played by Strother Martin and Denver Pyle, they offer a moment of comic relief for Marlowe and his men as they capture and interrogate the deserters. Yet, when they act disrespectfully to Miss Hunter, Marlowe dons gauntlets to punch each of the "gentlemen" in the mouth. There will be no other punishment for them by these Union cavalrymen, except to turn them back over to an elderly sheriff. Unlike in the historical raid, the sheriff remains unmolested and there is no government money on him for the raiders to confiscate.

Ironically, a greater sense of diversity seems to characterize the Union officers leading the raid. While dining at Greenbriar, Miss Hunter summarizes their backgrounds: "Major Kendall a doctor. And Colonel Secord almost a Congressman. And you an actor. And now all military men." She disdainfully concludes, "Such a waste of talent." Miss Hunter proves mistaken when she assumes that Marlowe is a professional soldier. He bluntly corrects the misimpression. "Prior to this insanity, I was a railroad engineer," he explains.

John Ford may have considered Grierson's actual civilian career as a music teacher to be inappropriate for John Wayne's character. Certainly, he did not want the audience to doubt Marlowe's credibility as a soldier and cavalry raider. In any case, the dilemma of a railroad builder now assuming the role of a railroad destroyer adds a useful dimension to the character and a sense of irony to the film.

Particularly with Wayne's Marlowe, but with the other principal characters as well, the movie allows only a gradual development. The colonel is depicted as a widower whose wife's death at the hands of a surgeon feeds his antagonism toward Kendall. By the end of the film, Marlowe will discover that he has fallen in love with his Southern captive, and he declares his feelings to her in a scene that is as incongruous to the central story as it is ludicrous for the real Grierson, who remained devoted to his wife.

The Horse Soldiers enjoys a good deal of creative license, yet it never seems to take itself too seriously. The battle scenes are quite tame, especially compared to those of the war films fifty years later. Words often replace the more powerful, but gruesome, visual images, as when Kendall and a local doctor treat the wounded at Newton Station or when Kendall removes a soldier's badly infected leg.

Ford uses the relationship between Colonel Marlowe and Miss Hunter, or the men detailed to guard her, to provide lighthearted moments along the way. Another such moment comes when a band of cadets at a military school and the venerable commandant march out to confront the raiders. A distraught mother approaches the old warrior to ask that her son be excused, explaining that she has already lost the rest of her family to the war. The commandant agrees and orders the lad out of ranks, but anxious to experience war at first hand, he climbs out of a window and races to rejoin to his colleagues as they march off to intercept the Federal invaders.

As the cadets stage their attack, the Union raiders pull out of their camp, lest anyone be hurt in the fray. Marlowe prevents one of his troopers from shooting the old schoolmaster. When one of his scouts brings in a prisoner and asks him what he should do with him, the cavalry commander replies, "Spank him." The young fellow must submit to the indignity of a whipping from the "dirty Yankee." It is, metaphorically, the same reaction that Grierson displayed when he confronted Southern civilians. He preferred to lecture them and send them home, much as he might have done to a recalcitrant student who had neglected his music lessons.

Then, as the charging youngsters rush against the Union troops, they encounter a large tree sprawled across their line of advance. Despite their warlike circumstances, some feel compelled to climb over or scamper under the limbs of the tree, as if on a backyard romp rather than on a battlefield. Finally, as the last cadet frees himself from the roots, the commandant strides into the scene wielding only a cane and a Bible.

The inclusion of the cadets from the Jefferson Military Academy suggests that John Ford, a devotee of the Civil War, wanted to put as much of the war as possible into the film, even when the connections were tenuous. Nothing like this occurred during Grierson's raid. Indeed, the most obvious historical parallel was the participation of cadets from the Virginia Military Institute in the battle of New Market in Virginia, both geographically and chronologically quite distant from the raid depicted on-screen.[2]

Ford includes various historical figures in the film. He opens with General Hurlbut introducing Colonel Marlowe to Ulysses S. Grant and William T. Sherman as they discuss the pending operation. During the raid itself, numerous references suggest that Confederate major general Nathan Bedford Forrest is tracking the column. In point of fact, Forrest was chasing a Union raiding force, but not Grierson's. His pursuit of Union colonel Abel Streight's command as it crossed northern Alabama ended in the latter's capture.[3]

Likewise, several characters suggest that, if captured, the raiders are doomed to spend time in Andersonville Prison in Georgia, despite the fact that the prison did not receive its first occupants until the end of February 1864.[4] Furthermore, captured officers such as Colonel Streight, or Marlowe and Kendall in the film, would not have gone to Andersonville in any case. Streight went to Libby Prison in Richmond.[5] Grant's reference in the movie to the officers going to the "hell hole" of Andersonville may have played well with audiences, but it did not fit well historically with the facts.[6]

The cavalry accoutrements and uniforms are generally true to the period. The insignia of rank for the officers on both sides is correct. Johnny Miles wears the three stars of a Confederate colonel, while Dr. Kendall wears the gold oak leaves of a Union major. Marlowe's insignia is more difficult to distinguish, but he appears to wear the oak leaves of a lieutenant colonel (which should be silver), rather than the eagles of a full colonel. The "butternut guerrillas" are appropriately dressed, although fewer in number than those Grierson employed in the raid. One of the Confederate deserters is barefoot.

Because John Ford could not handle the horses as they would have been treated in such a military operation, the animals do not demonstrate the wear and tear they would have shown over the course of a long and grueling campaign. The director attempts to compensate for this in part through his manipulation of music and imagery, with the best indication of this coming at the beginning of the raid. The men start off on the expedition jauntily, singing lustily, then as the hours in the saddle begin to show, the music and the singing lag, until the men are dismounted and leading their weary mounts.

Clearly, *The Horse Soldiers* is a work of entertainment. Still, the director occasionally chose reality over theatricality. Film historian J. A. Place observes, "*The Horse Soldiers* is an unusual cavalry picture for John Ford because its hero is not a career man."[7] To be true to Grierson, upon whom Marlowe is obviously based, the character could not be a career soldier. Furthermore, the raids that the fictional Marlowe and the real-life Grierson carried out fit the same basic profile by originating in LaGrange, Tennessee, and ending at Baton Rouge, Louisiana. Both the fictional and historical raids featured destruction of Confederate property and railroads that the Confederates were unable to prevent.

Still, the man who General Stephen Hurlbut selected to lead the force would not have been mistaken for John Wayne. Colonel Benjamin Grierson certainly must have seemed an unlikely choice, since he had no formal military training and had been a music teacher and businessman before the war. But Hurlbut registered no reservations for the record and in the course of the campaign observed, "I have full faith that he can cut through any force they can raise."[8]

Grierson may have lacked a West Point pedigree, but the Pittsburgh, Pennsylvania, native was a loyal soldier who had joined the war at the outset. Commissioned major of the Sixth Illinois Cavalry in October 1861, he quickly became the unit's colonel. The Sixth saw only sporadic service in 1862, but by the spring of 1863 Grierson was ready to do some raiding of his own.

In mid-April, Colonel Grierson assembled a force of 1,700 men drawn from his own unit, the Seventh Illinois, and the Second Iowa at LaGrange, Tennessee. This command and a battery of six light artillery pieces set out on April 17, 1863. Crossing into Mississippi at an easy pace, the Federals met no resistance on the first day. However, they encountered their first opposition on the 18th, and from that point, Grierson had to assume that the Confederates knew of his raid and would expend every resource to intercept it.

The Union colonel proved more than equal to the challenge. On two occasions, he split off portions of the command to return to LaGrange for the purpose of deceiving the enemy into thinking the entire raiding force had turned back. The first of these parties left on April 20, carrying the "least effective" 175 men, one of the guns, and all of the prisoners taken to that point. The second left on the 21st, with orders to raid the Mobile and Ohio Railroad near the town of West Point and do as much damage as possible before returning to LaGrange.[9]

The ruse worked better than Grierson could have hoped. A substantial Confederate cavalry force pursued the smaller force, leaving the main column free to continue its march more or less unmolested. Indeed, the only resistance Grierson's command faced for most of the raid consisted of guerrillas and home guards. The latter, citizens who organized to protect their communities, proved the least effective, often scattering at the first sign of the approaching raiders.

As the command moved deeper into Confederate territory, Grierson used a small force of scouts, dubbed the "butternut guerrillas," to provide himself with information and to confuse the enemy. The force of eight troopers and a sergeant served superbly throughout the expedition, at one point sending a force that would have collided with the raiders scurrying down the wrong road.[10]

A second device Grierson employed proved just as effective. On several occasions, he broke off small detachments to hit the rail lines at some distance from the main column. These units aided in confusing the enemy as to the location of the main body of raiders. Confederate colonel Wirt Adams expressed his frustration when he complained to Lieutenant General John C. Pemberton in Vicksburg, "Notwithstanding I marched over 50 miles per day, and moved during day and night . . . [yet] I found it impossible, to my great mortification and regret, to overhaul them."[11]

The main Union force reached the rail line leading into Vicksburg early on April 24. Grierson sent volunteers with the scouts to seize Newton, on the Southern Mississippi Railroad. The scouts determined the Confederate defense of Newton to be negligible, it having no troops other than those in a military hospital there. The town fell quickly into Union hands before Grierson and the larger portion of the command had time to arrive. In fact, when two Confederate supply trains stumbled into the Federals' possession, the lieutenant colonel commanding the detachment had them blown up. The resulting explosion caused Grierson to race to his troops' relief, believing them to be under attack.

When he arrived, Colonel Grierson assumed command and directed the destruction of the remaining public property. As he explained in his report, "Here the track was torn up, and a bridge half a mile west of the station destroyed." Grierson concluded, "Having damaged as much as possible the railroad and telegraph, and destroyed all Government property in the vicinity of Newton, I moved about 4 miles south of the [rail]road and fed men and horse."[12]

A major element of the raid accomplished, Grierson still had a force to extricate from deep in Southern territory. Once more, he considered his options and determined his best course would be to continue south. The scouts paved the way, suggesting routes by which the raiders could bypass places containing larger Confederate forces. Grierson recalled in his postraid report, "Colton's pocket map of Mississippi, which, though small, is very correct, was all I had to guide me; but by the capture of their couriers, dispatches, and mails, and the invaluable aid of my scouts, we were always able by rapid marches to evade the enemy when they were too strong and whip them when not too large."[13]

As the expedition neared its end, the pressure became greater than ever. The raiders dispersed bands of armed civilians, usually capturing large amounts of weapons, ammunition, and equipment in the process. Although Grierson often sent the older citizens home with a stern lecture, he saw to it that private property, excluding food and forage, remained protected. On one occasion, the Federals captured a sheriff of a local county and confiscated the $3,000 in government funds in his possession. Still, Confederate General Pemberton had reason to boast to President Davis that, "all the cavalry I can raise is close on their rear."[14]

Despite their success thus far, Grierson began to run into more and more opposition. At Brookhaven, he encountered "about 500 citizens and conscripts . . . organized to resist us" and dispersed them, capturing "over 200 prisoners." Still, the command was suffering from the long hours in the saddle. Men and horses were wearing out, just as the last and most dangerous leg of the raid was being undertaken.[15]

On May 1, the Federals found a bridge over the Tickfaw River being guarded. The same lieutenant colonel who had dashed into Newton led a bold, but reckless charge against the defenders. The Confederates repulsed the assault, killing one and wounding several, including the Union commander of the detachment. However, Grierson arrived with the main column, deployed his artillery, and sent out forces to hit the Southerners in the flanks. Under this pressure, the smaller Confederate force withdrew, leaving the bridge under Union control.

Placing the wounded under the care of a surgeon from the Seventh Illinois, Grierson ordered the column to proceed. Ironically, under the desperation to escape, Grierson won his greatest military successes of the campaign. Spending the "last twenty-eight hours" traveling seventy-six miles, the Federals fought "four engagements with the enemy."[16] One of Grierson's victims, Captain B. F. Bryan, had the misfortune of having to file a report explaining how he and most of his command (thirty-eight men, thirty-eight horses, and so forth) fell into Union hands without resistance.[17] Confederate colonel R. V. Richardson tried to put a more positive face on the setbacks, considering the failure to stop the raid due to the unwillingness of the Union forces to stand and fight. "It was not his desire to fight," that officer lamented of his opponent. "He wanted to make observations, destroy railroads and telegraphic communications."[18]

Whatever the Southerners might think of his intentions, when Grierson drove off the last Confederates barring his way to Baton Rouge, he had completed an enviable military coup. Carrying his command across the face of Mississippi, over some six hundred miles in sixteen days, he managed to bring the substantial portion of his men back safely behind Union lines while capturing some five hundred Confederates, wrecking miles of railroad, and confiscating weapons, horses, and mules.[19] The psychological impact, particularly on Mississippians, was also substantial. One Southerner confided in his diary, "It was a bold and daring raid. Where were our authorities? 'Asleep?'"[20] Most importantly from a strategic view, the raid tied up the cavalry that might have been used against Grant's operations near Vicksburg.[21]

Grierson's accomplishments, at a loss of three killed, seven wounded, and fourteen either missing or left behind sick, were phenomenal.[22] Even the Confederates had to acknowledge the feat. "He has made a most successful raid through the length of the State of Mississippi and a part of Louisiana," Colonel Richardson admitted, "one which will exhilarate for a short time the fainting spirits of the Northern war party."[23]

Union authorities were especially pleased. General Hurlbut called "this gallant exploit of Colonel Grierson" "unequalled in the war."[24] William T. Sherman labeled the raid, "the most brilliant expedition of the war."[25] Admiring spectators lined the streets of Baton Rouge when the raiders reached the town, while the music-teacher-turned-cavalry-raider received his commission to brigadier general the following month.[26]

The Horse Soldiers is good fun, particularly if one is a fan of either Wayne or Holden. Yet, as a reflection of historical reality, it comes up well short. The inclusion of stock characters and out-of-place historical incidents clouds the real story of Grierson's successful raid. Likewise, the dramatic need for the Hannah Hunter character defies historical or military logic. To carry a Southern woman in a Union raiding expedition as a foil for Wayne's character is one thing; to jeopardize the raid by her presence is quite another. Still, if one wants a demonstration of the élan of the cavalry, or a rather sanitized sense of the drama of a cavalry raid against an enemy's lines of communication and supply, this one will offer a glimpse. If one wants a more realistic understanding of this raid or the use of cavalry in the war, he or she should consult one of the historical works on the subject.

CHAPTER 11

A Stomach for War

Copyright © 1966 Columbia Pictures Corporation. All Rights Reserved · Printed in U.S.A. · Permission is hereby granted to newspapers, magazines and other periodicals to reproduce this photograph for other than advertising purposes. Must not be sold, leased or given away.

Colonel Tom Rossiter (Richard Widmark, l.) and Alvarez Kelly (William Holden, r.) ponder their reluctant partnership in a scheme to capture a herd of Union cattle to feed General Robert E. Lee's hungry army in *Alvarez Kelly*.

130

It was a fair capture, and they [the cattle] were sufficiently needed by the Confederates.

—Union general Ulysses S. Grant

LVAREZ KELLY (1966) takes its historical basis from the operations of Confederate generals Wade Hampton and Thomas L. Rosser in September 1864. Popularly referred to as the "Beefsteak Raid," the effort secured almost 2,500 head of Union cattle for the Confederacy, giving Robert E. Lee's men a badly needed boost in morale as well as sustenance for his hungry army.[1]

Alvarez Kelly glamorizes the historical cavalry raid. It features a charming, but roguish, William Holden as the title character and Richard Widmark as the battle-scarred but devoted Confederate officer. Kelly (Holden) is a self-serving and self-absorbed entrepreneur who wants nothing more than to sell his herd to the most dependable bidder and pocket his profits in peace. But fulfilling that desire proves elusive as the Confederates intervene to steal the cattle and force Kelly to assist them in shooing the animals safely behind Southern lines.

As the film opens, a word scroll establishes its theme. "In every war . . . in every age . . . the forgotten weapon is . . . food. For to kill, a soldier must live . . . to live he must eat. And a herd of cattle is as vital as a herd of cannon." Yet for all of its relevance to conflict "in every age," this motion picture is not about just any war or any herd of cattle; it is set in "the United States in 1864."

Alvarez Kelly moves his cattle from Mexico toward a rail line and a rendezvous with a Union officer with the authority to purchase and ship the animals to Virginia. The Union officer, Major Albert Steadman (Patrick O'Neal), deliberately antagonizes the cattleman, who inquires coyly, "Is it Vermont or Massachusetts?" The major responds that he is a lawyer from Boston. When Kelly suggests that he might see how the other side might treat him, Steadman responds sanctimoniously, "You'd do business with the Confederates?" Kelly pauses only momentarily, "No, their money's no good."

Kelly and his men move the cattle by train to Virginia and then drive them onto a local plantation "thirty miles south of Richmond." The Federals have need of the beef to sustain an army that is planning for the final campaign of the war. "The war's going to a new phase," Steadman explains to Kelly. "We're concentrating on Richmond. And when we take it, we've won." This is the reason for Kelly's beef to be sent there and for him to be personally responsible for the herd's delivery. The Union officer insists that the contract between them specifies, "in rather small print I'll admit," that he drive the herd to Virginia himself in order to receive payment. "I prepared it myself, even in specifying the size of the print. Now those steers are going east Mr. Kelly."

When the cattle arrive at the Virginia plantation, the mistress, Charity Warrick (Victoria Shaw), directs them to be placed in the "north pasture."

The Union officer makes arrangements for the cattle and invites himself to dinner.

At the same time, hungry Confederates watch as the herd reaches its destination. A one-eyed Southerner, Colonel Tom Rossiter (Richard Widmark) allows his men to cut out a steer. "There's enough down there to feed a lot of people," the Confederate observes. The Rebels knock out a drover, grab a steer, and then inexplicably cook the meat by fire within sight of the plantation and its visitors. Just as incredibly, the Federals initially fail to detect either the Confederates or their fallen comrade.

In the meantime, Steadman pays Kelly the $50,000 owed him for bringing the cattle to Virginia. "So now you go to some nice, safe place and count your profits," he sneers. "Money, whiskey, and women, your three deities." The cattleman takes the slight in stride. "Do you object to someone making money Miss Charity?" "In wartime?" she responds, "I think so." Kelly's rejoinder reveals a great deal about what drives him. "Making money out of war is an act of nature." To the major, he inquires, "But what about a colonel's salary? Prestige after. You'll carry that rank into every courtroom for the rest of your life." Touching a nerve, Kelly's observation elicits an immediate denial. "I didn't go to war for that!" "No, but you'll use it. . . . Every man in his own special way takes care of number one." Therein lies the mantra of Alvarez Kelly—figure out how to take care of yourself first.

Charity suggests she has no respect for such a man. Kelly calls her hand on her own hypocrisy, pointing out that she had wanted the cattle to be placed in the overworked "north pasture" so that the fertilizer that results would help to replenish it. A soldier interrupts to tell the major that they have found the drover. Kelly and Charity are left to themselves. "I should think your sympathies would be with us," she prods. "I have no sympathies," he answers, "just instincts, and they shy away from losers." Despite the dismissing comment, she and Kelly embrace and kiss. Confederates suddenly appear while Kelly is thus occupied.

Rossiter and his men capture him. "I warn you, I'm a Mexican national," he argues. "Doing business with the Yanks," the Confederate officer replies. Kelly cannot help but wonder what interest the Southerners might have in detaining him rather than simply taking his money and departing. "For some reason you want me alive and in one piece. Why?" The answer will come soon enough. They carry him to Richmond by a skiff that the captive dismisses contemptuously: "Confederate man-of-war?"

In the Confederate capital, Kelly and Rossiter meet with Secretary of War Harrison and disclose their scheme to capture the herd. Kelly balks. "How are you going to get 2,500 head of cattle over Grant's lines?" Posted on the wall behind them is the first Confederate national flag to add a sense of official status to an otherwise nondescript room.

"You know there's a small army guarding those steers? Now how do you expect to get them without a fight?" Rossiter is unfazed. "I'll handle the military end. You'll handle the herd." Kelly remarks, "Fair division," but otherwise remains unconvinced. "I do not intend to die from a Yankee bullet, so I say the hell with it Colonel."

The Southerners hold Kelly in prison, hoping to convince him to change his mind. Rossiter explains that his men will suffice as drovers, noting that they are all "Top riders. Fought under Jeb Stuart." But when Kelly leaves his cell to evaluate their capabilities in that capacity, he judges the men to be less than adequate. The Southerners learn that the task of herding cattle is not as easy as it looks. Disgustedly, Rossiter yells out, "Sound retreat," but Kelly has decided to have nothing to do with the experiment. "You can train us," the Southerner implores to no effect, before finally ordering Kelly, "Back to jail."

Rossiter returns to visit the incarcerated cattleman. "General Lee has approved the raid; that makes you the missing link." Kelly remains unmoved. "Missing is the word." Finally, the Confederate plays to Kelly's greed by burning some of his confiscated cash. When this latest ploy fails to have the desired effect, Rossiter turns to more drastic measures. "Ten days before we start," he remarks, and shoots off one of Kelly's fingers. "Ten days. You used to have ten fingers, now you've got nine. Tomorrow you'll have eight. You stay stubborn, the day after that you'll have seven. The day after that. . . . It's up to you. You decide whether you want to end up with a pair of stumps or lend us your talent. You decide." Kelly has already observed, "God deliver me from dedicated men," but there will clearly be no deliverance unless he agrees to cooperate. "You gentlemen have a way of making it hard for me to refuse," he says as he finally accepts the assignment to train the Southerners for their cattle raid. Secretary Harrison devises the recruit's cover as a rich Mexican speculator and invites him to a soiree. Rossiter has obtained Kelly's services, but under extreme duress, and assigns a subordinate, Sergeant Hatcher (Richard Rust), to watch the entrepreneur closely, lest his newfound loyalty begin to waver.

The dance in full dress is not unlike that seen in *Gone with the Wind*. Rossiter's fiancée, Liz Pickering (Janice Rule), arrives. "That is what I hate most about the Yanks," she tells him. "They keep us apart." But all is not as congenial between them as it seems. Kelly quickly assesses the situation. Sensing a distance between the two, he sees his opportunity for a measure of revenge on Rossiter, if by no other means than by lavishing attention on Pickering. "You're gallant enough to be a Virginian," she remarks shortly after meeting him. "And your beauty goes beyond the bounds of geography," Kelly suavely replies. She clearly has something in mind, and asks him to meet with her later to discuss an urgent matter.

"Playing with fire, aren't you lad?" a sea captain and blockade runner he has met at the gathering asks when Kelly returns to his seat. "It's not my house," he coldly replies. Kelly plans to slip out of his residence for the covert meeting with Pickering, but finds his intentions complicated by Sergeant Hatcher, who Rossiter has assigned to keep an eye on him. Unfazed, Kelly concocts an idea, and soon he and his Confederate watchdog head out to locate a "house of joy." "Let's be off," he tells the Southerner in mock camaraderie. "Two men of the world."

At the house of prostitution, Kelly searches for a way to divert the sergeant from his trail. He chooses one of the courtesans and heads for an upstairs room, managing to convince the sergeant that he will be occupied for the rest of the evening. When they reach the room, he asks her, "You lonely?" "Not really," she replies. "Friendly?" "Not very." "Thirsty?" "Not especially." Kelly has found what he wants. As he opens the window to leave, he gives her money. "Now look, I want you to stay here all night," he explains. Then handing her a book to help her wile away the time they would ordinarily be employing in another fashion, he instructs, "Improve your mind. Your body's already perfect."

Kelly is now free to have his clandestine meeting with Liz Pickering. He learns that she wants his help in getting out of Richmond. With Rossiter's reaction in mind, the cattleman agrees. The next day, Kelly meets with the sea captain and arranges for Pickering's transportation, paying an extra sum for her travel "with maid servant." She thanks him and apologizes for taking advantage of him. "As for using me," Kelly responds, "it seems to be the national pastime of the Confederate States of America."

In the meantime, Kelly works with the Confederates. They balk when he insists they sing "Dixie" to soothe the cattle and prevent a stampede. Secretary Harrison is less concerned with appearances and observes lightly, "Mr. Kelly, I'd give you the Richmond symphony if they weren't already in the army." But the Confederate official is not the only one witnessing the preparations. A Union spy watches as well, and rushes to Major Steadman to report on Kelly and his association with the Southerners. He theorizes as to the cattleman's scheme: "Alvarez Kelly is planning to import herds of Mexican beef into the Southern states by sea." Steadman replies that the "theory is idiotic." He conjectures, "Amusing picture, boatload of seasick cows all standing with their heads over the rail." Yet Steadman thinks there may be something to the notion. The plan may not be so much to bring cattle from Mexico into the Confederacy as to obtain a herd "closer to home."

He takes his theory to a superior, who scoffs at the idea. "Grant has an army around Richmond. Rossiter has to get his cavalry out and the cattle in. Now plead your case." Once he has done so, the general notes wryly, "Major, if anyone tries to steal one of your precious cows, telegraph me and I'll come a running."

Rossiter makes Kelly his temporary lieutenant colonel. Kelly informs him that he has paid to get Pickering out of the country. It is too late to stop her, and the cattleman's cooperation is still too important to be discarded. The men report, and Rossiter lays out the plan. "We'll head for Grant's backdoor, through Blackwater Swamp. About a fifty mile route. . . . Cavalry under General Hampton will cover our flank on return." Having dispensed with military matters, Rossiter is still in no mood to forgive, assuring Kelly, "that book's not closed, yet." The Confederate instructs Hatcher, "If anything happens to me, kill him." The sergeant will stick close to Kelly, with the justification, "Colonel Rossiter detailed me as your aide."

The raiders set out. Men test a crucial bridge and determine that it needs to be improved. The troops shore up the bridge so that it will stand the weight and punishment when hundreds of cattle cross. Kelly tries to get away, but Rossiter catches him. The bulk of the command rides on to the plantation and takes refuge in a fruit cellar. Hatcher kills a sentry, tries on his boots, and rifles his body.

In the meantime, Rossiter gathers information on the force that he will face. "How many men?" he asks. "Two hundred at the very least." "Any idea what regiment they are?" "Pennsylvania Twelfth." "We fought them in the Wilderness Colonel, remember? They've equipped with them new repeating rifles." Rossiter orders the telegraph line cut so that word of the operation will take longer to get out to units that might ride to the rescue.

In the meantime, the Federals find and kill a Confederate. His suspicions aroused, Steadman probes for intelligence of his own. Under interrogation, a servant says she does not know the Confederate, and she covers an apple core that might give away their hiding place in the fruit cellar. "I don't understand," Steadman observes. "We're down here fighting for you. Fighting to free you. Ruth, how can you be so loyal to someone who wants to keep you a slave?"

As a detail takes the Confederate for burial, a storage apple falls from his haversack. Steadman sees it, makes the appropriate deduction, and orders the Confederates out of the cellar. But just as it seems that the Union major has stymied the Southern scheme, other Confederates appear to disarm his men and take them captive. Steadman grabs the slave woman to use as a shield until he can get clear and escapes. The Southerners capture the other Union troops, collecting their weapons and the cattle.

The Union major reaches headquarters and reports to the general. Far from being upset at the news, the general is elated. "I gambled Lee would risk his cavalry and he did. He did. The herd is bait for Rossiter, and Rossiter is bait for Hampton. . . . I knew what that beef meant to the Rebs." He orders six thousand men of the Second New York to move down the Jerusalem Plank Road to intercept the herd and the Rebel wranglers. The general gives Steadman his reserves, consisting of three hundred men and a howitzer battery.

The cattle move through the swamp toward the bridge. The Confederates scout the approaches and find Federals arriving under Steadman. Kelly decides to use the cattle to punch through the blocking force, and Rossiter lets him take over the operation from this point. Steadman waits at the river crossing, where his men apparently have enough time to improve their defensive works with head logs.

The Southerners stampede the cattle in the direction of the Union defenses at the bridge. Federal troops break and run. The Confederates have rigged canteens with black powder to be employed as homemade bombs. The cattle rumble across the bridge. In the meantime, the Confederates set powder to blow it when the cattle are across.

Some of the men and cattle go down under the Union fire. Kelly goes back for a lieutenant who has been unhorsed. Hatcher sees his opportunity to rid himself of the troublesome cattleman and shoots at Kelly. A wounded Rossiter sees what the sergeant is doing and fires at him. Although he is now severely wounded, Hatcher manages to fire the powder trail. Kelly races for safety and dives into the river as the bridge explodes.

Now that Steadman's force has been scattered, the injured Rossiter exults, "Clear sailing to Richmond." The tally of casualties for the raid is fairly light: eight dead and twenty wounded, with some forty steers lost. The narrator concludes, "For once the soldiers of the Confederacy and the people of Richmond would eat their fill. What General Grant had to say when he heard that his prize herd was raided is unquotable. President Lincoln's comment, however, is a matter of record. Lincoln called it 'the slickest piece of cattle stealing I ever heard of.'"

Like *The Raid* and *The Horse Soldiers*, *Alvarez Kelly* is one of the few Civil War motion pictures to examine a specific military operation or campaign. Historically, the Beefsteak Raid had its inception in the early fall of 1864, when General Robert E. Lee suggested that Wade Hampton consider an attack on Ulysses S. Grant's headquarters at City Point, Virginia. He instructed the successor to Jeb Stuart, killed earlier at Yellow Tavern, to "have the matter closely inquired into and the roads and distances you would have to travel." Lee may even have dared to hope that a well-coordinated lightning strike might catch the Union commander himself. At any rate, he was convinced that "a sudden blow in that quarter might be detrimental to him."[2]

With these ideas percolating in his mind, Hampton dispatched a Southern agent, Sergeant George Shadburne, to examine the Union lines as Lee desired. The scout subsequently notified General Hampton of Federal troop dispositions in the area he had recently scouted. Buried in his report, but as future actions would indicate, not lost in it, was the location of a vast herd of cattle near the Union supply center of City Point on the James and Appomattox Rivers. "At Coggins' Point [there] are 3,000 beeves," the Southerner estimated, "attended by 120 men and 30 citizens, without arms."[3] The number of troopers guarding the herd was invitingly small, supplemented only by a few unarmed drovers to handle the herd. According to one of the general's biographers, "the idea of rustling cattle from under Grant's nose tickled Hampton's fancy and appealed to his sense of the absurd."[4]

Still, a swift cavalry raid behind Union lines would be required to snatch the prize. Robert E. Lee communicated his concern to Hampton on the 9th. "The only difficulty of importance I see to your project is your return." Asking the cavalryman to speak with him further on the subject, the Confederate army commander must have been satisfied with what he heard, for he subsequently assented to the operation.[5] Confederate generals Wade Hampton and Tom Rosser set the plan into motion on September 14.

As in the film, the Confederates had to cross the Blackwater River on a bridge that had to be rebuilt. While the raiders plunged ahead with Shadburne as a guide, other Southern commands under Major General William H. F. "Rooney" Lee and Brigadier General James Dearing fanned out to provide protection on the flanks.[6]

The soldiers settled in for the night within a short ride of the cattle pens that contained the prize they hoped to acquire. Rosser's men made contact with well-armed Union troops from the First District of Columbia Cavalry early on the 16th. A swift dash among them by the Southerners neutralized the firepower advantage that newly acquired Henry repeating rifles gave to the Federals. The Confederates experienced more trouble subduing the members of the Thirteenth Pennsylvania Cavalry, responsible for guarding the herd, but managed to overcome them as well. Impressing the civilian drovers into the service of the Confederacy, Rosser and his men pushed the nearly 2,500 head of cattle toward Southern cook stoves. As the herd spread out, it covered approximately seven miles of ground.

Belatedly, the Federals sought to intercept the herd. Apparently not as well prepared as the general in the movie, brigadier generals August V. Kautz and Henry E. Davies mounted a pursuit. A flurry of communications between the Union commanders attested to the chase, the messages sometimes occurring on almost an hourly basis.[7] Finally, late in the afternoon, Davies's efforts to overtake the Confederates required them to fight, but the raid had been accomplished with such rapidity that there was actually little the Federals could do to stop it. The operation cost the Southerners ten killed, forty-seven wounded, and four missing, a larger number than the film seemed to indicate. The Confederates netted 2,468 of the available 2,486 head of valuable beef cattle.[8] The Northerners suffered approximately three hundred casualties, mostly in missing or captured. General Kautz reported the D.C. Cavalry tally alone at four killed, one wounded, and two hundred and twelve missing, while Davies placed his losses at twenty-five total casualties.[9]

By all accounts, the Beefsteak Raid of Hampton and Rosser had been an overwhelming success. Robert E. Lee reported the news to Secretary of War John Seddon on the 17th, observing simply, "Everything was brought off safely."[10] A Union commissary officer reported the next day, "The enemy got off with the whole herd at Coggin's Point, 2,486 head. None [have] been re-captured."[11] Although he was in error slightly on the latter point, the staff officer's assessment was essentially correct.

In addition to the coveted steers, Wade Hampton accepted one of the captured Henry repeaters, which Edward Longacre explained, "he carried through the rest of the war and into whose stock he proudly carved his name."[12] Hampton and his men had reason to be pleased. They had completed a complicated mission successfully.

Army of the Potomac commander George Meade offered his regret to his superior, Ulysses S. Grant. "I hoped the difficulty of driving the cattle and the chances of war might prove more favorable to us," he explained.[13] Clearly, neither those factors nor the belated and poorly coordinated pursuit redounded to his or his chief's credit. In his memoirs, written just before his death, Grant referred to the raid. "It was a fair capture," he explained of the pilfered beef, "and they were sufficiently needed by the Confederates."[14] President Lincoln was supposed to have observed simply, "It was the slickest piece of cattle stealing I ever heard of."[15] As for Thomas Rosser, the inspiration for the Thomas Rossiter of *Alvarez Kelly*, although wounded numerous times, like his screen counterpart, he continued to serve the Confederacy. The headstrong Southerner refused to surrender at Appomattox and outlived the war by forty-five years.[16]

Of course, the film version could not help but slide history into the background when the story line required embellishment. The destruction of the bridge that allows Kelly, Rossiter, and their Confederate beef wranglers to escape Steadman's grasp with a dramatic and screen-filling explosion did not take place, at least in the manner depicted. According to one account, the Confederates could not blow the bridge because they did not have any powder available. Instead, they had the much more laborious and cinematically less glamorous task of tearing it down, and barely completed the task as the Federal pursuit caught up with them.[17]

In the end, the operation did more than just fill Confederate bellies; it provided a badly needed boost to Southern morale. War Clerk John B. Jones exuded in his diary on the 18th, "We have intelligence of another brilliant feat of Gen. Wade Hampton. Day before yesterday he got in the rear of the enemy, and drove off 2500 beeves and 400 prisoners. This will furnish fresh meat rations for Lee's army during a portion of the fall campaign." The usually optimistic Confederate bureaucrat felt even more reason for celebration. "I shall get some shanks, perhaps," Jones hungrily anticipated.[18]

The ravenous men of the Army of Northern Virginia enjoyed the feast, particularly with the awareness that the beefsteaks had been meant to fill Union stomachs. Their opponents across the way had to eat something else, both literally and figuratively, in the sense that for some time after the raid, whenever the Southerners wanted to gall the Federals they would bellow like cattle.[19] Alvarez Kelly and Thomas Rossiter would have been particularly pleased at the sound.

CHAPTER 12

Enough Glory for All

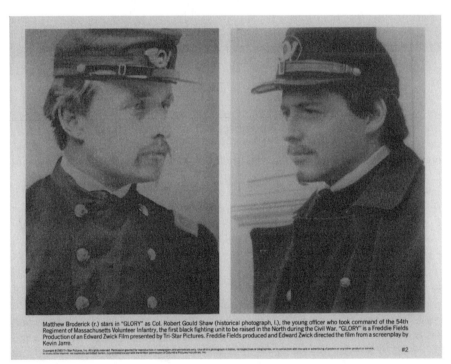

Matthew Broderick (r.) stars in "GLORY" as Col. Robert Gould Shaw (historical photograph, l.), the young officer who took command of the 54th Regiment of Massachusetts Volunteer Infantry, the first black fighting unit to be raised in the North during the Civil War. "GLORY" is a Freddie Fields Production of an Edward Zwick Film presented by Tri-Star Pictures. Freddie Fields produced and Edward Zwick directed the film from a screenplay by Kevin Jarre.

Copyright © 1989 Tri-Star Pictures, Inc. All rights reserved. Permission granted for reproduction in newspapers and periodicals only. Use of this photograph in books, retrospectives or biographies, or in connection with the sale or advertising of posters or any other product or service, in any other manner not expressly permitted herein, is prohibited except with the written permission of Columbia Pictures Industries, Inc. #2

In *Glory*, actor Matthew Broderick (r.) assumes the persona of Colonel Robert Gould Shaw, the white officer who led the black Fifty-Fourth Massachusetts Infantry.

Men of Color! To Arms!

—Frederick Douglass

Let every man of color consider that *he* has an interest in this war as well as the white man, and it will be well with him.

—Corporal James Henry Gooding, Fifty-Fourth Mass.

The greatest difficulty will be to stop them.

—Corporal Gooding

O N JANUARY 1, 1863, Abraham Lincoln's Emancipation Proclamation went into effect, freeing the slaves in territories that remained in rebellion against the Union. It also provided for the raising of black troops for the Union armed forces.[1] Those acts bestowed upon President Lincoln the title of "Great Emancipator" and solidified the administration's record on freedom, culminating a process that had begun with gradual, compensated emancipation, then continued with confiscation of slaves as "contraband of war" and finally freedom for slaves held in Confederate-controlled areas.

Hollywood would understandably wish to avoid controversial subjects that might have a backlash at the box office, but slavery remained for moviemakers, as it had been for the Antebellum world itself, the one immutable fact that could not be ignored about the American Civil War. But film producers who have taken up the subject of the South's "peculiar institution" have done so under the shadow of white supremacy and Jim Crow segregation. After 1915, films operated under the influence of *The Birth of a Nation*, and twenty-four years later they labored under the conceptions of race presented by *Gone with the Wind*. The result was stereotyping of the most egregious order, with "happy darkies" depicted working or singing and "Mammy" raising the children and running the household in her own inimitable fashion.

It would be some time before Hollywood would try to break the mold of the "plantation myth." Warner Brothers tries to tackle the thorny issues of slavery, miscegenation, and emancipation with *Band of Angels* (1957), based on a Robert Penn Warren novel. *Journey to Shiloh* (1968) introduces moral questions regarding slavery and freedom to a group of young soldiers on their way to war. But it is not until 1989 that *Glory* attempts to analyze these issues in the context of the war. Although the story of the Fifty-Four Massachusetts is seen largely from the perspective of its white commander, Robert Gould Shaw, the film raises the perspective of black service. *Gangs of New York* (2002) illustrates the broader divisions of wartime American society between the nativists and immigrants against the backdrop of the New York City draft riots

140

of 1863 and the racial undertones that permeated Northern society, regardless of the tenets of Free Labor ideology.

Band of Angels (1957) brings Clark Gable back onto the big screen as a figure from the Civil War era. But the movie should not be misunderstood to be a remake of *Gone with the Wind*. Hamish Bond (Gable) is a planter whose vast holdings in Louisiana include human property and a black overseer named Rau-Ru (Sidney Poitier). At auction, Hamish purchases a mulatto slave woman, Amantha Starr (Yvonne De Carlo). Although she has believed herself to be white, she learns that she is actually the product of a union between a white father and a black mother.

As war erupts, Rau-Ru escapes from the plantation, only to return as a Union soldier. Hamish draws the attentions of the Federals by burning his plantation so as to deny its resources to the Northerners. Union soldiers sweep the grounds attempting to locate and detain him. Despite his enmity for his master, the freedman allows Hamish to slip through and escape on a vessel with Amantha.

With *Band of Angels*, the film's producers were trying to portray a different plantation South than seen earlier. Edward D. C. Campbell has observed, "*Band of Angels* was a turning point of sorts in that it was the first movie to portray white and black as neither all good nor all evil under the system of slavery."[2] However, in doing so, the film departed from the comforting, or at least familiar, stereotypes that audiences had come to accept and expect. As Jack Kirby notes, "The break with the Old South sentimentalist tradition which had sold so many movie tickets was difficult."[3] Although the movie was supposedly based on Robert Penn Warren's 1955 novel, "Hollywood took little of the book except its opening device and its title," according to one observer.[4]

Glory opens on the battlefield of Antietam as Robert Gould Shaw leads his men against the Confederate lines. A destructive shell fire rains on them from their adversaries. His commander dies dramatically, while Shaw suffers a painful, but not serious wound.

Shaw returns to New England to recover, where the local civilians and his parents fete him. The young, ambitious officer desires a command of his own and uses his connections with Governor John Albion Andrew to obtain one. The catch is that this unit is to consist of black troops. Shaw hesitates only briefly before accepting the assignment and the rank of colonel.

The Fifty-Fourth undertakes a rigorous training regimen under Shaw's watchful eye and an Irish sergeant's intense supervision. The men must be whipped into fighting shape, especially in the case of Shaw's friend, Thomas Searles (Andre Braugher). The colonel intervenes when he considers the treatment unnecessary, but backs off when the sergeant makes him aware of the legitimacy of his methods.

The choice of an Irishman as a modern-style drill sergeant for the unit is interesting on a several counts. First, it plays to the notion that Irish "were not fond" of African Americans, as Major Cabot Forbes (Cary Elwes) observes.

Second, it allows Shaw to evolve as a commander, taking increasing interest in his men. Third, and most importantly, it allows the colonel to remain free of any taint in command. When he punishes Private Trip (Denzel Washington) for being absent without leave to obtain shoes, military regulations require a flogging, which the Irish sergeant administers. Shaw is the one who sends his personal surgeon to attend to the man, and he then raids a military warehouse to obtain shoes for his command. Likewise, he wins the affections of his troops by refusing to accept his pay voucher and tearing it up before them to protest their inferior pay.

The Fifty-Fourth sees its first military action in South Carolina. Shaw's fanatical Union superior forces the command to participate in the destruction of nearby Darien, Georgia. Then the first fighting comes outside Charleston. After this brief but bloody inauguration, the colonel realizes that he and his men are indeed prepared for combat, and he volunteers to send them against Battery Wagner, a Confederate stronghold guarding access to Charleston.

In one of *Glory's* more passionate scenes, the men of the Fifty-Fourth gather in something of an impromptu tent revival, to thank the Almighty for his blessings and to share their hopes and fears for the action shortly to come. Each who wishes to do so may speak and when he has finished blend his voice into the chorus that follows.

The last and most dramatic segment of the film features the futile assault against the formidable Confederate earthwork. Shaw and his men march through a cordon of Union troops, amid flowing national banners and barking artillery pieces. The scene is clearly contrived, but glory for the Fifty-Fourth awaits and demands appropriate framing. Amazingly, the bombardment stops whenever a statement has to be made.

Shaw passes letters to a newspaper correspondent and releases his horse as if he understands that this fight will be his last. Then, as the command gathers on the beach before Battery Wagner, he calls upon his men to follow him and to pick up the flag if it should fall. Searles, now hardened into a soldier and prepared to do battle, steps forward to insist that he will do so.

The charge is a desperate one. Artillery fire pins the troops against the sand dunes to await advance under darkness. When the opportunity arrives, Shaw leads his men to the ditch and plunges into it before attempting to climb the parapet wall. The fire is so intense that the men hesitate. Casualties mount among the exposed Union troops. Shaw girds himself, clears his weapons, and surges forward, calling on the troops to follow. Confederate fire riddles him, and he falls backward. Trip lurches ahead with the flag he earlier refused to carry, shouting encouragement, but quickly meets the fate of his commander.

But the deaths of these leaders inspire the troops to storm the parapet. They force their way onto the summit of the works and struggle toward the interior of the fort. However, as the survivors press forward, they find that the

Confederates have reversed artillery and are poised to blast them into submission. The fort remains indisputably in Southern hands, as the raising of the Confederate national flag demonstrates the next morning. As what they deem to be a final indignity to the brave Union colonel, the Confederates bury him on the field in a mass grave with his own men. Shaw and his men have paid a high price, but have gained glory through the costly assault and helped to establish the legitimacy and wisdom of arming blacks in the name of liberty.

Glory has garnered extensive praise for its groundbreaking portrayal of black troops and its appropriate historical symbolism. Historian William C. Davis terms it, "probably the most historically sound and reliable dramatization of genuine events yet put on the screen."[5] Yet, as a docudrama of the Fifty-Fourth Massachusetts, *Glory* falls short. Robert Brent Toplin observes, "As in all cinematic views of the past, *Glory*'s presentation includes manipulations of the evidence."[6] One would be better served historically by the companion documentary, *The True Story of Continues* (1991). But, as a reflection of the attitudes and actions of the many African Americans who served the Union cause when the government finally offered them the opportunity to do so, the feature film is unparalleled.

Pulitzer Prize–winning historian and author James M. McPherson describes the movie in glowing terms. "Not only is it the first feature film to treat the role of black soldiers in the American Civil War, but it is also one of the most powerful and historically accurate movies ever made about that war."[7]

Even so, the prolific writer had to admit that most of the specifics of *Glory* were less accurate concerning the famed Fifty-Fourth Massachusetts than one might be comfortable with otherwise. "Except for Shaw, the principal characters in the film are fictional," he explains. "The movie gives the impression that most of the Fifty-Fourth's soldiers were former slaves. In fact, the atypical regiment was recruited mainly in the North, so most of the men had always been free."[8]

On this point, most historians concur that the motion picture falls short of the mark for accuracy. The Fifty-Fourth was largely composed of free men of color. Yet a student of the regiment found that the portrayal of slaves, or at least former slaves, as members of the regiment was not as far off the mark as would seem to be the case. "Direct, written evidence," Edwin Redkey observes, "shows that at least thirty men of the Fifty-Fourth had been slaves." Looking at the locations of their births, he notes that approximately a fourth of the men came from the South.[9]

The same issue has arisen when historians have considered individuals in the movie command. Historian Martin Blatt notes that the figure most representative of the men in the unit, Thomas Searles, appears "as pathetically effete and incompetent."[10] This is certainly true of the scenes depicting the unit's training period, as Sergeant Mulcahy is particularly hard on the would-be soldier. But, training faux pas notwithstanding, Searles emerges in the film as a stouthearted warrior who suffers wounds in two of the regiment's engagements and bravely carries the regimental standard onto the parapet of Battery Wagner in the final assault.

Just as with any other regiment, the Fifty-Fourth contained men who were not suited to the rigors of military life, and the drills helped to weed them out. In May 1863, Corporal James Gooding noted that "there is about a dozen or more who, by the trying effects of camp life, are not physically able to be retained as good soldiers." But he did not despair about the condition of the men generally, expressing his confidence that the Fifty-Fourth "will compare favorably" with any other regiment raised in Massachusetts.[11]

Historian William McFeely has noted that the historical Shaw was "a vastly different man from the one played by Matthew Broderick in the film *Glory*."[12] Yet Shaw suffered a slight wound in the battle of Antietam as depicted in the opening scenes. Following the engagement, he wrote his father, "It was at this time that Lieutenant-Colonel Dwight and three other officers were hit. . . . I was struck once by a spent ball in the neck, which bruised, but didn't break the skin." The young officer also talks of burial and hospital parties working the battlefield the next day, after he and the troops had been required to sleep among the casualties through the night, mirroring the introduction of the Shaw character to the gravedigger John Rawlins (Morgan Freeman).[13]

In the training of the command, Matthew Broderick's Shaw comes across as sympathetic and willing to intervene to prevent unnecessary cruelty. Ironically, this was apparently not reflective of the real colonel's attitude toward such matters. In a letter to his mother in March, Shaw confessed, "One trouble, which I anticipated, has begun—viz: complaints from outsiders of undue severity [toward the troops]. But I shall continue to do, what I know is right in that particular. . . . I have treated them much more mildly, than we did the men of the 2d" (the Second Massachusetts, a white regiment in which Shaw had served previously).[14] The complaints seem to have been substantiated among officers and men of the regiment, although Shaw's motivation was sound in wanting his troops to represent themselves well before the eyes of the world. In a biographical sketch, Russell Duncan observes that Shaw "understood in these early stages [that] appearance meant everything."[15]

The men themselves seem to have understood that the eyes of an often disapproving world were upon them. James Henry Gooding, a corporal in the Fifty-Fourth, wrote in early April 1863, "It really makes one's heart pulsate with pride as he looks upon those stout and brawny men, fully equipped with Uncle Sam's accoutrements upon them, to feel that these noble men are practically refuting the base assertions reiterated by copperheads and traitors that the black race are incapable of patriotism, valor, or ambition."[16]

Shaw understood that his regiment reflected on him as commander as well as on the men themselves. Corporal Gooding attributed praise the unit received from others as belonging especially to Shaw's vigilance and diligence. Such compliments were due to "Col. Shaw, whose quick eye detects anything in a moment out of keeping with order or military discipline."[17] This occasionally led to excesses. As Russell Duncan has observed, "Yet, in an effort to prevent ridicule and instill discipline, Shaw went too far." The colonel's punishments reflected typical army rigor, including having offenders "stand on barrels for hours" and endure "bucking and gagging," as the culprits sat "gagged and had their hands and feet bound with their arms stretched around heavy sticks."[18] Even so, the fictional Sergeant Mulcahy was clearly a device for demonstrating the rigors of such military training while deflecting less than sympathetic attention away from the colonel.

One antagonist of the Fifty-Fourth was also more a dramatic convention than a historical reality. In *Glory*, a supply officer refuses to give the unit the equipment to which it is entitled. In reality, the unit's quartermaster "kept up with the supply needs of the men."[19] But a developing and maturing Colonel Shaw needs a foil to work against on behalf of his men—just as he will when the command travels into the South to put down the rebellion, only to learn that prejudice flourishes in the hearts and minds of other Union commanders there. Shaw has to accept these prejudices temporarily and reluctantly instruct his men to assist in the burning of Darien, but his chance for a form of retribution will come. He threatens to expose corruption among the same commanders in order to secure permission to put the unit into combat.

Likewise, the film depicts the soldiers as using pikes for a time before they receive more conventional arms. Shaw complained that there were plans "to arm the Negroes with pikes," but these did not materialize.[20] Russell Duncan notes that the men "drilled through the winter with old muskets, having to wait until one thousand Enfield rifles became available in May."[21] Corporal Gooding recorded on the 4th: "Yesterday the men received their new arms. We are supplied with the Enfield rifle, made in 1853, so you may suppose they intend us to make good use of them; and I doubt not if the opportunity presents itself, they *will* be made good use of."[22]

The Union colonel also warned his father of discrepancies over pay for his unit. "You may have perhaps heard that the colored troops are to receive $10 instead [of] $13 per. mo. It is not yet decided that this regt comes under the order." Certainly Shaw would do everything in his power to prevent such an order from applying to his men, since he had every assurance that their pay would be equivalent to that of other volunteer units from Massachusetts.[23]

Frederick Douglass appears briefly in the film as the command marches off to war. His inclusion is certainly appropriate. He visited with the unit prior to its departure, when it received its battle flags on May 18, and then saw them off aboard their transport vessel when they left Boston.[24] Yet the Frederick

Douglass of *Glory* is silver-haired and strangely quiet. What ought to be a young and dynamic individual who has recruited heavily for the regiment and established a strong reputation as a powerful orator instead actually looks as he would many years after the war when a popular photograph of the era caught his visage whitened with age.[25]

Ironically, *Glory* fails to use the historical connection to the Douglass family that was at once poignant and historically significant. The former slave and well-known abolitionist sent two sons into the regiment and bore the responsibility for helping to recruit many others as well.[26] Indeed, it was Frederick Douglass's sons who assailed the Confederate position at Battery Wagner, along with their commander, Robert Gould Shaw. The film would have been better served historically by including Sergeant Lewis Douglass in place of the fictional Sergeant Major John Rawlins, although Morgan Freeman would have been hard-pressed to play the considerably younger man instead.

Corporal James Gooding had watched as the regiment honed its fighting trim in such an abnormally short time. Yet he was not concerned for the preparedness of the men to fight. As the unit received its marching orders, he paused to record his thoughts. "There is not a man in the regiment who does not appreciate the difficulties, the dangers, and maybe [the] ignoble death that awaits him." The willingness to expose themselves to these elements of war against the Confederacy was not the issue. "The greatest difficulty will be to stop them," he concluded.[27]

Upon arriving in South Carolina, Colonel Shaw sought service for his unit, but was appalled at the excesses he witnessed in a Union raid on Darien, Georgia. The attitude portrayed in the film genuinely reflected the concerns he expressed over the incidents of looting and burning in the Southern town by order of James Montgomery. Montgomery was a zealous commander with a background in Kansas and an Old Testament notion concerning rebellion.

After the raid, in a letter to his wife Annie, Shaw remained particularly strong in his condemnation. "But I think now, as I did at the time, that it is cruel, barbarous, impolitic, and degrading to ourselves and to our men; and I shall always rejoice that I expressed myself so at the time of the destruction of Darien."[28] A month later, with his soldiers having exhibited themselves well in combat, Shaw exuded, "what we have done to-day wipes out the remembrance of the Darien affair."[29]

At the same time, Colonel Shaw could hardly contain his satisfaction with the combat performance of his command. "We have at last fought alongside of white troops," he remarked happily.[30] Three days after sending his wife this correspondence, Shaw would have his men drawn up on the beach before Battery Wagner for an attack upon that strong point.

As the men gathered for the fateful assault, they received encouragement from Brigadier General George Strong. An after-action report, filed by Colonel Edward N. Hallowell (a lieutenant colonel at the time of the attack

146

on Wagner) recorded that Strong "presented himself to the regiment and informed the men that he contemplated assault upon Fort Wagner and asked them if they would lead it." Hallowell recalled, "They answered in the affirmative." Thus it was that Strong, not Shaw (as no reference is given to any speech he might have made), who inspired the Fifty-Fourth to answer destiny's call on the sandy South Carolina soil.

The regiment then formed into two wings for the attack, with Shaw on the right and Hallowell on the left: Hallowell reported afterward, "In this formation, as the dusk of the evening came on, the regiment advanced at quick time, leading the column; the enemy opened upon us a brisk fire; our pace now gradually increased till it became a run." So often, soldiers recorded that when they advanced against an enemy position they bent forward as if moving against a stiff rain. So it must have been that day, for as the Federal lieutenant colonel explained, "Soon canister and musketry began to tell on us. . . . [T]he havoc made in our ranks was very great." The Southerners fought desperately to hold their works, the Northerners as intensely to take them. "It was here," Hallowell explained, "on the crest of the parapet, that Colonel Shaw fell." Other officers and men fell, too, including the severely wounded lieutenant colonel. The survivors struggled to hold what they had taken before finally being pushed back, the blue tide receding as it had earlier advanced against the earthen walls of Battery Wagner.[31]

Historians have cited the requirements of filming on modern Georgia's Jekyll Island, which sent the black troops against Confederate-held Battery Wagner in the wrong direction. Instead of approaching the position from the South to the North as they did in 1863, in order to pull the cordon tighter around the port city of Charleston, the troops in the movie attack from North to South.[32] Yet the essence of the assault remains true to form, and the courage and tenacity the soldiers displayed in the fruitless attack is no less accurate.

Certainly, *Glory* depicts rather well the enormous sacrifice asked of and given by the members of the Fifty-Fourth Massachusetts. Approximately 600 of these African American soldiers stormed the fort, suffering 272 casualties, including 34 officers and enlisted men killed. Less well represented in the film is the sacrifice of their white compatriots, whose losses swelled the human toll for the Union at Battery Wagner to 1,515.[33] For their part, the defenders lost 174 men in the bloody fray. A few days after the fight, Confederate general Pierre G. T. Beauregard reported to Adjutant General Samuel Cooper "about 150 killed and wounded, noting that the Confederates had buried eight hundred Union soldiers under a flag of truce." He added matter-of-factly, "Colonel Putnam, acting brigadier, and Colonel Shaw, commanding negro regiment, were killed."[34]

The Federals put the best face on the costly repulse. Union generals Quincy Gilmore and Truman Seymour submitted reports that noted the success of the Union troops in breaching the southeast portion of the earthwork, for a time, before circumstances required them to withdraw.[35] *Glory* depicts this temporary victory, before Confederate forces rallied to drive the Northern troops back from the Southern works.

But even *Glory* stops short of a full account of the fighting as Major Forbes, Sergeant Rawlins, and the handful of men with them finally become engulfed in the black powder smoke of the Confederate artillery pieces arrayed against them. No depiction is made of Sergeant William Carney, who won the Medal of Honor for cradling the regiment's riddled battle flag in his arms, despite being desperately wounded in the attack, and bringing it and himself safely back to his camp.[36]

Such discrepancies as exist between the fictional and nonfictional components of the story do not take away from the value of the film. It is a powerful portrayal of the contribution that 200,000 African Americans made to winning their own or their brothers' and sisters' freedom. This is reflected in the joyous response the gravedigger-turned-soldier Rawlins gives as black children swirl around him once the regiment arrives in the Deep South. "We run away slaves and come back fighting men."

The film does much better in presenting the trials of men learning to be soldiers and of the rampant air of racism and discrimination they faced on a constant basis from their friends as well as their foes. One of the best scenes remains the confrontation between Union troops, white and black, in which Shaw and his black sergeant defuse hostilities between men wearing the same uniforms and fighting for the same cause.[37]

Historian Jim Cullen points out that *Glory* misses one extremely important historical event in Civil War America: the New York draft riots of July 13–16, 1863. He terms this as "perhaps the most significant omission" in the film. He notes that members of Colonel Shaw's family had to flee for safety and that a relative of one of the Fifty-Fourth's soldiers died in the chaos, then suggests that despite these personal connections to those distant events, "no mention" is made of the "disorder in New York." He undergirds his case by observing, "By contrast, Union victories at Gettysburg and Vicksburg are mentioned, though these took place weeks, not days, before."[38] Yet it is precisely because those events have taken place with sufficient time to filter into the part of the South in which the Fifty-Fourth has found itself that it is entirely plausible that the unit would have heard of the great Union victories and be ignorant of what was transpiring virtually simultaneously in distant New York City. Aside from some vague reference to dissatisfaction with the draft, it would not appear so out of the ordinary that men consumed with military operations—the fighting for Battery Wagner had begun only days before—would not have much to say about such recent, and ongoing, events.

Glory, then, was an unlikely vehicle for including the New York draft riots in more than even a cursory fashion. The same could not be said concerning *Gangs of New York*. The riots of July 1863 are a key element of the Martin

Scorsese film, which opens in the years before the Civil War in a New York City deeply divided by ethnic differences between Irish Catholic immigrants and Protestant nativists in the notorious Five Points section of the city. Rival "gangs" clash with each other in vicious street fighting that leaves broken bodies and mangled corpses sprawling on the snow-covered streets. The fighting leads to the death of the "Priest" Vallon (Liam Neeson) and the triumph of Bill the Butcher (Daniel Day-Lewis) and his nativists.

In a superb establishing shot, New York City 1846 gives way to the city in the midst of the Civil War. The orphaned boy has grown into a young man. A minister admonishes the fellow, "You go forth to a country torn apart by civil strife." The words ring in his ears as he passes Chinese laborers. "Lend your hand to the work that yet remains that this war may end. And the plague of slavery that brought this conflagration down upon us vanish forever from the earth."

But Amsterdam Vallon (Leonardo DiCaprio) has another crusade in mind: revenge over Bill for the death of his father. He discards the Bible he has been given and heads out into the city. Vallon provides context through a voice-over. "In the second year of the great Civil War, when the Irish Brigade marched through the streets, New York was a city full of tribes, war chiefs, rich and poor." A wide cacophony of voices cascades through the streets, with people representing diametrically opposite positions shouting and waving placards: "The President's Proclamation—Slavery Abolished in States in Rebellion." "Lincoln will make all white men slaves." "Jefferson Davis our brother." "New York to secede from the Union." "The Union forever." Bill the Butcher walks among them, fireworks booming behind him as he greets the marching soldiers with derision: "That's the spirit boys, go off and die for your blackie friends." To his own cronies he mumbles, "We should have run a better man against Lincoln when we had the chance." One of them attacks two well-dressed black men who have been watching the proceedings, assailing them with racial epithets as well as with their fists. "Go back to Africa, nigger!" "We free," they reply, but the cry falls on ears deaf with racial hatred.

Once more, Vallon's voice provides an overview of the turmoil that lies just beneath the surface: "The angriest talk was of the new Conscription Act. The first draft in Union history." As if to emphasize his position on such matters, Bill deftly puts his knife between the eyes of a poster of Abraham Lincoln. A copy of the *New York Tribune* offers further context: "An Irish Invasion. While the North invades the South, the Irish Invade New-York."

Ships bring Irish immigrants into the city by the score. Military recruiters, political opportunists, and angry nativists greet the new arrivals. "Join the army, lads. Three square meals a day and good pay," a recruiter calls out to entice the newcomers to enlist. Shouts of "Vote Tammany" mix with those demanding "America for Americans." William Marcy Tweed, Tammany Hall's great manipulator, is among the greeters offering handouts for the favor of future votes. "Go back to Ireland, you dumb Mick. Get back on the boat, Paddy," the nativists cry out, tossing objects into the mass before them. All the while the boats off-load immigrants from Ireland and coffins from the battlefields of the Civil War.

Tweed tries to win over Bill the Butcher to use his people as the "muscle" to match Tammany's "spirit." "The appearance of the law must be upheld," Tweed explains, "especially while it is being broken." The Irish lieutenant Happy Jack Mulraney (John C. Reilly) is now a policeman. He extorts loot from the thieves. Bill sets the boys up with a boat to raid. They pass more coffins being unloaded. A plaintive voice explains, "I lost my own eldest at Antietam."

As Bill, Tweed, Vallon, and the rest vie for position in the streets, New York City continues to seethe with antiwar sentiment. Again, the catalyst for an upheaval comes to the fore: "Avoid the draft!" "Volunteer and get your $50 bonus," comes from the recruiting office. Vallon observes: "Everywhere you went people talked about the draft. Now you could buy your way out for $300. But who had $300? For us it might as well have been three millions." So Vallon chooses to concentrate on his own agenda of vengeance. "Besides," he observes quietly, "we never dreamt the war would ever touch New York." But the time is rapidly approaching when the war, or at least a violent component of it, will settle on the city.

As Election Day draws near, Tweed tries to convince Bill to help get the Irish to the polls, but the Butcher has decided that his interests lie elsewhere, and the tenuous alliance dissolves. But the Tammany chief has new constituents arriving every day: that is, if the military does not get to them first. "That document makes you a citizen," a recruiter explains to one of them. "This one makes you a private in the Union army. Now go fight for your country." A ballad plays over the scene: "When we got to Yankeeland, they shoved a rifle into our hands, saying Paddy you must go and fight for Lincoln." One of the newly minted soldiers inquires, "Where are we going?" His companion responds, "I heard Tennessee," and perplexed the first replies, "Where is that?" Now it is the soldiers' turn to go on ships for the fighting down in Dixie, while still more coffins come off.

For the time being, Vallon pretends to side with Bill. When a man comes forward and tries to assassinate the Butcher, Amsterdam saves Bill's life. In the aftermath of the attack, Bill describes the secret of his success to his young protégé: "Fear. That's what preserves the order of things." In the course of their discussion, Bill thinks back to 1846: "I killed the last honorable man fifteen years ago." He adds, "The priest and me lived by the same principles. It was only faith that divided us." Finally, the Butcher concludes, "He was the only man I ever killed worth remembering."

Young Vallon and Bill will soon clash, with the older man winning temporarily. The Butcher burns Amsterdam's face as a permanent mark of his dominance over him. But, when he has recovered sufficiently from the assault, Vallon renews his father's old challenge. Bill is unwilling to back down to his former associate, targeting even the Catholic Church being constructed in the neighborhood. Vallon and his friends stand up to Bill, who withdraws for the moment to bide his time.

But time is a luxury in New York City. "One night you look up," Vallon tells the audience. "One spark and the sky's on fire." That spark is conscription. "You all have to register," an enrolling officer tells the Irish residents of one tenement. "You can't force me to join no army," one replies. "Have you got $300?" the official rejoins. "Of course not. Who the hell's got $300?" "If you are drafted, release from military service can only be secured with $300, according to the Conscription Act, otherwise you have to serve." Then the underlying sentiment begins to boil to the surface: "I was born in this country, sir. You immigrated to this country. You will fight for this country, sir." "Who the hell has $300?" an Irishman repeats as another yells at the enrolling officer, "Go back uptown"; another observes, "$300 is a rich man's war."

In the meantime, neither Tweed nor Vallon seem aware of what is about to transpire in their city. The Tammany politico only knows that he needs Vallon and offers to form an alliance with the Irish. "I need a new friend in the Five Points, son. I'd like that friend to be you." "Why should so many Irish die down South, when the first war to win is not down in Dixie, but right here in these streets."

Election Day arrives. A soldier angrily protests to blacks, "I fought for you, nigger. I lost an arm for you." There is considerable election fraud on all sides. But, when Tammany and the Irish win, Bill cannot accept the outcome and slaughters the newly elected Irish sheriff. Bill and his nativists and Amsterdam and his Irish set the terms for a renewal of the battle that began in 1846.

Once more the film offers context, this time with a newspaper whose headlines read: "Casualties." "Army of the Potomac." "And then it came," Vallon's voice explains. "the first day of the draft." The tribes gather for their confrontation as people begin to attack the draft station: "Kill the rich bastards." For the moment, the police seem to have everything in hand: "Uptown at the draft office, the cops broke a few skulls and the people ran away."

Seemingly safe in their posh homes in the upscale part of the city, newspaperman Horace Greeley and wealthy Mr. Skimmerhorn expect that the worst is over. "Just a brief burst of anger over Mr. Lincoln's draft." Besides, as Skimmerhorn observes, "You can always hire one half of the poor to kill the other half."

The message filters out into the city that if you support the protest against the draft you should light a candle and place it in the window. Skimmerhorn believes that the city will remain dark, but candles soon fill the windows of the Five Points. The next morning, angry people fill the streets determined to force an end to the hated draft. "Nobody goes to work today," a voice calls out from among the mob, "We'll shut the factories down." In voiceover, Vallon reflects the prevailing sentiments: "Let the sons of the rich go and die."

The film now cuts between three separate scenes, and three very different prayers. Bill and Vallon pray for victory and vengeance, while Skimmerhorn offers a conventional mealtime prayer as he presides at the head of the bounty of his ample dinner table. The mob suddenly attacks his house, sending the family shrieking in paroxysms of fear. Skimmerhorn rushes to his cabinet to extract two pistols, but the mob quickly overwhelms him and ransacks the house.

Gangs of New York now employs the technique of using a telegraph operator to provide the voice-over historical context: "The mob is sacking houses." "The rioters are attacking colored boarding houses, robbing them and setting them on fire." "The blacks are being attacked all over the city." "Gunboat *Liberty* and ironclad *Passaic* now lying off Wall Street. They are ready to open fire on mob." "The mob is attacking *Tribune* office." "The Seventh regiment has arrived." "The mob is about 4,500 strong." "There's a mob headed for the Colored Orphans Asylum."

Amid the chaos of the news reports come brutal assaults on the wealthy and blacks particularly as the mob gives vent to its social and racial frustrations and prejudices. "Get the nigger!" "Did your daddy buy you out of the army? Can he buy me out of the army, too?"

The response of the military commanders in the city is to crush the rebellion: "Put the mob down. Don't take a prisoner in until you put the mob down." The telegraph agent continues with his regular updates, providing street numbers that lend authenticity to actions being described.

Finally, the troops arrive. When the mob does not disperse, the soldiers fire. The gunboats also open fire on the city streets.[39] Amid heavy smoke, Bill and Amsterdam both go down. Vallon is dazed, but the Butcher is badly wounded. "Thank God I die a true American," he calls out, and Amsterdam kills him.

In the aftermath, the Five Points is a bloody mess. There is a long shot of the city on fire. Bodies are being tossed into mass graves. "We are burying a lot of votes tonight," Tweed remarks. "Friend or foe, it didn't make no difference now." The boss of Tammany wants to rebuild with the new immigrants coming into the city, just as he has done before.

Once more, Vallon's voice offers context. "It was four days and nights before the worst of the mob was finally put down. We never knew how many New Yorkers died that week before the city was finally delivered." He had survived the turmoil in the streets and the combat with the Butcher, but Amsterdam recognized that everything would be different from this time. "It was like everything we knew was mightily swept away." A scene of Vallon at the graveside of his father gives way to the ever-changing progress of New York from nineteenth-century metropolis to the modern one that features the twin towers of the World Trade Center, not yet victims of their own appointment with fate on September 11, 2001.

Gangs of New York gets a great deal right about the piece of Civil War history that it explores and the significance of these events make them worthy of study as well as dramatically powerful for the screen. Author Harry Stout explains, "The draft riots provide a unique window into the violent tensions that lurked beneath the surface of Northern society."[40] Edward Spann narrows the scope, but hardly the importance of the riots to the city itself. "Even more than most great cities," he observes, "New York had the prime ingredient for violence: a large floating population of unattached males."[41] He notes that in addition to the prevalent social factors, "The most important spark was the National Enrollment (Conscription) Act of March 1, 1863."[42] James McPherson concurs: "Nowhere was the tinder more flammable than in New York City, with its large Irish population and powerful Democratic machine."[43] Indeed, for McPherson, these political elements in the city turned the motto "Rich man's war, poor man's fight" into "a powerful symbol to be manipulated by Democrats who made conscription a partisan and class issue."[44]

As the film illustrates, recruiters attempted to use the threat of the draft as an inducement to stir up volunteers for the army. Even so, with a cause that many did not support in the first place and the threat of being forced to fight for it anyway, as well as the uneven ability to avoid it if you could produce $300 or hire a substitute, the draft was bound to stir emotions and resentments to the boiling point, and it did.[45] The resulting violence tended to focus on the draft apparatus, Republican newspapers, and prominent citizens, as well as blacks and any institutions associated with them. The final toll was variously thought to be as high as a thousand, although later studies placed the casualties at just over a hundred, most of them among the rioters.[46]

In the final analysis, the epic of life on the streets of New York City that Martin Scorsese directs has less to do with the Civil War distinctions between the North and South than with the ethnic and religious divisions that separated all Americans from each other. These divisions, like the large ones between the sections, had to be expunged in order for a better New York City and a greater United States to emerge.

CHAPTER 13

The Angels of Gettysburg

Photo: Merrick Morton

Turner Home Entertainment releases on home video the Turner Pictures' presentation of the Civil War epic, *Gettysburg*. Confederate soldiers: (Back row from left) Colonel Freemantle (James Lancaster); Jim Kemper (Royce Applegate); Veneable Marshall (Tim Ruddy); Lewis Armistead (Richard Jordan); T. J. Gorce (Ivan Kane); James Longstreet (Tom Berenger); Moxley Sorell (Kieran Mulroney); Harrison, the Spy (Cooper Huckabee); and A. P. Hill (Patrick Falci). (Sitting, Front Row from left): George Pickett (Stephen Lang); Robert E. Lee (Martin Sheen); and Walter Taylor (Bo Brinkman).

TURNER HOME ENTERTAINMENT

GETTYSBURG

©1993 Turner Pictures, Inc.
All Rights Reserved.

Based on the novel *The Killer Angels*, the motion picture *Gettysburg* depicts Robert E. Lee (Martin Sheen, center, first row) against George G. Meade in the pivotal battle of the Eastern Theater of the war. Here, Confederate leaders have gathered in a Matthew Brady–style photograph that features George Pickett (Stephen Lang, l., first row), Lewis Armistead (Richard Jordan, fourth from l., second row), and James Longstreet (Tom Berenger, third from r., second row).

I tell you today of the most horrible thing I can. Murder on the worst scale I could ever dream.

—Union soldier at Gettysburg after Pickett's charge

ELEVISION MAVERICK Ted Turner has generated several projects that relate to various aspects of the American Civil War. In 1993, he turned his eyes to the greatest land engagement of the conflict: the three-day battle in and around Gettysburg, Pennsylvania, that most see as the turning point of the war, particularly in the Eastern Theater. The film was to be based on Michael Shaara's popular Pulitzer Prize–winning novel *The Killer Angels*, which historian Gary Gallagher has termed, "By far the most widely read of Civil War novels published in the last quarter century."[1]

Nevertheless, Gallagher finds that the novel, as well as the movie *Gettysburg*—"the sprawling four-hour film based closely on its text—would by turns delight and upset Lost Cause adherents."[2] Indeed, *Gettysburg* is Michael Shaara's movie as much as it is anyone else's. The Ron Maxwell film is a faithful adaptation of the sentiments and character portrayals found in the novel.

Presented in three distinct parts that coincide with the three days of the battle itself, the film identifies key individuals from both sides around which to tell its story. The first part focuses on the events of July 1, day one of the monumental struggle in and around Gettysburg as the antagonists advance to their rendezvous at the small Pennsylvania crossroads town. The hero of this initial fight is John Buford (Sam Elliott), the Kentucky-born Union cavalry commander whose men delay the Confederate advance sufficiently to allow the Union infantry of John Reynold's I Corps to come up. Although ultimately unsuccessful in preventing the Southerners from driving them back through the town, the Union defenders are able to secure the crucial heights of Cemetery Hill, "the high ground," as Elliott's Buford tells the audience repeatedly.

The second part of the film shifts the action on day two of the battle to the Round Tops, two hills that anchor the Union left flank. The hero in this portion of the film is the professor-turned-soldier Joshua Lawrence Chamberlain (Jeff Daniels). His men hold their positions against incredible odds in the form of repeated assaults by Lee's finest shock troops under James Longstreet (Tom Berenger) and John Bell Hood (Patrick Gorman).

The third part focuses on the charge of the Confederates against the Union center on July 3. Here the heroes are friends and old army colleagues, now on opposite sides: Lewis Armistead (Richard Jordan) and Winfield Scott Hancock (Brian Mallon). Former brother officers, they are pitted against each other in the great battle that will decide the outcome of the struggle, and in which both will be struck down, although only Armistead's wound proves mortal. The grand assault of the troops under Confederate generals George Pickett (Stephen Lang), Isaac Trimble (Morgan Sheppard), and Johnston

Pettigrew (George Lazenby) occupies center stage as the Southerners batter and bend, but fail to break, the Union line.

In the wake of the repulse, Robert E. Lee must regroup and prepare to return to Virginia. Despite the horrific human cost of this battle, the war and its terrible bloodshed will continue. Lee's battered army remains intact and will return safely to the Old Dominion.

Gettysburg attempts to establish its historical credentials from the outset. With an outstanding score as background, images of the leading historical figures of the drama blend with those of the actors who portray them. Then a voice-over by Morgan Sheppard informs the audience of the situation in the summer of 1863, against a backdrop of a map with lines representing the antagonists that coil like bony fingers to reach the town of Gettysburg:

> In June 1863, after more than two years of bloody conflict, the Confederate Army of Northern Virginia, Robert E. Lee commanding, slips across the Potomac to begin the invasion of the North. It is an army of seventy thousand men. They move slowly behind the Blue Ridge using the mountains to screen their movements. The main objective is to draw the Union army out into the open where it can be destroyed.
>
> Late in June, the Union Army of the Potomac, eighty thousand men, turns north from Virginia to begin the great pursuit up the narrow roads across Maryland on into Pennsylvania. General Lee knows that a letter has been prepared by the Southern government, a letter which offers peace. It is to be placed on the desk of Abraham Lincoln, president of the United States, the day after Lee has destroyed the Army of the Potomac somewhere north of Washington.

As Robert E. Lee, veteran actor Martin Sheen took the brunt of criticism for his portrayal of the general in *Gettysburg*. But the Lee of the film posed an insurmountable hurdle for him that he may not have anticipated when he accepted the role. The Lee of *Gettysburg* is Michael Shaara's Lee. He is certainly not the central character or even a particularly strong peripheral one, in either *The Killer Angels* or *Gettysburg*. Yet this was the General Lee that Sheen was called upon to portray. Had the actor established his highly successful role as a president in the television drama *The West Wing* prior to taking the role of the South's most esteemed general, he might have experienced less censure. Still, Sheen did not enjoy the luxury of being seen as someone fit to play such a venerable character, and confined to the Lee he was given he might not have escaped criticism in any event.

To be sure, Sheen's Lee is given little film exposure, but what there is to be seen is nuanced. From the show of confidence in his army to succeed against the enemy, to the display of anger at Jeb Stuart for arriving so late on the battlefield, to the final demonstration of resignation in the wake of the Union defeat of George Pickett's charge, viewers can see hints of the complexities of the Confederate commander.

What the fictional Lee says to Stuart is not out of character for the general or the situation on that July 2 afternoon as Lee contemplated his next move against his adversary. When the cavalryman reported, General Lee is supposed to have admonished him: "Well, General Stuart, you are here at last."[3] The rebuke, such as it was, could hardly have been gentler concerning the cavalryman's feelings. Stuart had failed in the vital function of scouting for the main force. Lee and the Army of Northern Virginia had been left blind. It would have been foolish of the army commander to allow the lesson to go unmentioned or unlearned, even for so trusted and capable a commander as his cavalry chieftain.

Afterward, General Lee, who assumed all responsibility for the actions of his army and its component parts as any good commander would do, noted simply: "The movements of the army preceding the battle of Gettysburg had been much embarrassed by the absence of cavalry."[4] Stuart biographer Emory Thomas describes the cavalryman's report of his role in the Gettysburg campaign as "unfortunate." Thomas explains, "He clearly underestimated the need for speed, and he gravely miscalculated the effect of his tardiness upon the campaign."[5]

No one took the loss at Gettysburg harder than Marse Robert, and Sheen captures the pathos well on screen. As a stunned George Pickett absorbs the shock of the setback his men have just experienced, the army commander calls upon his subordinate to rally his men in the face of a potential Union counterstroke. "General Lee, I have no division," comes the hasty reply, and Lee responds as he will to everyone else in the aftermath of the defeat: "It is all my fault." These sentiments and the deep angst that they represent translate from the historical page to celluloid with great accuracy and force.

Other features of the novel ensure that certain individuals will be enhanced on-screen and others diminished. Chief among the former on the Union side is Joshua Lawrence Chamberlain (Jeff Daniels), the Bowdoin professor and commander of the Twentieth Maine. His stand on the Union left is crucial, but little is done to credit Gouverneur Warren with seeing the necessity of defending this part of the line and securing troops to do so. Without Warren, Chamberlain would not have had the opportunity for the distinction he gained from defending the Union flank on the second day of the battle. Yet the vigilant New Yorker enjoyed prominence in neither the novel nor the film and thus has fallen in the shadow of his colleague from Maine.

Likewise, good Confederates from outside the confines of the Commonwealth of Virginia, and particularly those from North Carolina, will lament the fact that Virginia's George Pickett was still the leader of the charge on the third day, and not one of a group of commanders that included Isaac Trimble and Johnston Pettigrew. As Carol Reardon has written, "'Pettigrew' appears only briefly, primarily to accept the compliments about his grades at the University of North Carolina and to promise Longstreet a copy of his book."

Then, as if to add insult to Tar Heel injury, Berenger's Longstreet scratches the wrong formation into the dirt when he demonstrates how he wants the troops to advance.[6]

Yet the battle scenes themselves are well executed. Hosts of reenactors made authenticity of uniform, weaponry, and military drill possible in a way that extras without their knowledge and understanding would not have been able to do. The vast numbers enable the director to give the film a scope it could not have attained with a handful of "troops" on a studio back lot. The smoke and chaos of the fighting is also true to form in the days of black powder, but even then the viewer has advantages that the participants did not. Recalling the great charge at Gettysburg as his men swept forward with two other Virginia brigades, James L. Kemper observed, "You doubtless realize how an officer in battle is absorbed in his own separate duties and how oblivious he is of the separate operations of other commands."[7] Thus the audience member, unburdened and undistracted by responsibilities other than consuming popcorn and a drink, can watch the panorama unfold and take in more than the commander in the field could do, even with the smoke and pyrotechnics replicated on-screen.

For the historical participants, the scene they saw play out before them on the third day of the momentous engagement was unforgettable, seared into their consciousnesses in an early and quite different version of "shock and awe." From his "Camp Above the Field," one Union soldier paused on July 3 to commit his observations to paper for the benefit of a brother. "I tell you today of the most horrible thing I can," he began simply enough. "Murder on the worst scale I could ever dream." But such words were insufficient to convey that horror, and the soldier felt compelled to continue. "The Rebels, blessed souls of glory came at us in a massive line of pomp and glory, only to meet their maker with comrades aplenty to go with them. Our cannon ripped through them like a scythe in a field of dry wheat, and they still kept coming at us." The scene was disturbingly stirring for the blue-coated soldier who explained that he continued to fire his weapon until he could no longer hold it in his hands. The Southern advance left him as impressed as he was dazzled by the terrible spectacle that stretched before him. "What men are these we slaughter like cattle," he concluded, "and still they come at us?"[8] Although it does not portray its subject in the graphic manner of such productions as *Saving Private Ryan*, *We Were Soldiers*, or *Black Hawk Down*, and it certainly does not reflect the destructiveness this soldier and his comrades actually witnessed, the film succeeds in capturing the enormity of the Confederate assault and something of the sacrifice of humanity entailed by it.

Approximately a decade after *Gettysburg*, Ron Maxwell would release a film designed to lay the foundation for his 1993 motion picture. As prequel to *Gettysburg*, *Gods and Generals* (2003) is essentially the story of Thomas Jonathan "Stonewall" Jackson, with the occasional nod to Robert E. Lee, Joshua

Lawrence Chamberlain, and a handful of others. *Gods and Generals* follows Jackson, portrayed ably by Stephen Lang (the man who gave life to George Pickett in the earlier film), from the classroom of the Virginia Military Institute to the battlefield of First Manassas (Bull Run), where he earns his famous sobriquet. The film ends with the depiction of the opening scenes of Chancellorsville, Jackson's spectacular flank march, his assault on Oliver O. Howard's Union XI Corps, and his tragic wounding at the hands of his own men. Along the way, the Federals futilely smash themselves against the Confederate defenses on Mayre's Heights at Fredericksburg. Other scenes, including the important battle of Antietam, or Sharpsburg, are left in the drawer, if not on the cutting room floor.

The most poignant scenes of the film are associated with Jackson and his relationship with death: that of the little girl he befriended during the winter of 1862–1863 and the facing of his own mortality following his accidental wounding, the subsequent loss of his arm, and the development of the pneumonia that finally took his life after Chancellorsville.

Jackson emerges as powerfully real, not the stoic image on a Confederate $500 bill. *Gods and Generals* is at its best when he is on-screen, but gets lost when he is not. Thus the film suffers from its inability to focus on one story. Because of its connection to *Gettysburg*, the film seems obliged to introduce the future Union heroes Joshua Chamberlain, Buster Kilrain, and Winfield Scott Hancock. But it cannot both allow these characters to develop and keep the story of the film moving simultaneously. *Gods and Generals* simply tries to cover too much ground. In the process, except for Jackson and the people with whom he associates, the audience finds it difficult to identify with the characters.[9]

When the film tackles the issues of slavery and race, it is on particularly shaky ground. The most incongruous scene in this regard is the exchange between General Jackson and his personal servant, Jim Lewis (Frankie Faison), as they journey toward Fredericksburg. Jackson pauses to pray, and Lewis seizes the opportunity to express his views on slavery. "How is it a good Christian man like some folks I know can tolerate their black brothers in bondage? How is it, Lord, they don't just break them chains?"

Yet Jackson is unfazed by the inquiry. "Jim," he offers quietly, "you must know that there are some of us in the army that are of the opinion that we should be enlisting Negroes. . . . General Lee is among them." Then, reflectively, "Stonewall" concludes, "Your people will be free one way or the other. The only question is whether the Southern government will have the good sense to do it first, and in so doing seal a bond of enduring friendship between us." The words almost exactly mirror the sentiments Robert E. Lee will express, but in January 1865, long after Jackson is gone from the scene.[10]

Gods and Generals gets much right. Thomas Jackson comes across as far more human than the labeling of "Stonewall" ordinarily allows. Yet the film does not take advantage of opportunities to develop many of the interesting relationships Jackson experienced with others. He is kind and solicitous to a dying Maxcy Gregg at Fredericksburg, with only a passing reference made to the differences the men had felt previously.[11]

The brief scene after the battle between the dying general and his superior officer is typical of the exactitude with which Ron Maxwell directs and the actors, in this case Stephen Lang and Buck Taylor, portray their characters in situations where historical dialogue has been recorded. The language and tone of the scene fit the historical record perfectly as Lang's Jackson calmly asserts that the men should forget their past differences under the circumstances: "The doctor tells me that you have not long to live. Let me ask you to dismiss this matter from your mind and turn your thoughts to God and to the world to which you go." The accuracy is just as present in Stonewall's reaction when he leaves the stricken man's side:

Jackson: How horrible is war!

Dr. McGuire: Horrible yes, but we have been invaded. What can we do?

Jackson: Kill them, sir! Kill every man![12]

At another point, early in the war, Stonewall exhibits this same Old Testament–style ferocity in words that accurately reflect the historical record: "General Stuart, if I had my way we would show no quarter to the enemy." He is prepared to raise "the black flag, sir," and sees the conflict as more quickly ended if the Confederates were to show "No quarter to the violators of our homes and friends." Not surprisingly, Jackson insists, "We should look to the Bible" for examples of how war ought to be waged.[13] In his "moral history" of the Civil War, Harry Stout maintains that "Stonewall" Jackson "brought a prophetic rage to the battlefield that was fearless in the face of death and sought not only to conquer his—and God's—enemies but to annihilate them."[14]

Thomas Jackson comes across on the screen as the complex man he most assuredly was. Yet *Gods and Generals* can reveal but so much of that complexity beyond the contradictions of an intensely private man in a public arena, and a religious man in the sphere of death and war. The less flattering side of Jackson's approach to command relationships would have given his character more development than the film allows and would have made scenes such as the one with Gregg more understandable to a general audience.

Likewise, although the enigmatic Jackson and his commander, Robert E. Lee, shared an almost symbiotic relationship, there is no real connection between them on the screen. For instance, *Gods and Generals* does not take advantage of the last meeting between the two great Southern commanders before Lee sent his subordinate on a flanking march that threatened the Union right at Chancellorsville the next day. This may have been because so little was actually recorded about what the two men said. As historian Stephen Sears has explained, "Afterward, when the full significance of this conference in the Wilderness had become apparent, men would scour their recollections for the exact words Generals Lee and Jackson spoke in those evening hours." Sears notes the length of their time together and the general ebb and flow of visitors and concludes, "in later years it was hard to remember just who said what or when they said it."[15]

The film does an admirable job establishing the attack Jackson makes after leading his troops on a circuitous route to approach the Union flank. In real life, as the lengthening shadows of a receding day began to gather, Jackson determined that all was in order and sent his men forward.[16] As the movie depicts, Jackson accompanied his troops as they advanced, relishing in the success the attacks were enjoying in the fading light and admonishing his men to "press on."[17]

Darkness and the disorganization of troops in the chaos, even in a successful attack, eventually brought the Confederate advance to a halt. Jackson remained anxious to keep the pressure on the Federals and sought to learn more about their intentions on his front by reconnoitering the Union lines. What he heard, again depicted accurately on-screen, disturbed him greatly. The enemy troops were busy improving their lines, rendering any assault the Confederates carried out against them the next day more difficult and deadly.

By approximately 9:00 p.m., Jackson had heard enough. He and his staff, accompanied to the front by Ambrose Powell Hill and his staff, rode back toward Confederate lines. Already there had been much confusion on the lines in the twilight.[18] A single shot rang out, followed in rapid succession by several shots and then a volley as the blasts moved down the line and lit up the darkness. Some of these shots penetrated the thick growth of woods and found their marks among the Confederates. Robert Krick observes, "Only seven of the nineteen [Southern riders] came back untouched, man or horse."[19] Jackson was not one of them. "Stonewall" had been struck three times.

Gods and Generals presents these scenes realistically, from the confusion attendant in the incident to the frantic attempts to get the general out of harm's way. Ironically, it may have been these efforts that ultimately contributed to Jackson's death. Twice the litter bearers fall with the stricken general, not only causing him excruciating pain, but also further damaging his wounded left arm and shoulder. Krick recognizes that pneumonia was the direct factor in Jackson's death on May 10, but attributes it to the falls the general had endured during his evacuation from the area between the opposing lines.[20]

Jackson's final scenes are superbly presented. Again, the adherence to the historical record is substantial. What Lang's Jackson says and how he acts are faithful to the records that exist of that fateful period. This was undoubtedly the case because the general's distinguished biographer, James I. "Bud" Robertson, served as one of the film's historical consultants. Robertson's influence, particularly with regard to the words that the actors and actresses use in these closing scenes of the film, is unmistakable. A few examples will suffice.

A fading "Stonewall" Jackson observes to his beloved wife, Anna: "I know you would gladly give your life for me, but I am perfectly resigned. Do not be sad. I hope I may yet recover. Pray for me, but always remember in your prayers to use the petition, 'Thy will be done.'"

In turn, she feels deeply the need to fulfill the obligation she has accepted to tell him when the end was near: "Do you know the doctors say you must very soon be in Heaven?" She also reminds him that it is a Sunday and that he had always expressed the hope that he would die on a Sunday.

"I prefer it."

"Well, before this day closes, you will be with the blessed Savior in His glory."

"I will be the infinite gainer to be translated."[21]

In each instance, the words spoken on screen essentially mirror those of the historic persons who uttered them. Even Robert E. Lee's rather quixotic response to Jackson's wounding, amputation, and death are faithful to the sources. Although Duvall's Lee speaks to the Reverend Lacy about Jackson at a different point in time and under different circumstances than the general did in reality, in connection with a worship service on the Sunday Jackson died, his words are true to form: "Surely General Jackson must recover. God will not take him from us, now that we need him so much." Then his final, heartfelt, and heart-rending gesture: "When a suitable occasion offers, tell him that I prayed for him last night as I have never prayed, I believe, for myself."[22]

One aspect that no motion picture can ever hope to cover in any substantial way is the offering of alternative interpretations. If film producers try to inject other possible explanations, they invariably do so to the detriment of good storytelling and overall continuity. This is the charge that Robert Brent Toplin levels against Ang Lee and *Ride with the Devil*, and that he saw as fatal to the box office success of the film.[23] However, it could be said in the director's defense that this movie suffers from especially poor timing. Had Lee's motion picture appeared after Tobey Maguire's success and exposure in the *Spiderman* series and *Seabiscuit*, or after James Caviezel's gritty performance in *The Passion of the Christ*, *Ride with the Devil* obviously would have benefited more from the presence of those actors in the film.

Yet, in the case of *Gods and Generals*, the lack of complexity, even in an extended format, does not allow the film to explore alternative explanations— a luxury that historians have and indulge in with regularity. Thus James I.

Robertson speculates that Robert E. Lee did not go to see Jackson personally because he could not have trusted his emotions under the circumstances, one of two reasons tendered by Douglas Southall Freeman for Lee's decision.[24] Lee biographer Emory Thomas argues that "Lee knew that Jackson was lost to him for an indefinite period; that was enough. He would not allow himself to dwell upon pain; he would think about Jackson whole or not at all."[25] Duvall's Lee captures this sense of discomfort, almost as if the great Southern chieftain thinks that by refusing to see his stricken lieutenant he will not actually lose him.

Perhaps the most energetic pastime among many Civil War aficionados relates to the death of Thomas Jackson and the absence of his genius and martial capabilities from later battlefields. A favorite speculation of alternate historians puts Jackson at Gettysburg, a theory that works if the Stonewall of the Shenandoah appears, and not the one who proved lethargic in the Seven Day's battles around Richmond. In any case, one of the general's biographers has observed, "The wealth of Jackson legends and his near apotheosis began immediately."[26] *Gods and Generals* has certainly done nothing to harm that process.

Indeed, while the motion picture is not exclusively about the Confederate commander, *Gods and Generals* is as close as moviegoers have gotten to an adequate screen portrayal of the enigmatic Jackson. Ironically, because of its heavy inclusion of his story and the depiction of the string of Southern victories ranging from Manassas to Chancellorsville, *Gods and Generals* has been susceptible to the charge that it is too pro-Confederate. Undoubtedly, the anticipation of this criticism prompted Ron Maxwell to introduce future *Gettysburg* heroes Chamberlain, Mulroney, and Hancock and film so many of the Fredericksburg scenes from the Union perspective. However, it should be remembered that in the first years of the war, particularly in the Eastern Theater, the results were consistently positive for the Confederates. At least the director was kind enough to spare the audience of such Federal command failures as George B. McClellan, John Pope, and except for a small glimpse at Chancellorsville, "Fighting Joe" Hooker.

If the Ted Turner/Ron Maxwell Civil War trilogy sees its third installment, a similar opportunity for featured status will be available for Ulysses S. Grant. Even so, it is probably safe to assume that neither Martin Sheen nor Robert Duvall will appear with the victorious Union commander in Wilmer McLean's parlor at Appomattox Court House. It is also unlikely that the focus on action in Virginia will allow viewers to learn of the subsequent surrenders of Confederate commanders in other theaters well after Lee had offered his sword to his counterpart in the Old Dominion.

Still, *Gettysburg* and *Gods and Generals* (with *Last Full Measure* if it is made) constitute the most extensive cinematic examination of the Eastern Theater of the Civil War (outside of the television miniseries *Blue and Gray*). No such treatment exists of the other theaters of operation, although anyone who tries to depict the war in the West with the ill-starred Confederate Army of Tennessee and generals such as Braxton Bragg and Leonidas Polk will surely draw the ire of Southern viewers over alleged bias. In any case, until such motion pictures appear, Hollywood's depiction of the war (even with Ted Turner's assistance) remains incomplete.

CHAPTER 14

The Plight of the Prisoners of War

Photo courtesy Andersonville National Historic Site.

Photo by Doug Hyun. ©1994 Turner Pictures, Inc. All Rights Reserved.

ANDERSONVILLE

Emmy Award-winning director John Frankenheimer executive-produces and directs ANDERSONVILLE, a four-hour original miniseries about the legendary Confederate prisoner of war camp and the Union soldiers who lived and died there. (Top photo) Prisoners' shebangs along the "Dead Line" within the prison walls of Andersonville in 1864. (Bottom photo) The prison camp as recreated for ANDERSONVILLE in 1994. The TNT Original premieres Part I Sunday, March 3, and Part II Monday, March 4, 1996.

TNT

Contrasting images of the Confederate prison camp at Andersonville, Georgia (top), and the version constructed for the Ted Turner production of the same name attest to the overcrowded conditions for Union prisoners unfortunate enough to be held there.

165

I was dying by inches.

—Confederate prisoner of war at Rock Island

Same old story—coming in and being carried out.

—Andersonville captive John L. Ransom

Andersonville became, in effect, the fifth largest "city" in the Confederate States of America.

—Historian Lonnie R. Speer

APPROXIMATELY 400,000 soldiers on both sides endured wartime captivity at the hands of their opponents at some point in the conflict. Of this number, some thirty thousand of the Federals and twenty-six thousand of the Confederates held in these prison camps never left them. Those who did were often shattered wrecks, battered by cold and disease, threatened by malice and malnutrition, broken in body if not in spirit. Some 150 prison camps and compounds stretched across the landscapes of both antagonists, representing for those unfortunates incarcerated in them, as one historian has termed it, "the portals to hell."[1] In the popular mind at least, the worst of these were Andersonville in Georgia and Rock Island in Illinois, but the men held at Elmira in New York, Libby Prison in Richmond, Salisbury in North Carolina, Point Lookout in Maryland, Camp Douglas in Chicago, or any of the other major prison facilities would have disputed the notion that conditions there were any better.[2]

Yet, until 1993, Civil War cinema had largely ignored the plight of the prisoners of war. Except for the occasional references to such individuals found in Civil War westerns, usually concerning the conditions that caused them to fight alongside their former enemies or attempt to flee from confinement, no detailed examination of prisons and their inhabitants existed. The closest to a historical representation to appear was *The Andersonville Trial* (1970), adapted from the stage to the small screen with Richard Basehart as the notorious prison warden, Henry Wirz. But this treatment was a courtroom drama that relied on testimony to convey the horrible reality of the notorious Southern prison compound rather than attempt to recreate the physical dimensions of the camp.

Of the films that tackle the subject even tangentially, several refer to historical prisoner-of-war compounds, while others create fictional ones to meet their cinematic needs. The camp in *Rio Lobo* (1970) in which the Confederate prisoners Captain Pierre Cordona (Jorge Rivero) and Sergeant Tuscarora Phillips (Christopher Mitchum) find themselves confined after robbing a Union payroll train is unidentified. *Shenandoah* (1965) does not follow prisoners into one of the established camps, but is one of the few films that illustrates the methods of transportation that the Federals in particular used to get their prisoners to the more permanent facilities. Thus "the boy" (Phillip Alford) and his comrade Carter (James Best) escape as they are being loaded onto steamboats, while the Anderson party rescues Sam (Doug McClure) from train boxcars in which captured Confederates are being moved. The experience of the fictional characters being carried northward on steamboats certainly mirrors that of real Southerners such as those who surrendered at Fort Donelson in 1862.[3]

The "Galvanized Yankee" westerns of the 1950s in particular use prisons as the means by which Northerners and Southerners can unite against common opponents. *Escape from Fort Bravo* (1953) features John Forsythe as Captain John Marsh, a disgruntled Confederate prisoner held "in a sun-baked stockade at Fort Bravo, Arizona Territory." The Union officer in charge of the prisoners, Captain Roper (William Holden), has already proven ruthlessly efficient at guarding his charges, although the prison contains no walls beyond a corral fence and no guard towers. In a conversation with a curious visitor, he explains that the prisoners do not require guards. "Where would they go without arms or horses?" he observes about the vast hostile territory that surrounds them.

"Do any of them ever try to escape?" she asks. "Sometimes," he replies.
"What happens?"
"I find them."

Yet the captain betrays a sense of ambivalence toward his duties when he observes to his commander, "Colonel, I don't know who's going to win this war, the North or the South, but we're here to hold this country for one of them, even if we have to arm these Reb prisoners." Indeed, Confederate captain Marsh succeeds in escaping from the Union officer's clutches, only to die in fighting alongside his captors against their common foe: the Apache Indians.

The prison depicted in *Two Flags West* (1950) features captured Confederates held at "the Prison Camp at Rock Island, in Illinois, in Autumn of 1864." The premise for the story scrolls across the screen: "On December 8th, 1863, President Abraham Lincoln issued a Special Proclamation whereby Confederate prisoners of war might gain their freedom provided they would join the Union Army to defend the frontier West against the Indians."

The impression of prison life at the Rock Island compound is appropriately grim. An officer sent to recruit volunteers under Lincoln's proclamation explains, "My offer's a way out of this stinking pesthole." As the Southerners contemplate their choices, one of them observes, "We're just rotting in here. If it ain't the fever, it's the dysentery." Indeed, the blankets and the buildings provide poor protection against the cold and conditions that are almost palpable on-screen.

"I understand you men were all part of General Jeb Stuart's own cavalry," the Union recruiter notes. "I reckon we still are," comes the reply meant to illustrate that while these men may have been captured, they are not defeated in their spirits. But the offer is tempting, and the officer suggests that the officer-in-charge, Colonel Clay Tucker (Joseph Cotten), has an obligation to consider the well-being of the men. "And you say we Southerners won't be asked to fight against our own?" "That's right." Then the Colonel quickly retorts, "You fail to mention how many Northern troopers we'll be relieving to do just that." But the bandaged officer replies, "There are no troops out West who can be relieved; they're either greenhorns or casualties like me." He concludes, "It's no charity picnic you're invited to," the officer observes. "It's a soldier's life at 40 cents a day."

After trying to woo Confederate prisoners, the recruiting officer notes, "General Grant's order of August 19th is final." This refers to the refusal to exchange further prisoners. Ironically, on that same day, the Federals reopened draft facilities in a still-simmering New York City.[4]

Created in the aftermath of the failure of the commissioners of exchange to reach an agreement, the Rock Island compound featured crude barracks and brutal conditions.[5] Orders for construction called for eighty-four barrack buildings that would hold sixty bunks, or 120 residents each. These were to be arrayed in six rows of fourteen barracks, each encased in a stockade wall with guard or sentry towers spaced at approximately one-hundred-foot intervals.[6] The camp became available in early December 1863, but quickly turned into a haven for disease. Initially, 5,592 prisoners transferred to the new facility from Camp Douglas, near Chicago, when barracks burned there, leaving them without shelter. Many of these men, captured at Lookout Mountain and Missionary Ridge, brought smallpox with them that continued to ravage their ranks.[7] In the first three months of 1864, better than six hundred of the over seven thousand Confederate prisoners housed there succumbed to exposure and smallpox.[8] The toll of disease for the twenty months the prison remained open ran to 1,960.[9]

The film correctly notes President Lincoln's December 8, 1863, amnesty decree, although the enlistees in the movie have an easier transition than the first ones in reality. Those individuals, numbered at 1,797, became caught in a bureaucratic vacuum. They no longer counted as prisoners who would receive issues provided to captives, nor were they yet fully mustered Union soldiers provisioned by the quartermaster and commissary departments.[10] The numbers of Confederates willing to take the oath to the Union and "galvanize" from Rock Island rose to as many as four thousand.[11] Yet not all desirous of taking this opportunity could do so. As one writer explains, "life on the island was not calculated to keep a man fit for combat."[12]

Two Flags West does an admirable job illustrating the dilemma that such a decision posed for the Southern prisoners. One soldier sent a letter home describing the agony, as well as the necessity, of the decision he felt had been forced upon him: "I know that I have disgraced myself in the eyes of honorable people, but it was because of starvation and to escape a miserable death, I took the course I did." He recognized, too, that some at home would think "I would better have died than dishonor myself. I would have said so too, a year ago, but no one who has not been placed as I have been placed, should judge us harshly." Whether or not he expected such clemency from the home folks, he added, "I had lingering starvation before me, from day to day, from week to week, until I scarcely knew what I was doing. I was dying by inches." Under such conditions, he had accepted the Union offer, but only after receiving the assurance "expressly stated in my enlistment that I am not to fight against my own people, but only against Indians."[13]

Imprisoned loyal Confederates tried to offset this Union recruitment scheme by staging a reenlistment effort of their own. Their work produced 1,300 reenlistees for service in the cavalry, but the war ended before an exchange could be reopened and the reenlistees could return to Confederate field service.[14] Even so, the incident reflected the bitterness, portrayed best in the film by Corporal Cy Davis (Noah Beery), that many Southerners felt about reaching any accommodation with the North short of exchange or unconditional release.

The film's worst historical element is the association of the name "Jeb Stuart" with the Rock Island prisoners at various points. The first comes when the Union recruiter appears at the opening, but the most extensive occurs in a heated exchange between the commander of Fort Thorn, Major Henry Kenniston (Jeff Chandler), and the former Confederate colonel, now a Union lieutenant, Clay Tucker (Cotten).

After preliminaries at the officer's mess table, the dinner conversation quickly devolves between the two men. When a guest offers, "But the lieutenant's on the right side now. Aren't you Lieutenant Tucker?" He responds curtly, but politely, "Just here to fight Indians." Another asks if he had been in prison long, to which he answers, "Any time in prison is a long time." Then, noticing the commander's discomfort, Tucker inquires if he had been in Libby Prison himself. The commander fires back concerning his freedom: "I didn't bargain for mine, I escaped."

The heat of the discussion swells:

"Were you with Jeb Stuart from the beginning?"

"Yes sir, I was with General Stuart right up to Yellow Tavern."

Then, in a steady drumbeat Kenniston badgers Tucker. "Were you at First Bull Run?" "At Gaines' Mill and Savage Station?" "At Crampton's Gap and Fredericksburg?"

But each time the reply to the inquiries is a restrained, "Yes, sir."

"Were you at Chancellorsville?" the Union commander reaches the heart of his interrogation. "At Chancellorsville when Stuart made his charge against Brown's Brigade?"

"My squadron had the honor to lead that charge, sir."

"My brother, Elana's husband, was killed in that charge."

But the personal losses have not been one-sided. Tucker fires back, "My brother was killed at First Manassas, my cousin at Vicksburg, another cousin," as he allows the litany of losses to trail off.

The exchange produces a number of verifiable facts. One reason the alignment of Tucker and his men to Jeb Stuart works in the film is that, as the Union recruiter first indicates, although his offer is "technically open to all prisoners," the army wants cavalrymen. Of course, given that the captives at Rock Island tended to come from the Western Theater, they would not in all likelihood have ridden with Stuart. Finally, despite service in most of the engagements listed, Stuart and his men were otherwise occupied when Lee's troops tangled with McClellan's Federals in the battles of the Peninsula campaign that Kenniston cites.[15]

Like their counterparts in *Two Flags West*, the Confederates held in *A Time for Killing* (1967) are also horse soldiers. Captain Dorrit Bentley (George Hamilton) and his comrades escape from their captors by way of a tunnel that runs beneath the cookhouse. Their prison differs little in appearance from the wooden forts of the standard western, with two observation towers converted to use for sentries and wire fencing to contain the prisoners. The number of prisoners, all ostensibly captured Virginia cavalrymen, cannot exceed thirty.

When the Southerners make their break, they seem remarkably free to move about in the stockade without being detected. The Confederates easily overpower their guards. Then, while some of the sick or injured Southerners remain behind to keep the Union garrison occupied, the escapees use the tunnel to reach the river, where they employ logs to float to freedom. The remainder of the film follows Major Charles Wolcott's (Glenn Ford's) pursuit of the fugitives through a series of running skirmishes that end with a final gun battle in Mexico in which most of the remaining soldiers on both sides are killed.

Director Sergio Leone places "the good" Blondie (Clint Eastwood) and "the ugly" Tuco Ramirez (Eli Wallach) in a prison dominated by "the bad" Angel Eyes Sentenza (Lee Van Cleef) that writer Jay Hyams has observed, "resembles Auschwitz more than Andersonville."[16] Indeed, it is in this facility that Tuco endures a torture session while a band of prison musicians play a serenade designed to mask the proceedings. Instigated by Sentenza to extort information about hidden gold, the scene smacks more of the sadism of Idi Amin or Saddam Hussein than of a Civil War prison compound.

Likewise, the prison that viewers see in the opening scenes of *Macho Callahan* (1970) is a cross between a World War II German stalag, with its "coolers" for unruly inmates, and the tents and lean-tos that could be found in South Georgia during the Civil War. Clearly, Andersonville was the inspiration for the latter elements of this prison, although the inmates in this stockade include Confederate deserters as well as Union prisoners. Labeled as a deserter after being railroaded into military service, Diego Callahan (David Janssen) escapes from the compound in a dramatic, if highly implausible, fashion when he places dynamite in the coffin of a dead comrade. The resultant explosion blows open the gates and sets off a free-for-all that allows the prisoner to slip away and spend the remainder of the movie seeking revenge for his false imprisonment.

While Andersonville is only one influence on the look of Callahan's prison, the Georgia facility is the focus of a 1996 Ted Turner production. *Andersonville* tells the story of the infamous prisoner of war camp and the conditions of the Federal troops imprisoned there. The credits contain sketches from *Harper's Weekly* to offer authenticity from the outset.

The action opens at Cold Harbor, Virginia, on June 1, 1864. The Confederates capture most of the members of a company of Union troops from the Nineteenth Massachusetts. The captors separate the men and noncommissioned officers from their superiors and place them on a train that passes by devastated areas and slaves still picking cotton in the fields. When the prisoners finally arrive at their destination, they walk past guards with dogs and watch as a patrol brings in some would-be escapees. "What do you call this little piece of heaven?" one of them asks. "This? This is Andersonville."

The compound is already jammed with humanity. The ones already there ask for news, while some eye the new arrivals with anticipation. "Nice fresh fish," one of them remarks. The new arrivals reunite with a comrade they thought was killed at Antietam. He serves as a transitional guide for them. "Dick, they got kids watching us here?" Dick answers, "The Rebs are moving out men. They are robbing the cradle and the grave to guard us." The situation is a deadly one. When one of the guards lures a prisoner too close to the "dead line," he shoots the man almost for sport. The message is clear that life is cheap at the prison.

The new prisoners quickly learn the ropes. It will cost two dollars to get a letter out of the prison camp. Veterans advise them not to drink the water from the swamp that gathers at one end of the compound. Then they learn the most difficult lesson of all. They must be as wary of some of their fellow prisoners as they are of some of their guards.

These Union prison raiders strike seemingly at will, beating, robbing, and killing to obtain what the men have brought with them into the compound. "Get everything they got," one of them calls out. "Stick with Collins boys you'll live like kings," the leader exhorts. Collins and his men celebrate their latest triumphs, gloating over the spoils they have accrued and the broken bodies from which those spoils were taken. Andersonville Prison is the cruelest example of "survival of the fittest."

The prisoners soon discover a traitor in their midst. Some of the Union men catch one of their own trying to inform on his colleagues to the guards. He is a "tunnel traitor," punished with the letters "TT" cut into his forehead.

Nevertheless, men continue to try to escape. One dies at the hands of the guards. Another turns back and is recaptured. Hound dogs track a corporal and sergeant, treeing them until their handlers arrive to take the men back into custody.

A Confederate colonel travels to Andersonville to inspect the prison, chiding Henry Wirz (Jan Triska), the commandant, for the poor conditions there. Wirz, a Swiss national who has come to the South and sided with it in the war, has had his arm shattered at Seven Pines and carries the wounded limb in a sling. He protests that the conditions in the facility are beyond his control.

Finally, the camp rises against the raiders and takes them into custody. Wirz agrees to let the prisoners decide their fates and promises to carry out whatever sentence they designate. The trial begins. Six of the ringleaders will hang. In a significant sense, purging the population of these thugs, or at least their ringleaders, eases the situation for the prisoners. But other conditions in the camp continue to deteriorate. Scurvy ravages the men. New arrivals inquire if Andersonville is as bad as they say, and they are told, "No. Worse." A prisoner can take no more and crosses the dead line to get shot, a suicide by guard.

At length, another Confederate colonel arrives to address the men with a similar offer to that made to the Southern occupants of Union prison camps such as Rock Island. "You men. You prisoners," he begins. "It must be clear to you by now that your government has cruelly abandoned you. As you know, they have turned down all of our efforts to exchange you. They know of your suffering, which though terrible is no worse than the suffering of our men in Northern prisons." The colonel asks for volunteers from among them to leave the prison to enter Confederate service. The unanimous answer of the captives is to turn about face in silent refusal. Even in their desperate straits, the men choose continued imprisonment to dishonor.

With the war winding down, Wirz comes in to tell the prisoners that they are at last to be exchanged. It is too late for many of them, including Martin Blackburn, who dies. As his comrades leave the compound, they carry his body out to be left for burial as the survivors trudge past to an uncertain fate.

The film's ending provides context for the brutality of life as a prisoner of this notorious camp:

In 1864–5 more than 45,000 Union soldiers were imprisoned in Andersonville. 12,912 died there.

The prisoner exchange never happened. The men who walked to the trains were taken to other prisons, where they remained until the war ended.

After the war, Wirz was hanged, the only soldier to be tried and executed for war crimes committed during the Civil War.

Yet even these facts contain errors and historical limitations. Henry Wirz was executed by hanging in November 1865 for the excesses at Andersonville, but he was not "the only soldier" to meet that fate. Historian Lonnie Speer has argued that at least two other individuals should join Wirz in that dubious honor.[17] Certainly this was true for the Kentucky guerrilla Champ Ferguson, although the Federals did not capture him until May 1865. Subsequently tried in a military court that found him guilty of murdering over fifty Union soldiers, Ferguson met his end on the gallows in Nashville, one month before Wirz stepped onto the scaffold at Old Capitol Prison.[18]

Andersonville has done more to illustrate the plight of at least some of the prisoners of war than any other film had done previously. Yet it also demonstrates the limits of the ground any one film can cover. This is a story that reflects the horrors of just one prisoner-of-war facility, albeit the one most familiar to the audience.

Originally named Camp Sumter, the prison stockade was designed initially to hold only ten thousand occupants. The first Union prisoners arrived from Belle Island in Richmond, Virginia, on February 24, 1864.[19] One historian places the prisoner population at 7,160 on April 1, before swelling to 12,213 by May 8, with 728 men having died and six having escaped successfully out of thirteen attempts in just over a month's time.[20] By the end of July, a staggering 29,998 men were sweltering under the Georgia sun as prisoners at Andersonville.[21] By the time the course of the war finally compelled the Confederates to remove the prisoners from the stockade, approximately forty-one thousand Union soldiers had been held there.[22]

Situated in remote southwestern Georgia, the camp offered greater security for the burgeoning prisoner-of-war population than locations closer to the front lines. This became all the more necessary when large-scale military actions produced substantial numbers of prisoners on both sides, particularly following Confederate victories such as Chickamauga. Union armies continued to penetrate deep into Southern territory, adding to the need for secure locations for Union prisoners. The Federal decision not to exchange prisoners also contributed to the pressure to which a woefully unprepared prisoner-of-war system had to respond.

As James McPherson writes in his widely read and acclaimed *Battle Cry of Freedom*, "The camp at Andersonville in southwest Georgia became representative in northern eyes of Southern barbarity."[23] Then he adds in a footnote that this was not the Confederacy's worst prison. "That dubious distinction belonged to Salisbury, North Carolina, where 34 percent (compared with Andersonville's 29 percent) of the total of 10,321 men incarcerated there died." Finally, McPherson notes, "The highest death rate in a northern prison was 24 percent at Elmira."[24] Thus neither side could truly claim the moral high ground in its treatment of the men who ended up as its war captives.

Andersonville remains the best known of Civil War prisons on either side.[25] It is a story at once compelling and heartbreaking. Yet were that story continued, it is likely that it would be surpassed by what happened to some of the prisoners who survived that terrible experience only to board an over-crowded steamer, the *Sultana*, to meet their doom on their way home.[26] Hollywood has yet to tackle that sad corollary to the story of Andersonville in a disaster whose death toll in all likelihood surpassed even that of the often-depicted sinking of the *Titanic*.[27]

CHAPTER 15

The War and the Waves

The Hunley features the Confederate vessel that became the first submarine to sink an enemy ship in combat. Here the crew, led by George Dixon (Armand Assante), prepares to take the vessel out.

In the name of Virginia, let every man do his duty.

—Confederate captain Franklin Buchanan, CSS *Virginia*

SWASHBUCKLING FILMS and grand naval engagements have always seemed to find ample room on Hollywood's big screen. Errol Flynn virtually made a living as a pirate, while Laurence Olivier brought the British naval hero of Trafalgar, Lord Horatio Nelson, to life. Robert Stack did the same for the American Revolution's John Paul Jones. Yet few films, with the prominent exception of the 1936 motion picture *Hearts in Bondage*, have attempted to put Civil War naval warfare, or even major components of it, on celluloid until Ted Turner did so for cable television in the 1990s. In 1991, in *Ironclads*, Turner tried his hand at depicting the revolutionary naval engagement between the ironclads *Virginia* and *Monitor*. The confrontation between these vessels in March 1862 in Hampton Roads changed naval warfare forever.[1] Turner followed this in 1999 with a film devoted to *The Hunley*, the Confederacy's submarine that in 1864 became the first such vessel to sink an enemy ship in combat.[2]

The historical aspects of *Hearts in Bondage* revolve around the development of ironclad vessels early in the American Civil War and culminate in the historic showdown between the USS *Monitor* and the CSS *Virginia* at Hampton Roads in March 1862. Labeling itself the "story of ships and men—iron ships and men of iron," the movie prominently features the *Monitor* and is largely cast from a Northern point of view. Indeed, the motion picture is dedicated to this first Union ironclad, and "to the gallant men who fought for and against her."

The film opens with seamen who are proud to serve on the USS *Merrimack*, but are oblivious to the signs of impending sectional troubles that threaten to change their lives and the national registry of their warship. "The *Merrimack*'s mighty seaworthy," one of the men gushes in a bit of foreshadowing irony.

But the fate of the vessel and those who will serve on her in one incarnation or another are already being decided. A sense of urgency grips some of the more established figures in the U.S. Navy. Captain Franklin Buchanan, portrayed by the familiar silent screen star of *The Birth of a Nation*, Henry B. Walthall, is summoned with his friend and fellow Virginian, Commodore Jordan, to a meeting with Secretary of the Navy Gideon Welles, President Abraham Lincoln, and other naval officers. The secretary informs the gathering that six of the cotton states have seceded from the Union, forming a government in Montgomery, Alabama, and that Virginia has called a convention of its own. Under such circumstances, he must be sure of the loyalty of every officer who remains in the U.S. Navy.

Buchanan is decisive in his response. "The question raised by Mr. Secretary has been weighing heavily upon me these past few months," he admits. "I was born in Virginia, the son of Virginians. Birth has determined my decision. As my state goes, so must I." In apparent anticipation of the Old Dominion's choice, he adds, "It is with regret that I am compelled to tender my resignation from the United States Navy." There is no rancor in the decision, or bitterness in the reception of it by those in the room. All eyes then turn to Buchanan's friend, Commodore Jordan.

Jordan is also a Virginian, but he has determined that his loyalty lies with the Union. "Any section of the land over which Old Glory waves is my home," he explains. President Lincoln accepts the statement with gratitude, paraphrasing in reply a toast made by the hero of the Tripolitan War and War of 1812, Stephen Decatur: "Our country . . . may she always be in the right; but our country, right or wrong."[3] Jordan's answer is simply to say to the chief executive, "Mr. President, I'm at your service." Lincoln understands that many will face the same dilemma in the war that looms over the nation.

Union lieutenant Keith Reynolds (James Dunn), a nephew of the eccentric inventor John Ericsson and the beau of Constance Jordan (Mae Clark), the daughter of the commodore, is destined to face a difficult choice himself. But his is not one of personal duty; it is one of romance. Unlike their father, Constance's brother Raymond (David Manners) chooses Virginia and the Confederacy. This puts an understandable strain on the relationship between Reynolds and Constance Jordan. She fears that Reynolds may be called to action against her brother if hostilities break out.

In the meantime, Southern sympathizers are anxious to seize naval facilities in and around Norfolk, Virginia. The Federal authorities at Gosport Navy Yard are equally determined to prevent such facilities from falling into Confederate hands intact. The commandant orders the yard to be destroyed, and flames, explosions, and destruction soon fill the screen. Of just as much importance are the vessels. Yet Reynolds refuses to burn the *Merrimack* as instructed. Instead, he scuttles her in the hopes that she can be raised for future service in the Union Navy. Unfortunately, his decision lands him in trouble with his superiors and prompts his dismissal from the service. Eventually, he will find his way back into the navy's good graces by volunteering for duty on an odd-looking vessel developed by his uncle, John Ericsson.

While his counterpart and friend struggles with his status in the Union Navy, Raymond joins the crew of a regenerated wooden ship that Confederate engineers have raised and turned into an ironclad vessel. The *Virginia* is no longer the *Merrimack*, nor is it operating under the U.S. flag. On March 8, Confederate commodore Buchanan, the commander of the vessel, speaks to his crew before sending them on a mission against the enemy's wooden vessels anchored in the Chesapeake Bay as part of a blockading force. "Our mission is to clear the harbor of enemy craft," he tells them. "And remember what you do today will be the history of tomorrow. Our homes, our women, our children shall be free if we succeed."

Thus, the Confederate ironclad steams out to confront the USS *Cumberland*, the USS *Congress*, and the USS *Minnesota*. The Southern vessel rams the first Union ship and sinks the second before Buchanan is knocked from action by shell fire. Lieutenant Jones assumes command, and the decision is made to save the third enemy warship, the *Minnesota*, for the following day.

In the meantime, a strange craft slips alongside the *Minnesota*. Derisively termed a "cheesebox on a raft" for its rotating turret and low-lying deck, the *Monitor* will clash with her adversary on March 9 in an action that will change naval history. During the fight, the Confederates succeed in injuring the Union commander, Lieutenant Worden, but fail to take the vessel with a boarding party. Raymond Jordan is one of the fatalities of the failed attempt.

By the time *Hearts in Bondage* ends, reconciliation has replaced the rancor of loss. A chance meeting with a solitary Abraham Lincoln (Frank McGlynn Sr.) by the couple divided by their loyalties, but united by their love for each other, shifts the message and reminds the audience that there were good people and sacrifices on both sides.

It will not be until 1991 that another motion picture features the historic confrontation between the opposing ironclads highlighted in the 1936 production. As if to lend veracity to that film's treatment of its pivotal historical event, *Ironclads* carries the statement: "This motion picture is based upon actual events which took place during the American Civil War. The producers have endeavored to accurately recreate the battles and all vessels portrayed in the film; however, certain characters and the roles they played in this historic period have been fictionalized."

With a disclaimer in place, the film opens in Gosport Naval Yard in Virginia on April 20, 1861, after the state has voted to secede from the Union. The *Pawnee* arrives with orders to destroy the dry dock to prevent it from falling intact into Southern hands. In the ensuing firefight, the Federals fail to blow the dry dock, thwarted by one of their own. The commanding Union naval officer waits in vain for the explosion, finally accepting that it will not come as he had hoped and expected. "So they get the only first-rate dry dock South of the Mason–Dixon line," he observes angrily to a colleague.

When confronted with his act of disobedience, Quartermaster's Mate Leslie Harmon (Reed Diamond), the man assigned with the task, confesses that he chose not to complete his mission because he had made friends among the people in the vicinity of Gosport while stationed there and did not wish to see them harmed by the huge stone blocks of the dry dock that a blast would have hurled in the air.

Southerners have a different view of young Harmon. He is the "Hero of Gosport." But, for all their adulation, Harmon is no traitor to the Union. To pay penance for his decision, he agrees to become a spy and learn all he can about the Confederacy's naval developments.

Because she does not agree with the institution of slavery, beautiful Southern belle Betty Stuart (Virginia Madsen) is also a spy. Yet she is torn between her efforts on behalf of the Union and her love for Confederate naval officer Catesby Jones (Alex Hyde-White).

Both North and South scramble to develop a weapon that will revolutionize naval warfare. The Confederates raise the burned-out hulk of the USS *Merrimack* and begin to outfit her with armor plating and heavy guns. At the same time, the Federals press the implementation of the plans of the eccentric Swedish inventor John Ericcson for an ironclad that will operate its guns with a rotating turret.

Confederate secretary of war Stephen Mallory officiates as the officers and crew man the renamed CSS *Virginia*. In the meantime, a Confederate intelligence officer, having held Betty Stuart under suspicion for some time, arrests her for espionage.

Unfortunately, Turner turned history on its ear for cinematic purposes by inserting scenes that had no place in the story depicted by *Ironclads*. One of these scenes features the captured Union spy Betty Stuart, watching from her comfortably situated cell as a spy is brought to the gallows to be hanged.

The Confederate officer who walks with him to the place of execution asks him to confirm his full name: Spencer Kellogg Brown. The man offers the confirmation and ascends the steps. He removes his hat to allow the noose to be placed over his head. The Confederate shakes the spy's hand and steps away. As the sentence is about to be carried out, he glances up at Betty Stuart to see that she is aware of the consequences of treachery. In short order, the floor is swung open and the spy falls calmly and quietly to his death.

The *Virginia* steams out to engage the Union blockading fleet on March 8, 1862. "The Confederacy expects every man to do his duty," the commander tells the crew. By every measure, they face a formidable foe. The Union's massive wooden vessels have an impressive array of firepower available to them: the *Cumberland* carries twenty-four guns, the *Congress* fifty, and the *Minnesota* forty-seven.

Yet the day belongs to the Confederates. The Southern ironclad sinks the *Cumberland* and compels the *Congress* to lower its colors in surrender. In the process the *Virginia* takes fire from troops on shore who are either unaware or unconcerned with these developments. The Confederate skipper, Captain Franklin Buchanan, angrily denounces the treachery, as he sees it, of violating the rules of war by firing once the colors of the enemy ship have been struck. The old warrior grabs a weapon and goes on deck to return the fire of the offending parties personally, and he receives a disabling wound in the process that will require him to pass command to Catesby Jones.

Although the *Congress* has not participated in further aggression, Buchanan's last order before passing command is for heated shot to be poured into the Union warship. In the meantime, the *Minnesota* has run aground trying to escape the Confederate craft, but the *Virginia*'s draft is too deep to allow it to pursue. Catesby Jones decides that the *Virginia* has done enough and will return the next day.

The *Monitor* arrives during the night and takes her place alongside the *Minnesota*. Acting as a pilot, the Union spy Leslie Harmon has brought the vessel to Hampton Roads to battle the *Virginia*. The next day, when the Confederate ironclad steams out to finish the task of clearing these waters of Union blockaders, she finds the *Monitor* waiting, and the stage is set for the historic encounter between the opposing ironclads.

Once the match between them has gotten underway, neither vessel seems able to gain a definitive advantage over the other. As the *Virginia* tries to ram the *Monitor*, it proves to be slow and unwieldy, running aground in the attempt. The *Monitor* tries to take advantage of the situation, but Catesby frees the vessel after redlining the pressure gauges and tying the valves off to prevent them from shutting the boiler down. A well-aimed shot from one of the *Virginia*'s guns strikes the *Monitor*'s pilothouse and blinds its commander John Worden. Both antagonists break off the engagement. Abraham Lincoln, played in this instance by James Getty, notes generously, "I would call it a draw."

In terms of the love story that burdens the film, Catesby returns to save Betty from the hangman, but then sends her North to "the side you chose." As *Ironclads* ends, it informs the audience of the fate of the two revolutionary vessels. "The Merrimack never saw action again. Two months after the battle, the Confederacy abandoned Norfolk, leaving the ship without a base. To keep her from falling into Union hands she was grounded and burned."

Nor is the outcome much better for the Union vessel. "The Monitor did not survive the year either. In December of 1862, she was ordered to join the Union attack on Wilmington, North Carolina. On December 31st in a storm off Cape Hatteras the Monitor went down with the loss of 16 lives."

The historical circumstances of the battle in Hampton Roads have their origin with the capture of Gosport Navy Yard in April 1861. Reacting to the firing on Fort Sumter and President Lincoln's subsequent call for volunteers to suppress the rebellion, the Commonwealth of Virginia opted for secession. Governor John Letcher then ordered the immediate seizure of Federal property in the state, including the facilities of Gosport Navy Yard near Portsmouth and across the Elizabeth River from the port city of Norfolk.[4]

As depicted, Confederate captain Franklin Buchanan really did have a flair for the dramatic, whether in addressing his crew or shouldering a musket to fire at the foe. When he sent his men into action against the Union blockading vessels in Hampton Roads, he drew upon the words Lord Horatio Nelson had used to inspire his men before the British victory at Trafalgar. Buchanan reminded his command of the larger stakes at play in the coming engagement:

180

"The eyes of the whole world are upon you this day, and in the name of Virginia, let every man do his duty."[5]

Buchanan also existed by a strict code of conduct that impelled him to take a rifle and exchange shots with soldiers on shore who fired at his vessel while a flag of truce flew. Although the old warrior paid personally with a wound in the left thigh that took him out of action, he had no doubt that his order to "fire" or burn the *Congress* in retaliation was fully justified in response to the treachery.[6]

Ironclads features scale models of the vessels filmed in a studio tank in England, yet the encounters between the *Merrimack* and the blockading vessels and the *Monitor* are relatively faithful to historical events.

For its shakedown cruise, the *Virginia* enjoyed an audience, as the film illustrates, although there were considerably greater doubts as to the outcome they expected to see from the ironclad's debut in combat. A witness, James Keenan, recorded the atmosphere among the spectators as they watched the real-life drama unfold:

> In an instant the whole city was in an uproar, women, children, men on horseback and on foot were running down towards the river from every conceivable direction shouting "the Merrimac is going down" and sure enough upon approaching the river I saw the huge monster moving loose from her moorings and making her way down the river with the gunboats Beaufort and Raleigh a little piece in the rear. A good portion of her crew were on top and received the enthusiastic cheers from the excited populace without a single response.

The crowd became uneasy as the *Virginia* held her fire while closing with the *Cumberland*, remaining silent as the Federals blazed away. Keenan recalled, "You may be able to partly imagine the great anxiety which prevailed along the shore now lined with thousands of anxious spectators. Everyone said why don't the Merrimac fire, the Cumberland will sink her, etc."[7]

The same adherence to history cannot be attributed to the love story that permeates the film. Not only was it superfluous to the military action, but it also served to discredit the work Turner and his compatriots put into depicting so accurately the naval scenes. The death of the spy Brown, ostensibly for the benefit of Betty Stuart, is a case in point. It is designed to awaken her (and the audience) to her possible fate and make her later salvation by Catesby Jones all the more satisfying. In point of fact, Spencer Kellogg, absent the Brown, died on the gallows at Camp Lee, "convicted of desertion and of being a spy," according to a Richmond newspaper, "in the presence of the military and a large concourse of citizens." As the film suggests, the report noted that, "He was cool, calm and collected up to the last minute, and gave the signal himself for the drop to fall."[8] It was only necessary to transfer this event, which actually happened a year later in 1863, to 1862, in a quiet ceremony that was designed to help Stuart see the error of her ways.

Turner was at his best while telling the naval story. He would return to the Civil War and the sea in 1999 with his strongest effort thus far in that regard, by depicting the saga of the Confederate submarine *Hunley* and the men who took her into another kind of naval history.

The Hunley opens as the vessel is being carried out on an experimental run. But, tragically, the submarine is stricken, takes water, and is flooded. It settles on the sediment of Charleston Harbor, claiming a crew that includes its inventor, Horace L. Hunley. Reluctantly, Confederate general Pierre Gustave Toutant Beauregard, stationed by this point in the war in Charleston, agrees to have the vessel raised, cleaned, and restored to service.

The new skipper of the craft will be an army officer, George Dixon (Armand Assante). His efforts to recruit a crew among experienced naval men meet with skepticism and rebuff. They know the reputation of the *Hunley* all too well and deem the service less an adventure to be coveted than a sure invitation to suicide. Nevertheless, Dixon succeeds in assembling a crew. A curious onlooker works mightily to gain the attention of the Confederate commander and anyone else to allow him to volunteer for service aboard the submarine. Ultimately, the transfer of Dixon's close friend and aide creates the necessary vacancy, and the young soldier becomes a part of the fateful team.

The craft continues to prove more threatening to the men who serve on it than to their opponents. An experiment with the *Hunley* and a floating torpedo, or mine, tethered to the vessel comes dangerously close to causing disaster for the submarine and its crew when it cannot be adequately controlled. Dixon and Beauregard decide to use a spar to hold the explosive device away from the vessel. Then the crew sets out on a final test run to establish whether they can remain below the surface long enough to reach the Union blockading fleet.

At last, the preparations are complete. Dixon informs the men that their target is the *Housatonic*. The crew members take their places at the crankshaft, and the vessel moves away from its moorings. As the *Hunley* closes on the Union vessel, the watch aboard the *Housatonic* notices what appears to be a large piece of driftwood floating in the water. He summons the officer of the day, who sounds the alarm. Men scurry about as they man the ship's cannons or shoulder muskets to repel the attack.

The *Hunley* benefits by being so low in the water and close to the vessel that the Union guns cannot be depressed sufficiently to damage or destroy her as she approaches. The *Housatonic* suddenly shudders as the spar strikes the side of the ship and takes hold. Dixon reverses his submarine, and the explosion from the mine shatters the night and rips a gaping hole in the side of the Union blockader. During the course of the attack, small arms fire penetrates one of the small observation windows and severely wounds Dixon. Nevertheless, the Confederate attack has been a success.

The *Hunley* surfaces and signals the shore, but begins to take on water. As she slips beneath the surface and plunges to the harbor floor, Dixon comes to the realization that there is nothing he can do to save the vessel or its crew. The men are faced with a terrible dilemma; they can either wait for the air to give out and suffocate, or they can open the sea cocks and allow themselves to be drowned when the submarine floods. The men make their choice, and Dixon opens the sea cocks as the *Hunley* claims her latest crew on this last mission. Ironically, much of the Union crew of the stricken *Housatonic* are able to save themselves by climbing into the rigging as the ship settles in relatively shallow waters.

Turner's film is one of the best devoted to a Civil War subject. The *Hunley* drowned not only the crew captained by Horace Hunley, but most of an earlier one as well. That accident had occurred when the wake of a passing ship spilled into the open hatchway of the submarine and caused her to plunge quickly. Only three men managed to escape before she disappeared completely, trapping a fourth with his leg caught by the hatch cover. That man, Charles Hasker, succeeded in freeing himself and swam to the surface, becoming the only man to go to the bottom with the vessel and live to tell the tale.[9]

The *Hunley* failed to lift the Union blockade of Charleston. But, in 2000, her last crew made the final voyage home. Raised from the murky depths, the silt-filled submarine has yielded treasures that both confirm and cause a reevaluation of the facts surrounding the historic vessel.[10]

Cinema has always shown a fondness for the seas. Tales of pirates and seafaring derring-do have filled the big screen with the likes of Douglas Fairbanks Sr., Errol Flynn, Tyrone Power, Burt Lancaster, and Yul Brynner.[11] Yet Hollywood has seldom ventured into the realm of traditional Civil War naval warfare, and nowhere has it done so with the realistic strokes of the 2003 film, *Master and Commander*, starring Russell Crowe. More exciting adventures as subjects for film are as near as the blockade runners that roamed the coastlines and the commerce raiders that traversed the seas. Films devoted to Raphael Semmes or David Glasgow Farragut could well join those depicting the naval heroes of other eras. Still, thanks in large measure to a maverick figure in the film industry, some portions of Civil War naval history have found their way onto celluloid.

Screening the "Real War"

The real war will never make it into the books.

—Walt Whitman

That a film carefully replicates the material culture of a period, however, is no guarantee that it conforms even vaguely to the historical
record.

—Mark C. Carnes

In the end, he who screens the history makes the history.

—Gore Vidal

THE POET Walt Whitman saw the American Civil War at its worst
while serving as a nurse for wounded soldiers. Whitman feared that the
"real war" that he and the people he treated had experienced would
never find its way into the history books.[1] For many years, as writings
centered on the lives of leaders, the famous poet's concerns must have appeared well founded. However, particularly with respect to the military history that has since focused on the ordinary soldiers and civilians, Whitman's
fears seem unfounded.

Had Whitman been able to follow the development of Civil War cinema,
he might have been less concerned. Throughout the years that began with
silent films, motion pictures have had a tendency to remember the soldiers
and civilians as well as the battles and leaders. To be sure, movies about Abraham Lincoln, William Clarke Quantrill, and others of significance abound,
but there are also the stories of the Andersons of Virginia, the Birdwells of Indiana, the boy soldier Henry Fleming, and of course, the trials and travails of
Katie Scarlett O'Hara. Historical films have featured Gettysburg, Petersburg,
and the burning of Atlanta; they have also made audiences aware of lesser-
known military operations such as the James J. Andrews and St. Albans raids

and the capture of cattle in Virginia, as well as the lesser-known war in places such as Kentucky and Missouri, or even in the distant West.

Yet, in a sense, it is evident how little the real Civil War has made it onto celluloid. The dependence on stereotypes and broadly drawn characterizations has left the nuances of history behind. Even when historical events make an appearance on the big screen, the history behind the events is often suspect. Pages could be written on the anachronisms and errors that appear in any film. Clearly, when the conflict between drama and historical accuracy plays out, the latter often takes a back seat. Still, the best films are those in which a general sense of history and a powerful story combine with good acting and directing to make a successful cinematic product.

Problems will always remain when trying to make a fictional story conform to historical reality. Studying history in film, Mark C. Carnes concludes: "That a film carefully replicates the material culture of a period, however, is no guarantee that it conforms even vaguely to the historical record."[2] In a conversation with historian Eric Foner, film director John Sayles observed rather pointedly, "If historical accuracy were the thing people went to the movies for, historians would be the vice presidents of studios. Every studio would hire two or three historians."[3]

Yet, if no motion picture–producing conglomerate is understandably prepared to submit its authority to one or more professional historians as CEOs, the former still have a compatible role to perform and an important contribution to make with regard to the work of the latter. As one historian explains, "It's our job as historians to deepen and add complexity to the story."[4] By offering even the shading of complication to an otherwise simple, even simplistic, story in a film, the historian as consultant will have provided an important service to filmmakers and movie audiences. As another student of film remarks, "When historians call for 'historical accuracy' in this context, what they want, more than precision of detail, is acknowledgment of the ambiguity and complexity of the past."[5]

The films examined in these pages confirm the sense that motion pictures tell us more about the times in which they appear than the periods being depicted on the screen. The better ones have transcended these limitations and still move audiences by the stories they tell. Whatever else might be said about them, images on the motion picture screen have proven themselves to be lasting and powerful ones, riveting a kind of history into audiences' minds. Thus the producers and directors, the screenwriters and technicians, the actors and actresses become the purveyors of a history that reaches more people than the monographs and biographies of trained historians or professional academics can. "In the end," as the writer Gore Vidal observes, "he who screens the history makes the history."[6]

APPENDIX A

Filmography

Abraham Lincoln (1930) Walter Huston, Una Merkel, Henry B. Walthall (Dir. D. W. Griffith, 97 min.)

Advance to the Rear (1964) Glenn Ford, Stella Stevens, Melvyn Douglas, Jim Backus, Andrew Prine, Joan Blondell, Alan Hale Jr., Whit Bissell, Michael Pate, Preston Foster (Dir. George Marshall, 97 min.)

Alvarez Kelly (1966) William Holden, Richard Widmark, Janice Rule, Patrick O'Neal, Richard Rust, Victoria Shaw, Harry Carey Jr. (Dir. Edward Dmytryk, 116 min.)

Arizona Bushwhackers (1968) Howard Keel, Yvonne De Carlo, John Ireland, Brian Donlevy, James Craig, Barton McLane, Scott Brady (Dir. Lesley Selander, 127 min.)

Arizona Raiders (1965) Audie Murphy, Buster Crabbe, Michael Dante, Ben Cooper, Gloria Talbott (Dir. William Witney, 88 min.)

Band of Angels (1957) Clark Gable, Yvonne De Carlo, Sidney Poitier, Efrem Zimbalist Jr., Torin Thatcher, Ray Teal, Raymond Bailey, Patric Knowles, Rex Reason (Dir. Raoul Walsh, 125 min.)

The Beguiled (1971) Clint Eastwood, Geraldine Page, Elizabeth Hartman, Jo Ann Harris, Matt Clark, Pamelyn Ferdin (Dir. Don Siegel, 109 min.)

Belle Starr (1941) Gene Tierney, Randolph Scott, Dana Andrews, Chill Wills, Louise Beavers, Mae Marsh, Charles Trowbridge, Hattie McDaniel (Dir. Irving Cummings, 87 min.)

The Birth of a Nation (1915) Henry B. Walthall, Lillian Gish, Mae Marsh, Ralph Lewis, George Siegmann, Walter Long (Dir. D. W. Griffith, 186 min.)

The Black Dakotas (1954) Gary Merrill, Noah Beery Jr., Robert Simon, Jay Silverheels, Clayton Moore (Dir. Ray Nazarro, 65 min.)

Cold Mountain (2003) Jude Law, Nicole Kidman, Renee Zellweger, Donald Sutherland, Philip Seymour Hoffman, James Gammon, Natalie Portman, Kathy Baker, Ray Winstone, James Rebhorn (Dir. Anthony Minghella, 155 min.)

Dances with Wolves (1990) Kevin Costner, Mary McDonnell, Graham Greene, Wes Studi, Robert Pastorelli (Dir. Kevin Costner, 181 min.)

Dark Command (1940) John Wayne, Walter Pidgeon, Claire Trevor, George "Gabby" Hayes, Roy Rogers (Dir. Raoul Walsh, 94 min.)

The Desperados (1969) Vince Edwards, Jack Palance, George Maharis, Neville Brand, Sylvia Sims (Dir. Henry Levin, 90 min.)

Drums in the Deep South (1951) Guy Madison, James Craig, Barbara Peyton, Barton MacLane, Craig Stevens (Dir. William Cameron Menzies, 87 min.)

Escape from Fort Bravo (1953) William Holden, John Forsythe, Eleanor Parker, William Demarest, Polly Bergen, William Campbell, Richard Anderson (Dir. John Sturges, 98 min.)

The Fastest Guitar Alive (1968) Roy Orbison (Dir. Michael Moore, 87 min.)

Finger on the Trigger (1965) Rory Calhoun (Dir. Sidney Pink, 87 min.)

Five Guns West (1955) John Lund, Dorothy Malone, Touch (Mike) Connors (Dir. Roger Corman, 78 min.)

Friendly Persuasion (1956) Gary Cooper, Dorothy McGuire, Anthony Perkins, William Schallert (Dir. William Wyler, 140 min.)

Gangs of New York (2002) Leonardo Dicaprio, Daniel Day-Lewis, Cameron Diaz, Jim Broadbent, John C. Reilly, Henry Thomas, David Hemmings, Liam Neeson, John C. Reilly (Dir. Martin Scorsese, 166 min.)

The General (1927) Buster Keaton, Marion Mack (Dir. Buster Keaton, Clyde Bruck-man, 74 min.)

Gettysburg (1993) Tom Berenger, Jeff Daniels, Martin Sheen, Sam Elliott, Richard Jordan, Brian Mallon, Stephen Lang, Kevin Conway, C. Thomas Howell, Royce D. Applegate, Patrick Gorman, Andrew Prine, Morgan Sheppard, John Diehl, Richard Anderson, Cooper Huckabee, Buck Taylor, James Lancaster, George Lazenby, Maxwell Caulfield, James Patrick Stuart, Ted Turner, Ken Burns (Dir. Ronald F. Maxwell, 145 min.)

Glory (1989) Matthew Broderick, Morgan Freeman, Denzel Washington, Cary Elwes, Jihmi Kennedy, Andre Braugher, Bob Gunton, Cliff De Young, Raymond St. Jacques, Jane Alexander, John Finn, Jay O. Sanders (Dir. Edward Zwick, 122 min.)

Gods and Generals (2003) Stephen Lang, Robert Duvall, Kali Rocha, Jeff Daniels, Brian Mallon, Kevin Conway, C. Thomas Howell, Matt Leitscher, Mira Sorvino, Karen Hochstetter, Lydia Jordan, Mia Dillon, Jeremy London, Sean Pratt, Stephen Spacek, Scott Cooper, William Sanderson, Bruce Boxleitner, Patrick Gorman, Morgan Sheppard, Buck Taylor, Royce D. Applegate, Frankie Faison, John Castle, David Carpenter, Christie Lynn Smith (Dir. Ronald F. Maxwell, 231 min.)

Gone with the Wind (1939) Clark Gable, Vivien Leigh, Leslie Howard, Olivia de Havilland, Thomas Mitchell, Hattie McDaniel, Butterfly McQueen, Victory Jory, Ward Bond, Harry Davenport, George Reeves (Dir. Victor Fleming, 222 min.)

The Good, the Bad and the Ugly (1966) Clint Eastwood, Eli Wallach, Lee Van Cleef (Dir. Sergio Leone, 161 min.)

The Great Locomotive Chase (1956) Fess Parker, Jeffrey Hunter, Jeff York, Kenneth Tobey, Harry Carey Jr., Slim Pickens, Morgan Woodward, John Lupton (Dir. Francis D. Lyon, 87 min.)

The Guns of Fort Petticoat (1957) Audie Murphy, Kathryn Grant, Jeanette Nolan, Ray Teal, John Dierkes (Dir. George Marshall, 82 min.)

Hangman's Knot (1952) Randolph Scott, Donna Reed, Frank Faylen, Lee Marvin, Richard Denning, Clem Bevans, Ray Teal, Jeanette Nolan, Guinn "Big Boy" Williams (Dir. Roy Huggins, 81 min.)

Hearts in Bondage (1936) James Dunn, Mae Clarke, Henry B. Walthall, Frank McGlynn Sr. (Dir. Lew Ayres, 72 min.)

The Horse Soldiers (1959) John Wayne, William Holden, Constance Towers, Althea Gibson, Willis Bouchey, Denver Pyle, Strother Martin, Ken Curtis, Hank Worden, Judson Pratt, Jack Pennick, Hoot Gibson, Carleton Young, O. Z. Whitehead, Chuck Hayward (Dir. John Ford, 119 min.)

How the West Was Won (1962) ["The Civil War" segment] George Peppard, John Wayne, Harry Morgan, Andy Devine, Willis Bouchey, Russ Tamblyn, Raymond Massey (Dir., "The Civil War," John Ford, 155 min. [total])

Jack McCall Desperado (1953) George Montgomery, Angela Stevens, Douglas Kennedy, John Hamilton, Jay Silverheels (Dir. Sidney Salkow, 76 min.)

Journey to Shiloh (1968) James Caan, Michael Sarrazin, Don Stroud, Harrison Ford, John Doucette, Noah Beery Jr., Jan-Michael Vincent, Michael Burns, Paul Petersen, James Gammon, Clark Gordon (Dir. William Hale, 101 min.)

Kansas Raiders (1950) Audie Murphy, Brian Donlevy, Marguerite Chapman, Richard Arlen, Tony Curtis, Richard Long, James Best, Richard Egan (Dir. Ray Enright, 80 min.)

The Last Outpost (1951) Ronald Reagan, Noah Beery Jr., Rhonda Fleming, Bruce Bennett, Hugh Beaumont (Dir. Lewis R. Foster, 88 min.)

The Last Rebel (1971) Joe Namath, Jack Elam, Woody Strode, Ty Hardin, Victoria George (Dir. Denys McCoy, 90 min.)

The Legend of Tom Dooley (1959) Michael Landon, Jo Morrow, Jack Hogan, Richard Rust, Dee Pollock (Dir. Ted Post, 79 min.)

The Lincoln Conspiracy (1977) John Anderson, Bradford Dillman, John Dehner, Robert Middleton, Whit Bissell (Dir. James L. Conway, 90 min.)

The Little Colonel (1935) Shirley Temple, Lionel Barrymore, Hattie McDaniel, Bill Robinson (Dir. David Butler, 80 min.)

The Little Shepherd of Kingdom Come (1961) Jimmie Rodgers, Luana Patten, Chill Wills, George Kennedy (Dir. Andrew V. McLaglen, 108 min.)

The Littlest Rebel (1935) Shirley Temple, John Boles, Jack Holt, Bill Robinson, Stepin Fetchit (Dir. David Butler, 70 min.)

Love Me Tender (1956) Richard Egan, William Campbell, James Drury, Elvis Presley, Debra Paget, Neville Brand, L. Q. Jones (Dir. Robert D. Webb, 96 min.)

Macho Callahan (1970) David Janssen, Jean Seberg, Lee J. Cobb, Pedro Armendariz Jr., David Carradine, James Booth, Bo Hopkins, Richard Anderson, Matt Clark, William Bryant (Dir. Bernard Kowalski, 99 min.)

Major Dundee (1965) Charlton Heston, Richard Harris, James Coburn, Jim Hutton, Michael Anderson Jr., Senta Berger, Brock Peters, Warren Oates, Ben Johnson, Slim Pickens, L. Q. Jones, R. G. Armstrong, Dub Taylor, Michael Pate, Mario Adorf, Karl Swenson (Dir. Sam Peckinpah, 124 min.)

The Man from Colorado (1948) Glenn Ford, William Holden, Ellen Drew, Ray Collins, Edgar Buchanan, Jerome Courtland, James Millican (Dir. Henry Levin, 100 min.)

No Drums, No Bugles (1972) Martin Sheen (Dir. Clyde Ware, 85 min.)

Of Human Hearts (1938) Walter Huston, Beulah Bondi, James Stewart, Charles Coburn, John Carradine, Gene Lockhart, Clem Bevans, Sterling Holloway, Ann Rutherford (Dir. Clarence Brown, 100 min.)

Only the Brave (1930) Gary Cooper, Mary Brian, Phillips Holmes, Guy Oliver, John H. Elliott (Dir. Frank Tuttle, 66 min.)

Operator 13 (1934) Gary Cooper, Marion Davies, Hattie McDaniel (Dir. Richard Boleslavsky, 86 min.)

The Outlaw Josey Wales (1976) Clint Eastwood, Sondra Locke, John Vernon, Bill McKinney, Chief Dan George, Woodrow Parfrey, Sheb Wooley, Royal Dano, Matt Clark, John Quade (Dir. Clint Eastwood, 135 min.)

Pharaoh's Army (1995) Chris Cooper, Patricia Clarkson, Kris Kristofferson, Will Lucas, Richard Tyson (Dir. Robby Henson, 90 min.)

The Proud Rebel (1958) Alan Ladd, Olivia de Havilland, David Ladd, Dean Jagger, Cecil Kellaway, Harry Dean Stanton, John Carradine (Dir. Michael Curtiz, 103 min.)

Quantrill's Raiders (1958) Steve Cochran, Diane Brewster, Leo Gordon (Dir. Edward Bernds, 68 min.)

The Raid (1954) Van Heflin, Richard Boone, Anne Bancroft, Lee Marvin, Peter Graves, Claude Akins, John Dierkes, James Best, Tommy Rettig (Dir. Hugo Fregonese, 83 min.)

Raintree County (1957) Elizabeth Taylor, Montgomery Clift, Lee Marvin, Rod Taylor, Eva Marie Saint, Agnes Moorehead, DeForest Kelley (Dir. Edward Dmytryk, 168 min.)

A Reason to Live, A Reason to Die (*Massacre at Fort Holman*) (1974) Telly Savalas, James Coburn, Bud Spencer (Dir. Tonino Valerii, 92 min.)

The Red Badge of Courage (1951) Audie Murphy, Bill Mauldin, Royal Dano, John Dierkes, Arthur Hunnicutt, Andy Devine, Whit Bissell (Dir. John Huston, 69 min.)

The Redhead and the Cowboy (1950) Glenn Ford, Edward O'Brien, Rhonda Fleming (Dir. Leslie Fenton, 82 min.)

Red Mountain (1951) Alan Ladd, Lizabeth Scott, Arthur Kennedy, John Ireland, Jeff Corey, Neville Brand, Carleton Young, Whit Bissell, Jay Silverheels, Iron Eyes Cody, Bert Freed (Dir. William Dieterle, 84 min.)

Revolt at Fort Laramie (1957) John Dehner, Frances Helm, Gregg Palmer, Harry Dean Stanton (Dir. Lesley Selander, 73 min.)

Ride a Violent Mile (1957) John Agar, Penny Edwards, Sheb Wooley (Dir. Charles Marquis Warren, 80 min.)

Ride with the Devil (1999) Skeet Ulrich, Tobey Maguire, Jewel, Jeffrey Wright, Simon Baker, James Caviezel, John Rhys Meyers, Mark Ruffalo (Dir. Ang Lee, 130 min.)

Rio Lobo (1970) John Wayne, Jorge Rivero, Jennifer O'Neill, Jack Elam, Christopher Mitchum, Mike Henry, Victor French, David Huddleston, Jim Davis, Edward Faulkner, Clint Walker, Hank Worden, George Plimpton (Dir. Howard Hawks, 114 min.)

Rocky Mountain (1950) Errol Flynn, Patrice Wymore, Scott Forbes, Slim Pickens, Sheb Wooley, Yakima Canutt, Guinn "Big Boy" Williams (Dir. William Keighley, 83 min.)

Santa Fe (1951) Randolph Scott, Jerome Courtland, Peter M. Thompson, John Archer, Warner Anderson, Roy Roberts, Jock Mahoney (Dir. Irving Pichel, 89 min.)

Santa Fe Trail (1940) Ronald Reagan, Errol Flynn, Raymond Massey, Olivia de Havilland, Alan Hale, Ward Bond, Van Heflin, Guinn "Big Boy" Williams, Charles Middleton (Dir. Michael Curtiz, 110 min.)

The Searchers (1956) John Wayne, Ward Bond, Jeffrey Hunter, Natalie Wood, Vera Miles, Harry Carey Jr., Ken Curtis, Hank Worden, Lana Wood, Henry Brandon, Pat Wayne (Dir. John Ford, 119 min.)

Secret Service (1931) Richard Dix, Shirley Grey, Gavin Gordon (Dir. J. Walter Reuben, 69 min.)

Shenandoah (1965) James Stewart, Phillip Alford, Doug McClure, Glenn Corbett, Patrick Wayne, Rosemary Forsythe, Katherine Ross, Charles Robinson, Tim McIntire, Paul Fix, Denver Pyle, George Kennedy, Strother Martin, James Best, Eugene Jackson Jr., Harry Carey Jr., Edward Faulkner, Warren Oates (Dir. Andrew V. McLaglen, 105 min.)

Sommersby (1993) Richard Gere, Jodie Foster, Bill Pullman, James Earl Jones, William Windom, Ronald Lee Ermey (Dir. Jon Amiel, 113 min.)

So Red the Rose (1935) Margaret Sullavan, Robert Cummings, Randolph Scott (Dir. King Vidor, 82 min.)

A Southern Yankee (1948) Red Skelton, Brian Donlevy, Arlene Dahl, George Coulouris, John Ireland (Dir. Edward Sedgwick, 90 min.)

Springfield Rifle (1952) Gary Cooper, Phyllis Thaxter, David Brian, Lon Chaney Jr., Fess Parker, Alan Hale Jr., Philip Carey, James Millican, Martin Milner, Guinn "Big Boy" Williams (Dir. Andre de Toth, 93 min.)

Stage to Tucson (1950) Rod Cameron, Roy Roberts, Charles Evans (Dir. Ralph Murphy, 81 min.)

The Tall Men (1955) Clark Gable, Robert Ryan, Jane Russell, Cameron Mitchell, Mae Marsh (Dir. Raoul Walsh, 122 min.)

The Tall Target (1951) Dick Powell, Adolphe Menjou, Will Geer, Marshall Thompson, Ruby Dee (Dir. Anthony Mann, 78 min.)

Tap Roots (1948) Van Heflin, Susan Hayward, Boris Karloff, Julie London, Ward Bond, George Hamilton, Richard Long, Hank Worden (Dir. George Marshall, 109 min.)

They Died with Their Boots On (1941) Errol Flynn, Olivia de Havilland, Arthur Kennedy, Stanley Ridges, Gene Lockhart, Sydney Greenstreet, Anthony Quinn, Hattie McDaniel (Dir. Raoul Walsh, 138 min.)

Three Violent People (1956) Charlton Heston, Anne Baxter, Tom Tryon, Gilbert Roland, Forrest Tucker, Bruce Bennett, Barton MacLane, Jamie Farr (Dir. Rudolph Mate, 100 min.)

A Time for Killing (1967) Glenn Ford, George Hamilton, Inger Stevens, Max Baer, Todd Armstrong, Kenneth Tobey, Harry Dean Stanton, Paul Petersen, Harrison Ford, Richard X. Slattery (Dir. Phil Karlson, 88 min.)

Two Flags West (1950) Joseph Cotten, Linda Darnell, Jeff Chandler, Cornel Wilde, Dale Robertson, Jay C. Flippen, Noah Berry Jr., Arthur Hunnicutt (Dir. Robert Wise, 92 min.)

The Undefeated (1969) John Wayne, Rock Hudson, Ben Johnson, Lee Meriwether, Roman Gabriel, Merlin Olsen, Bruce Cabot, Jan-Michael Vincent, Tony Aguilar, Edward Faulkner, Dub Taylor, Harry Carey Jr., Royal Dano, Paul Fix, Big John Hamilton, Richard Mulligan, James McEachin, Gregg Palmer, Kiel Martin, Guy Raymond, Pedro Armendariz Jr. (Dir. Andrew V. McLaglen, 119 min.)

Virginia City (1940) Errol Flynn, Miriam Hopkins, Randolph Scott, Humphrey Bogart, Alan Hale, Ward Bond, Guinn "Big Boy" Williams, Charles Middleton (Dir. Michael Curtiz, 121 min.)

Wicked Spring (2002) Brian Merrick, D. J. Perry, Terry Jernigan (Dir. Kevin Hershberger, 102 min.)

Woman They Almost Lynched (1953) Joan Leslie, Audrey Totter, John Lund, Brian Donlevy, Ben Cooper, Jim Davis, Ellen Corby (Dir. Allan Dwan, 90 min.)
Young Guns of Texas (1962) James Mitchum, Alana Ladd, Chill Wills (Dir. Maury Dexter, 78 min.)

Other Selected Films

Andersonville (1996) Jarrod Emick, Frederick Forrest, Cliff De Young, William H. Macy, Ted Marcoux, Jan Triska (Dir. John Frankenheimer, 168 min.)
The Andersonville Trial (1970) Richard Basehart, William Shatner, Cameron Mitchell, Martin Sheen, Buddy Ebsen, Albert Salmi, Jack Cassidy, Whit Bissell, Alan Hale Jr., Bert Freed, Kenneth Tobey, Woodrow Parfrey, William Bryant, Charles McGraw, John Anderson (Dir. George C. Scott, 150 min.)
The Hunley (1999) Armand Assante, Donald Sutherland (Dir. John Gray, 94 min.)
Ironclads (1991) Virginia Madsen, Alex Hyde-White, Reed Diamond, Philip Casnoff, E. G. Marshall, Fritz Weaver, James Getty (Dir. Delbert Mann, 93 min.)
Johnny Shiloh (1963) Kevin Corcoran, Brian Keith, Skip Homeier, Buck Taylor, Edward Platt (Dir. James Neilson, 90 min.)

Actors Who Wore the Blue

Dana Andrews, Major Thomas Grail, *Belle Starr*
Richard Boone, Captain Lionel Foster, *The Raid*
Willis Bouchey, Colonel Phil Secord, *The Horse Soldiers*
Matthew Broderick, Colonel Robert Gould Shaw, *Glory*
John Carradine, Abraham Lincoln, *Of Human Hearts*
Jeff Chandler, Major Henry Kenniston, *Two Flags West*
Montgomery Clift, John Wickliff Shawnessy, *Raintree County*
James Coburn, Colonel Pembroke, *A Reason to Live, A Reason to Die*
Chris Cooper, Captain John Hull Abston, *Pharaoh's Army*
Gary Cooper, Major Alex "Lex" Kearney, *Springfield Rifle*
Kevin Costner, Lieutenant John Dunbar, *Dances with Wolves*
Joseph Cotten, Lieutenant Clay Tucker, *Two Flags West*
Jeff Daniels, Colonel Joshua Chamberlain, *Gettysburg*
    Lieutenant Colonel Chamberlain, *Gods and Generals*
Royal Dano, The Tattered Soldier, *The Red Badge of Courage*
Clint Eastwood, Corporal John McBurney, *The Beguiled*
Sam Elliott, Brigadier General John Buford, *Gettysburg*
Paul Fix, General Joe Masters, *The Undefeated*
Errol Flynn, General George Armstrong Custer, *They Died with Their Boots On*
    Captain Kerry Bradford, *Virginia City*
Glenn Ford, Captain Jared Heath, *Advance to the Rear*
    Major Charles Wolcott, *A Time for Killing*
    Colonel Owen Devereaux, *The Man from Colorado*
Harrison Ford, Lieutenant Shaffer, *A Time for Killing*
Morgan Freeman, Sergeant Major John Rawlins, *Glory*
Sydney Greenstreet, General Winfield Scott, *They Died with Their Boots On*
Charlton Heston, Major Amos Charles Dundee, *Major Dundee*
William Holden, Captain Roper, *Escape from Fort Bravo*
    Major Henry Kendall, *The Horse Soldiers*
    Captain Del Stewart, *The Man from Colorado*
Arthur Hunnicutt, Bill Porter, *The Red Badge of Courage*
Walter Huston, Abraham Lincoln, *Abraham Lincoln*

Ben Johnson, Short Grub, *The Undefeated*
Brian Keith, Sergeant Gabe Trotter, *Johnny Shiloh*
George Kennedy, Colonel Fairchild, *Shenandoah*
Guy Madison, Will Denning, *Drums in the Deep South*
E. G. Marshall, Commander Smith, *Ironclads*
Lee Marvin, Orville "Flash" Perkins, *Raintree County*
Bill Mauldin, Tom Wilson, *The Red Badge of Courage*
Harry Morgan, General Ulysses S. Grant, *How the West Was Won*
Audie Murphy, Henry Fleming, *The Red Badge of Courage*
Patrick O'Neal, Major Albert Steadman, *Alvarez Kelly*
Fess Parker, James J. Andrews, *The Great Locomotive Chase*
George Peppard, Zebulon "Zeb" Rawlings, *How the West Was Won*
James Stewart, Lieutenant Jason Wilkins, *Of Human Hearts*
Denzel Washington, Private Trip, *Glory*
John Wayne, Colonel John Marlowe, *The Horse Soldiers*
    General William T. Sherman, *How the West Was Won*
    Colonel Cord McNalley, *Rio Lobo*
    Colonel John Henry Thomas, *The Undefeated*
Cornel Wilde, Captain Mark Bradford, *Two Flags West*

Actors Who Wore the Gray

Claude Akins, Lieutenant Ramsey, *The Raid*
Armand Assante, Lieutenant George Dixon, *The Hunley*
Max Baer Jr., Sergeant Luther Liskell, *A Time for Killing*
Noah Beery Jr., Sergeant Mercer Barnes, *Journey to Shiloh*
    Sergeant Calhoun, *The Last Outpost*
    Corporal Cy Davis, *Two Flags West*
Tom Berenger, Lieutenant General James Longstreet, *Gettysburg*
Ward Bond, Confederate Sergeant, *Virginia City*
James Caan, Buck Burnett, *Journey to Shiloh*
Joseph Cotten, Colonel Clay Tucker, *Two Flags West*
James Craig, Clay Clayborne, *Drums in the Deep South*
Royal Dano, Major Sanders, *The Undefeated*
John Dehner, Major Seth Bradner, *Revolt at Fort Laramie*
Brian Donlevy, William Quantrill, *Kansas Raiders*
    Quantrill, *Woman They Almost Lynched*
John Doucette, General Braxton Bragg, *Journey to Shiloh*
Robert Duvall, General Robert E. Lee, *Gods and Generals*
Clint Eastwood, Josey Wales, *The Outlaw Josey Wales*
Richard Egan, Vance Reno, *Love Me Tender*
Jack Elam, Matt, *The Last Rebel*
Errol Flynn, Captain Rafe Barstow, *Rocky Mountain*
Harrison Ford, Willie Bill Rearden, *Journey to Shiloh*
John Forsythe, Captain John Marsh, *Escape from Fort Bravo*
Clark Gable, Rhett Butler, *Gone with the Wind*
    Colonel Ben Allison, *The Tall Men*
Richard Gere, Jack, *Sommersby*
Peter Graves, Captain Frank Dwyer, *The Raid*
George Hamilton, Captain Dorrit Bentley, *A Time for Killing*
Richard Harris, Captain Benjamin Tyreen, *Major Dundee*
Van Heflin, Major Neal Benton, *The Raid*
Charlton Heston, Colt Saunders, *Three Violent People*
William Holden, Alvarez Kelly, *Alvarez Kelly*

Leslie Howard, Ashley Wilkes, *Gone with the Wind*
Rock Hudson, Colonel James Langdon, *The Undefeated*
Arthur Hunnicutt, Sergeant Pickens, *Two Flags West*
Jeffrey Hunter, William A. Fuller, *The Great Locomotive Chase*
Alex Hyde-White, Catesby ap-Jones Jones, *Ironclads*
John Ireland, Quantrill, *Red Mountain*
Ben Johnson, Sergeant Chillum, *Major Dundee*
Richard Jordan, Brigadier General Lewis A. Armistead, *Gettysburg*
Buster Keaton, Johnny Gray, *The General*
DeForest Kelley, Southern Officer, *Raintree County*
Alan Ladd, John Chandler, *The Proud Rebel*
    Captain Brett Sherwood, *Red Mountain*
Stephen Lang, George Edward Pickett, *Gettysburg*
    Thomas Jonathan "Stonewall" Jackson, *Gods and Generals*
Jude Law, Inman, *Cold Mountain*
Tobey Maguire, Jake Roedel, *Ride with the Devil*
Strother Martin, Virgil, *The Horse Soldiers*
Lee Marvin, Lieutenant Keating, *The Raid*
Audie Murphy, Jesse James, *Kansas Raiders*
Joe Namath, Captain Hollis, *The Last Rebel*
Jack Palance, Parson Josiah Galt, *The Desperados*
Fess Parker, Sergeant Jim Randolph, *Springfield Rifle*
Walter Pidgeon, William "Will" Cantrell, *Dark Command*
Andrew Prine, Brigadier General Richard B. Garnett, *Gettysburg*
Denver Pyle, Jackie Jo, *The Horse Soldiers*
Ronald Reagan, Captain Vance Britten, *The Last Outpost*
Michael Sarrazin, Miller Nialls, *Journey to Shiloh*
Telly Savalas, Major War, *A Reason to Live, A Reason to Die*
Randolph Scott, Sam Starr, *Belle Starr*
    Britt Canfield, *Santa Fe*
    Duncan Bedford, *So Red the Rose*
    Captain Vance Irby, *Virginia City*
Martin Sheen, General Robert Edward Lee, *Gettysburg*
Harry Dean Stanton, Sergeant Dan Way, *A Time for Killing*
Donald Sutherland, General Pierre Gustave Toutant Beauregard, *The Hunley*
Gene Tierney, Belle Starr, *Belle Starr*
Henry B. Walthall, Colonel Marshall, *Abraham Lincoln*
    Colonel Ben Cameron, *The Birth of a Nation*
John Wayne, Ethan Edwards, *The Searchers*
Richard Widmark, Colonel Tom Rossiter, *Alvarez Kelly*

The Best and Worst
of Civil War Cinema

The Best

The Birth of a Nation. This silent classic was a masterpiece of filmmaking with innovative techniques and a powerful, if significantly flawed, story line.

Glory. Although seen through the prism of the unit's white commanding officer and historically challenged in some of its detail, this film is a welcome exploration of one of the most celebrated African American units in the Civil War, with outstanding performances by the principals.

Pharaoh's Army. A fine examination of the Civil War on the small scale. The film depicts the troubled relationship between soldiers and civilians.

The Red Badge of Courage. John Huston's classic examination of the struggle of a young man facing battle for the first time remains one of the best films of its kind. Adhering faithfully to Stephen Crane's novel, it features compelling performances and powerful visual images of the common soldier's experience in war that resonate across the years.

Ride with the Devil. An outstanding and gritty treatment of the warfare in Kansas and Missouri, with strong performances by a young cast.

Two Flags West. This Civil War western depicts aspects of the war, including the issues of prison conditions and "galvanizing," better than its contemporaries.

The Worst

The Birth of a Nation. This innovative film's flawed history, based upon a notoriously racist novel, skewed generations of filmgoers' versions of the Civil War and Reconstruction Era, thereby tarnishing its place as a technical cinematic masterpiece.

The Last Rebel. A Joe Namath vehicle that simply does not run, the film is flawed, historically and theatrically, from the opening scene. Or, as Leonard Maltin has said succinctly, "Joe makes Ty Hardin look like John Gielgud" (Maltin's *Movie Guide*, 2001, 781).

Macho Callahan. Deserter turned fugitive, television star David Janssen spends most of the film chasing the man who helped put him in a prison, before hanging him and shooting virtually everyone else. The Confederate prison features World War II–style "coolers" and machine guns to keep the prisoners in line.

No Drums, No Bugles. This motion picture about a man who holes up in a West Virginia cave to avoid the Civil War is well-acted, but a remorselessly bad film dramatically with long periods of dead celluloid that make the viewer feel as if he or she would rather hide in a cave with the protagonist than endure this film.

A Reason to Live, A Reason to Die. The film's other title, *Massacre at Fort Holman,* better describes the action on which this campy Civil War film is based. Telly Savalas could not have saved this spaghetti western even if it had been an episode of *Kojak* instead.

Santa Fe Trail (1940). With little to do with the Civil War and much less still to do with history, this Michael Curtiz offering puts future president Ronald Reagan and actor Errol Flynn into the saddle as George Armstrong Custer and Jeb Stuart, respectively. Together they ride roughshod over the facts while indulging in the élan of the historical figures they are supposed to represent.

NOTES

Introduction: Hollywood's Civil War

1. For an overview of the Civil War in film and television, see Wills, "Films and Television," in *American Civil War*, 613–19.

2. Kinnard, *Blue and Gray on the Silver Screen*, 281–84, offers a list of silent films with Civil War themes for the years 1903–1929.

3. Campbell, *The Celluloid South*, 29.

4. For treatments of this nostalgia phenomenon in popular culture after the Civil War, see Silber, *Romance of Reunion*; Foster, *Ghosts of the Confederacy*; and Wilson, *Baptized in Blood*.

5. Henderson, *Griffith at Biograph*, 3, 111. A complete list of the Griffith Biograph films may be found in the appendix, 193–215, with 1910 highlighted on pages 204–8 and 1911 on pages 208–11.

6. Williams, *Griffith*, 61.

7. Heston, *In the Arena*, 317. Heston writes, "I wanted to be the first to make a film that really explores the Civil War," 326. Michael Munn, in his biography of the actor, recorded Heston's feelings regarding the matter: "I was very interested, and remain interested, in making a film about the American Civil War." Munn, *Charlton Heston*, 126.

8. Film critic Leonard Maltin noted caustically, "Joe [Namath] makes Ty Hardin look like John Gielgud." Maltin, *2001 Movie & Video Guide*, 781.

9. Of course, other American wars were also quite complex. One only has to consider the American Revolution, as loyalists battled patriots—each side American—at places such as King's Mountain and Moore's Creek Bridge.

10. From an academic standpoint, the only real drawback of this source is the lack of footnotes, but the publication is extremely informative and insightful.

11. Kinnard, *Blue and Gray in the Silver Screen*, is also a very handy reference guide to Civil War films.

12. See Cullen, "A Few Good Men: *Glory* and the Search for a Just War," chapter 5 in *Civil War in Popular Culture*, 139–71.

13. See Clinton, *Tara Revisited*.

14. See Davis, "The Civil War and the Confederacy in Cinema," chapter 12 in *Cause Lost*, 190–205.

15. Reardon, *Pickett's Charge in History and Memory*, 211.

16. Toplin analyzes *Mississippi Burning*, *JFK*, *Sergeant York*, *Missing*, *Bonnie and Clyde*, *Patton*, *All the President's Men*, and *Norma Rae*.

17. Clinton, *Tara Revisited*, 205.

18. Davis, *Cause Lost*, 193.

19. Munn, *Charlton Heston*, 9.

Chapter 1: The *Birth* of Civil War Cinema

1. See Henderson, *D. W. Griffith*, and Williams, *Griffith*, for examinations of this film innovator.
2. Litwack, "Birth," in *Past Imperfect*, 140.
3. Kirby, *Media-Made Dixie*, 13.
4. Kirby, *Media-Made Dixie*, 3.
5. Kirby, *Media-Made Dixie*.
6. Williams, *Griffith*, 62–63.
7. Cassidy, *Civil War Cinema*, 5.
8. Kirby, *Media-Made Dixie*, 6.
9. Kirby, *Media-Made Dixie*, 8.
10. See, Foner, *Reconstruction*.
11. Litwack, "Birth," in *Past Imperfect*, 139.
12. Campbell, *Celluloid South*, 46.
13. Blight, *Race and Reunion*, 395.
14. Noted Wilson biographer Arthur Link remained skeptical of the validity of the comment. He noted that the only individual present at the time who he could interview suggested that Wilson was silent in his response to viewing the motion picture. Link, *Wilson*, 253.
15. Thomas Dixon to Wilson, February 20, 1915. In *Wilson Papers*, 32:267.
16. Wilson to Griffith, March 5, 1915. In *Wilson Papers*, 32:325.
17. Wilson to Warren F. Johnson, March 29, 1915. In *Wilson Papers*, 32:454. See also Margaret Blaine Damrosch to Joseph Patrick Tumulty, March 27, 1915. In *Wilson Papers*, 32:455.
18. Tumulty to Wilson, April 24, 1915. In *Wilson Papers*, 33:68.
19. Wilson to Tumulty, April 25, 1915. In *Wilson Papers*, 33:68.
20. Wilson to Tumulty, ca. April 22, 1918. In *Wilson Papers*, 47:388n.
21. Griffith to Edith Bolling Galt Wilson, Los Angeles, Calif., June 14, 1918. In *Wilson Papers*, 48:314.
22. Link, *Wilson*, 252–54.
23. Gaughan, "Woodrow Wilson and the Legacy of the Civil War," 236.
24. Gaughan, "Woodrow Wilson and the Legacy of the Civil War," 237.
25. Litwack, "Birth," in *Past Imperfect*, 140.
26. Toplin, *Reel History*, 187.
27. Silverman, "Prohibition Propaganda," 29.
28. Quoted in Lang, ed., *Birth of a Nation*, 3.
29. Clinton, *Tara Revisited*, 204.
30. Conversations with various colleagues. A 1930s examination of the effects of the film on the attitudes of white middle and high school age students in an Illinois community found the same outcome in terms of attitudes toward African Americans. Quoted in Steiger, "Reception," 199.

Chapter 2: Victory Rode the Rails

1. See Turner, *Victory Rode the Rails*.
2. Pugh, *Sons of Liberty*, 122.

3. Hart, *Strategy*, 143.
4. Thomas, *Confederate Nation*, 156–58.
5. Turner, *Victory Rode the Rails*.
6. Wills, *Battle from the Start*, 296; Forrest Address, n.d., *The War of the Rebellion: A Compilation of the Official Records of the Union and Confederate Armies*, 45, pt. 2, 759–60.
7. For examinations of these men, see Thomas, *Bold Dragoon*; Ramage, *Rebel Raider*; and Wert, *Mosby's Rangers*.
8. For treatments of these individuals, see Leckie and Leckie, *Unlikely Warriors* (Grierson); Morris, *Sheridan*; and Longacre, *From Union Stars to Top Hat* (Wilson).

Chapter 3: The Romantic Era of Civil War Cinema

1. Curran, "*Gone with the Wind*: An American Tragedy," in French ed., *The South and Film*, 53.
2. Heston, *In the Arena*, 305.
3. Davis, *Cause Lost*, 194.
4. Roland, *American Iliad*, 4.
5. Clinton, *Tara Revisited*, 211.
6. Clinton, "Gone with the Wind," 134.
7. Wills, *Battle from the Start*, 251–61.
8. "Last Chance for the Confederacy" is the subtitle McMurry chose for his work on the Atlanta campaign. McMurry, *Atlanta 1864*.
9. Wills, *Battle from the Start*, 251–61.
10. Gorgas, *Journals of Josiah Gorgas*, 111.
11. Gorgas, *Journals of Josiah Gorgas*, 115.
12. Gorgas, *Journals of Josiah Gorgas*, 121.
13. See McPherson, *Battle Cry of Freedom*, 494, footnote; Roland, *American Iliad*, 91.
14. Kinnard, *Blue and Gray in the Silver Screen*, 43.
15. For historical examinations of conditions for Southern white civilians in the war, see Thomas, *Confederate Nation* and *Confederacy as a Revolutionary Experience*.

Chapter 4: The House Divided

1. Lincoln, *Fiery Trial*, 43.
2. Lincoln, *Fiery Trial*, 58–67.
3. Vidal, *Screening History*, 67.
4. McGlynn portrayed Lincoln in *Are We Civilized?* (1934), *The Littlest Rebel* (1935), *Hearts in Bondage* (1936), *Prisoner of Shark Island* (1936), *The Plainsman* (1937), *Wells Fargo* (1937), *Western Gold* (1937), *Lincoln in the White House* (1938), and *The Mad Empress* (1939).
5. See Donald, *Lincoln*.
6. See Neely, *Fate of Liberty*.
7. Chadwicke, *Reel Civil War*, 248.
8. Morris, *Sheridan*, 21–22; Warner, *Generals in Blue*, 437.
9. Warner, *Generals in Blue*, 430.
10. Examinations abound of George Custer in the West. For a study of his Civil War career, see Urwin, *Custer Victorious*. For a recent study of his life and military career, see Wert, *Custer*.

11. For the wide range of names applied to this conflict, see Pressly, *Americans Interpret Their Civil War*.

12. McPherson demonstrates this at the outset in *Battle Cry of Freedom*, 4–5, as does a cursory examination of the sketches provided in Warner's *Generals in Gray* and *Generals in Blue*.

13. Waugh, *Class of 1846*, xiv–xvi. James M. McPherson notes, "The description of the American Civil War as a war of brothers is more than a cliché." McPherson, *Battle Cry of Freedom*, ix.

14. Waugh, *Class of 1846*, x.

15. See Ramage, *Rebel Raider*.

16. Bynum, *Free State of Jones*, 2.

17. Bynum, *Free State of Jones*, 48.

18. McLemore, *History of Mississippi*, 1:525. Bynum uses the term *anti-Confederate* frequently to describe the political position of many of the Jones County resistors.

19. Bynum, *Free State of Jones*, 4, 94.

20. Polk to Maury, February 7, 1864, *The War of the Rebellion: A Compilation of the Official Records of the Union and Confederate Armies*, 32, pt. 2, 689. Hereafter cited as *OR*. All Series 1, unless otherwise identified.

21. Polk to Cooper, March 3, 1864, *OR* 32, pt. 3, 580.

22. Polk Report, March 17, 1864, *OR*, 32 pt. 1, 499.

23. Bynum, *Free State of Jones*, 125.

24. See Wills, *War Hits Home*, for similar difficulties in southeastern Virginia.

25. See Thomas, *Confederacy as a Revolutionary Experience*, and *Confederate Nation*.

26. Emory Thomas examines the bread riot in Richmond in several works. See *Richmond*, 119–20; *Confederate Nation*, 202–5; and "Bread Riot," 41–44.

27. See, for example, Blair, *Virginia's Private War*.

Chapter 5: The Personal War

1. Perhaps the most widely used example is Paludan's *Victims*. See also Noe and Wilson, eds., *Civil War in Appalachia*; Fisher, *War at Every Door*; Groce, *Mountain Rebels*; Weaver, *Civil War in Buchanan and Wise Counties Bushwhackers' Paradise*; Inscoe and McKinney, *Heart of Confederate Appalachia*; and McKnight, *Contested Borderlands*. An outstanding primary source of the war in the region is *Bluegrass Confederate*, Edward O. Guerrant's wartime diary.

2. Conti, "Seeing the Elephant," 19.

3. See Dean, *Shook Over Hell*, 75.

4. Long, *Civil War Day by Day*, 548.

5. McPherson, *Battle Cry of Freedom*, 760.

6. Meade to Burnside, July 30, 1864—5:40 a.m., *The War of the Rebellion: A Compilation of the Official Records of the Union and Confederate Armies*, 40, pt. 1, 140. Hereafter cited as *OR*.

7. Burnside to Meade, July 30, 1864—5:40 a.m., *OR*, 40, pt. 1, 140.

8. Humphreys to Burnside, July 30, 1864—5:40 a.m., *OR*, 40, pt. 1, 140.

9. See Burnside to Meade, July 30, 1864, *OR*, 40, pt. 1, 140; Meade to Burnside, July 30, 1864—7:30 a.m., *OR*, 40, pt. 1, 140; and Burnside to Meade, July 30, 1864—about 7:35 a.m., *OR*, 40, pt. 1, 143.

10. Finding, *OR*, 40, pt. 1, 127.

11. See the testimony of Major General Edward O. C. Ord and Brigadier General Adelbert Ames, for example. *OR*, 40, pt. 1, 83–84, 108–9.

12. Ulysses Grant observed to Henry Halleck, "I was strongly in hopes, by this means of opening the way, the assault would prove successful." Grant to Halleck, July 30, 1864—10 a.m., *OR*, 40, pt. 1, 17.

13. Kinard, *Battle of the Crater*, 53.

14. Jordan, North *Carolina Troops*, VII: 413. Major General Bushrod R. Johnson noted the role of the Twenty-Fifth North Carolina in the engagement, B.R. Johnson Report, August 20, 1864, *OR*, 40, pt. 1, 791.

15. Meade to Burnside, July 30, 1864—9:30 a.m., *OR*, 40, pt. 1, 144; Humphreys to Burnside, July 30, 1864—9:45 a.m., *OR*, 40, pt.1 144.

16. Casualties for the Ninth Corps as noted in General Burnside's testimony before the Court of Inquiry on the Mine Explosion, *OR*, 40, pt. 1, 60.

17. Grant to Meade, August 1, 1864—9:30 a.m., *OR*, 40, pt. 1, 134.

18. Grant to Halleck, August 1, 1864, *OR*, 40, pt. 1, 17.

19. Grant, *Memoirs of U.S. Grant*, 2:315.

20. Confederate Letter about Bascom Home Guards, Bess to Miss Katie, Bascom, May 10, 1861, in Bell I. Wiley Papers, Box 1, Folder 26, Woodruff Library, Emory University, Atlanta, Georgia.

21. Inscoe and McKinney, *Heart of Confederate Appalachia*, 194.

22. See Fisher, who employs the phrase for his title, *War at Every Door*.

23. Fisher, *War at Every Door*, 41–42, 68–69, 82–83, and 144–45; Inscoe and McKinney, *Heart of Confederate Appalachia*, 129–31, and 194–95.

24. Quoted in Inscoe and McKinney, *Heart of Confederate Appalachia*, 131.

25. Long, *Civil War Day by Day*, 710–12.

26. McPherson, *Battle Cry of Freedom*, 854; Roland, *American Iliad*, 255.

Chapter 6: A War without Boundaries

1. See Fellman, *Inside War*; Goodrich, *Black Flag*; Castel and Goodrich, *Bloody Bill Anderson*; Stiles, *Jesse James*.

2. One of the performers in *The Tall Men* was Mae Marsh, Flora Cameron in D. W. Griffith's *The Birth of a Nation*.

3. Shirley, *Belle Starr and Her Times*, 60–62, 66–70, 74–76, 137–41, and 214. Other historical inaccuracies exist as well, with Sam Starr's associate Blue Duck (Chill Wills) actually connected to Belle and her screen aversion to the Cole brothers not nearly as true as her historical links to Cole Younger suggest.

4. Shirley, *Belle Starr and Her Times*, 22.

5. "Jayhawkers" was a term applied to "bands of reckless young adventurers and abolitionists [in Kansas] who combined a hatred of slavery with a love of plunder." Castel, *William Clarke Quantrill*, 17.

6. The term "Red Legs," often seen synonymously with "Jayhawkers," applies to troops in the Kansas–Missouri region who favored red leggings as an adornment for their uniforms. See Castel, *William Clarke Quantrill*, 146 and 221, for examples. See also Albert Castel, "Kansas," in Faust, ed., *Historical Times Illustrated Encyclopedia of the Civil War*, 407.

7. See Castel, *William Clarke Quantrill*; Leslie, *Devil Knows How to Ride*.

8. See Goodrich, *Black Flag* and *Bloody Dawn*.

9. Carney to Stanton, August 22, 1863, *The War of the Rebellion: A Compilation of the Official Records of the Union and Confederate Armies*, 22, pt. 2, 467. Hereafter cited as *OR*.

10. Carney to Stanton, August 24, 1863, *OR*, 22, pt. 2, 470.

11. Carney to Schofield, August 24, 1863, *OR*, 22, pt. 2, 489.

12. Schofield to Ewing, August 24, 1863, *OR*, 22, pt. 2, 469.

13. Schofield to Ewing, August 25, 1863, *OR*, 22, pt. 2, 471–72.

14. Ewing to Schofield, August 25, 1863, *OR*, 22, pt. 2, 472–73.

15. Ewing to Schofield, August 27, 1863, *OR*, 22, pt. 2, 479–80.

16. Ewing to Schofield, August 27, 1863, *OR*, 22, pt. 2, 479.

17. Quantrill Report, October 13, 1863, *OR*, 22, pt. 1, 700–701. See also Lindberg and Matthews, "It Haunts," 42–53.

18. Castel, *William Clarke Quantrill*, 201–13.

Chapter 7: The West's Civil War

1. Former Confederate General Jubal Anderson Early helped to emphasize the importance of Virginia and the Eastern Theater in the Civil War.

2. Quoted in Hart, *Strategy*, 154.

3. Historian Thomas L. Connelly led the way in challenging the supremacy of Virginia and the Eastern Theater and establishing the West as primary. Connelly, *Army of the Heartland* and *Autumn of Glory*. More recently, this view has found support from historian Richard McMurry, in *Two Great Rebel Armies*.

4. Josephy, *Civil War in the American West*, xii.

5. Hyams, *Life and Times of the Western Movie*, 58–59.

6. For a complete treatment of this subject, see Brown, *Galvanized Yankees*. Brown observes that there were "Galvanized Confederates," as well (211–16).

7. Schickel, *Clint Eastwood*, 170.

8. Chadwick, *Reel Civil War*, 237–38.

9. Chadwick, *Reel Civil War*, 238.

10. Josephy, *Civil War in the American West*, 8.

11. Josephy, *Civil War in the American West*, 161.

12. Finch, *Confederate Pathway to the Pacific*, 26.

13. Josephy, *Civil War in the American West*, 269.

14. Warner, *Generals in Blue*, 69.

15. Josephy, *Civil War in the American West*, 269.

16. Josephy, *Civil War in the American West*, 272.

17. Josephy, *Civil War in the American West*, 276–77.

18. Josephy, *Civil War in the American West*, 281.

19. Josephy, *Civil War in the American West*, 290–91. Kit Carson received a promotion to brevet brigadier general in 1865 and died three years later in Colorado, on May 23, 1868. See *Encyclopedia of the American Civil War*, 1:367. Carleton's superiors relieved him of command in New Mexico in September 1866, but he remained in the army until his death on January 7, 1873. See Warner, *Generals in Blue*, 69.

20. Warner, *Generals in Blue*, 1–2.

21. Josephy, *Civil War in the American West*, 153.

22. Josephy, *Civil War in the American West*, 314.
23. Slotkin, *Gunfighter Nation*, 561–66.

Chapter 8: Shiloh's Bloody Harvest

1. For excellent studies of this battle, see Sword, *Bloody April*; Daniel, *Shiloh*; and McDonough, *Shiloh—In Hell before Night*. Casualty figures are from Long, *Civil War Day by Day*, 195–96.
2. Simpson, *Grant*, 134.
3. Sword, *Shiloh*, 434. In *How the West was Won* it is Sherman who shows the greatest determination, decisively insisting that Grant remain in command: "What is there to think about? Army's better off with you than without you. That's the test."
4. Ballard, *U.S. Grant*, 59; Simpson, *Grant*, 137; Daniel, *Shiloh*, 308.
5. Sword, *Bloody April*, 127.
6. Sword, *Bloody April*, 176.
7. Wiley, *Life of Billy Yank*, 297–98. Historian Timothy Smith disputes the Johnny Shiloh story and debunks a series of other myths associated with the battle of Shiloh in, "Oft-Repeated Campfire Stories: The Ten Greatest Myths of Shiloh," chapter 2 in *Untold Story of Shiloh*, 21–37.
8. Sword, *Bloody April*, 163.
9. Sword, *Bloody April*, 222.
10. Sword, *Bloody April*, 253, 306–7; Daniel, *Shiloh*, 207–14; McDonough, *Shiloh—In Hell before Night*, 133–36, 152–56, 162–67.
11. Sword, *Bloody April*, 270–72, 443–45; Roland, *Albert Sidney Johnston*, 336–39.
12. Roland, *Albert Sidney Johnston*, 260, 299, 347.
13. Long, *Civil War Day by Day*, 195–96.
14. Wills, *Battle from the Start*, 71.
15. Sword, *Shiloh*, 421, 441.

Chapter 9: Confederates Raid Vermont

1. Hoy, *Canadians in the Civil War*, 314.
2. A plaque on the wall attests to the posthumous award for valor at Gettysburg.
3. Kinchen, *Confederate Operations in Canada*, 127–28.
4. Stern, *Secret Missions of the Civil War*, 243.
5. Wilson, "Hit-and-Run Raid," 29.
6. Wilson, "Hit-and-Run Raid," 30–31.
7. Stern, *Secret Missions of the Civil War*, 243.
8. Hoy, *Canadians in the Civil War*, 318.
9. Stern, *Secret Missions of the Civil War*, 244.
10. Sharp, "The Spirit of Christian Warfare?," 37. Sharp also provides the ingredients for the substance, in the same work, 33.
11. Wilson, "Hit-and-Run Raid," 31.
12. Stern, *Secret Missions of the Civil War*, 243. The stricken citizen was a construction manager named Elinus J. Morrison, who died the next day of the wound he had received, making him the only civilian fatality of the operation. Wilson, "Hit-and-Run Raid," 90.

13. Wilson, "Hit-and-Run Raid," 90.

14. John A. Dix to Edwin M. Stanton, *The War of the Rebellion: A Compilation of the Official Records of the Union and Confederate Armies*, 43, pt. 2, 420. Hereafter cited as *OR*.

15. J. Gregory Smith to Stanton, October 19, 1864, *OR*, 43, pt. 2, 421.

16. Dix to Smith, October 19—9:30 p.m., 1864, *OR*, 43, pt. 2, 422.

17. R. Proctor to Dix, October 19, 1864, *OR*, 43, pt. 2, 422.

18. Dix to F. N. Clarke, October 19, 1864, *OR*, 43, pt. 2, 423.

19. Stern, *Secret Missions of the Civil War*, 244.

20. Smith to Eckert, October 19, 1864, *OR*, 423.

21. Dix to Provost Marshal [Rollo Gleason], October 20, 1864, *OR*, 43, pt. 2, 436.

22. Rollo Gleason to Dix, October 20, 1864, in Dix to Stanton, October 20, 1864, *OR*, 43, pt. 2, 435.

23. Stern, *Secret Missions of the Civil War*, 244.

24. Stern, *Secret Missions of the Civil War*, 245.

25. Stern, *Secret Missions of the Civil War*, 245–46.

26. Dix to Seward, October 20, 1864, *OR*, 435.

27. D. Thurston to Seward, October 20, 1864, *OR*, 43, pt. 2, 435.

28. Smith to Dix, October 20, 1864, *OR*, 43, pt. 2, 435–36. Historian E. B. Long suggests that the banks were able to recover approximately $75,000 of the money. Long, *Civil War Day by Day*, 586.

29. Wilson, "Hit-and-Run Raid," 90.

30. Crook, *North, the South, and the Powers*, 351–52.

31. May cites Robin Winks in his introduction to *Union, the Confederacy, and the Atlantic Rim*, 9, 25.

32. Winks, *Canada and the United States*, 306.

33. Gorgas, *Journals of Josiah Gorgas*, 144.

34. One account noted that Young "squired" a female resident around town in order to gain military intelligence for his operation. Papanek, ed., *Spies, Scouts and Raiders*, 60.

35. Wilson, "Hit and Run Raid," 91.

Chapter 10: The Music Teacher Raids Mississippi

1. Place, *Western Films of John Ford*, 162.

2. For more on the actual Virginia Military Institute cadets and the battle of New Market, Virginia, see Davis, *Battle of New Market*.

3. For more on Forrest and Streight, see Wills, *Battle from the Start*, 109–19.

4. William Marvel has the first Union prisoners arrive on February 24, and Ovid Futch places them at the facility on the 25th. Marvel, *Andersonville: The Last Depot*, 27; Futch, *Andersonville*, 10.

5. Colonel Streight did not remain indefinitely in Confederate custody in Richmond. He was one of over a hundred Union officers who successfully tunneled out of the prison in February 1864. Fifty-nine of these reached Union lines, while the Confederates recaptured forty-eight and two of the escapees drowned. This and John Hunt Morgan's escape from the Ohio Penitentiary in November 1863 are the stuff Hollywood ought to immortalize on celluloid. Long, *Civil War Day by Day*, 462.

6. There were some Union officers at Andersonville, such as Major Archibald Bogle of the First North Carolina Colored Infantry, but as a standard practice, the prison was meant for enlisted personnel. Marvel, *Andersonville: The Last Depot*, 41–42.

7. Place, *Western Films of John Ford*, 175. Chapter 12, 174–85, in this work deals with *The Horse Soldiers*.

8. Stephen A. Hurlbut to John A. Rawlins, April 29, 1863, *The War of the Rebellion: A Compilation of the Official Records of the Union and Confederate Armies*, Series I, 24, pt. 1, 520. Hereafter cited as *OR*.

9. Grierson Report, May 5, 1863, *OR*, 24, pt. 1, 523.

10. Leckie and Leckie, *Unlikely Warriors*, 89. The raid itself is discussed in chapter 4, 83–99. See also D. Alexander Brown, *Grierson's Raid*.

11. Wert Adams Report, May 5, 1863, *OR*, 24, pt. 1, 533.

12. Grierson Report, May 5, 1863, *OR*, 24, pt. 1, 524.

13. Grierson Report, May 5, 1863, *OR*, 24, pt. 1, 529.

14. John C. Pemberton to Samuel Cooper, April 29, 1863, *OR*, 24, pt. 3, 801.

15. Grierson Report, May 5, 1863, *OR*, 24, pt. 1, 527.

16. Grierson Report, May 5, 1863, *OR*, 24, pt. 1, 528–29.

17. B. F. Bryan Report, May 10, 1863, *OR*, 24, pt. 1, 537–38.

18. R. V. Richardson Report, May 5, 1863, *OR*, 24, pt. 1, 550.

19. Leckie and Leckie, *Unlikely Warriors*, 99; Ballard, *Vicksburg*, 208. William Shea and Terrence Winschel set the raid at 475 miles. Shea and Winschel, *Vicksburg Is the Key*, 93.

20. Quoted in Bearss, *Campaign for Vicksburg*, II, 235.

21. Bearss, *Campaign for Vicksburg*, 235–36; Shea and Winschel, *Vicksburg Is the Key*, 93; Winschel, *Triumph and Defeat*, 56.

22. Grierson Report, May 5, 1863, *OR*, pt. 1, 528–29. In *Grierson's Raid*, D. Alexander Brown accepts Grierson's numbers, 269, as do Leckie and Leckie, in *Unlikely Warriors*, 99. Shea and Winschel put Grierson's casualties slightly higher, at four killed, sixteen wounded, and seventeen missing in *Vicksburg Is the Key*, 93.

23. R. V. Richardson Report, May 5, 1863, *OR*, 24, pt. 1, 550.

24. Hurlbut, May 5, 1863, *OR*, 24, pt. 1, 521.

25. Quoted in Leckie and Leckie, *Unlikely Warriors*, 99.

26. Warner, *Generals in Blue*, 190.

Chapter 11: A Stomach for War

1. See, Boykin, *Beefsteak Raid*.

2. Robert E. Lee to Wade Hampton, September 3, 1864, *The War of the Rebellion: A Compilation of the Official Records of the Union and Confederate Armies*, 42, pt. 2, 1233. Hereafter cited as *OR*.

3. George Shadburne to Hampton, September 5, 1864, *OR*, 42, pt. 2, 1236.

4. Longacre, *Gentleman and Soldier*, 211. For other studies of the general, see Wellman, *Giant in Gray*, and Cisco, *Wade Hampton*.

5. Lee to Hampton, September 9, 1864, *OR*, 42, pt. 2, 1242.

6. Hampton Report, September 27, 1864, *OR*, 42, pt. 1, 946.

7. See numerous communications from 6 a.m. to 10:30 p.m., September 16, 1864, *OR*, 42, pt. 2, 868–78.

8. Hampton Report, September 27, 1864, *OR*, 42, pt. 1, 946.
9. August V. Kautz Report, September 19, 1864, *OR*, 42, pt. 1, 823; H.E. Davies to A.A. Humphreys, September 17, 1864—11 a.m., *OR*, 42, pt. 2, 891.
10. Lee to John Seddon, September 17, 1864, *OR*, 42, pt. 1, 852.
11. D. D. Wiley to M. R. Morgan, September 18, 1864, *OR*, 42, pt. 1, 898.
12. Longacre, *Gentleman and Soldier*, 213.
13. George Meade to U. S. Grant, September 17—2 p.m., *OR*, 42, pt. 1, 880.
14. Grant, *Memoirs of U. S. Grant*, 2:424.
15. Quoted in Brooksher and Snider, "Piece of Rebel Rascality," 18.
16. Warner, *Generals in Gray*, 265; see also Welsh, *Medical Histories of Confederate Generals*, 189–90.
17. Brooksher and Snider, "Piece of Rebel Rascality," 17.
18. Jones, John Beauchamp, *Rebel War Clerk's Diary*, 421.
19. Longacre, *Gentleman and Soldier*, 213.

Chapter 12: Enough Glory for All

1. For a concise examination of this important historical document, see Franklin, *Emancipation Proclamation*.
2. Campbell, *Celluloid South*, 166.
3. Kirby, *Media-Made Dixie*, 115.
4. Kirby, *Media-Made Dixie*, 115.
5. Davis, *Cause Lost*, 197.
6. Toplin, *Reel History*, 59.
7. McPherson, *Past Imperfect*, 128.
8. McPherson, *Past Imperfect*, 130.
9. Redkey, "Brave Black Volunteers," in Blatt et al., eds., *Hope and Glory*, 26.
10. Blatt, "*Glory*: Hollywood History," in Blatt et al., eds., *Hope & Glory*, 222.
11. Gooding, "Camp Meigs, Readville, May 9," in *On the Altar of Freedom*, 18.
12. See McFeely's foreword, Shaw, *Blue-Eyed Child of Fortune*, xiii.
13. Shaw to Father, September 21, 1862, in Shaw, *Blue-Eyed Child of Fortune*, 241. Shaw notes that his commander, Wilder Dwight, was killed.
14. Shaw to Mother, March 25, 1863, in Shaw, *Blue-Eyed Child of Fortune*, 313.
15. Shaw, *Blue-Eyed Child of Fortune*, 32.
16. Gooding, "Camp Meigs, Readville, April 3," in *On the Altar to Freedom*, 9.
17. Gooding, "Camp Meigs, Readville, April 25," in *On the Altar to Freedom*, 15.
18. Shaw, *Blue-Eyed Child of Fortune*, 33.
19. Shaw, *Blue-Eyed Child of Fortune*, 32.
20. Shaw to Father, July 1863, Shaw, *Blue-Eyed Child of Fortune*, 366. Duncan says that the proposal to use pikes "came to nothing." Shaw, *Blue-Eyed Child of Fortune*, 367.
21. Shaw, *Blue-Eyed Child of Fortune*.
22. Gooding, "Camp Meigs, Readville, May 4," in *On the Altar of Freedom*, 16.
23. Shaw, *Blue-Eyed Child of Fortune*, 366.
24. Shaw, *Blue-Eyed Child of Fortune*, 38–39.
25. Cullen points out this age discrepancy for Douglass in his examination of *Glory* in *The Civil War in Popular Culture*, 161.

26. Duncan attributes "over one hundred men" to Douglass's efforts. Shaw, *Blue-Eyed Child of Fortune*, 28.

27. Gooding, "Camp Meigs, Readville, May 24, 1863," in *On the Altar of Freedom*, 24.

28. Shaw to Annie, June 26, 1863, Shaw, *Blue-Eyed Child of Fortune*, 361.

29. Shaw to Annie, July 15, 1863, Shaw, *Blue-Eyed Child of Fortune*, 385.

30. Shaw, *Blue-Eyed Child of Fortune*. Shaw describes his losses in the fighting on James Island as "seven killed, twenty-one wounded, six missing, supposed killed, and nine unaccounted for. These last are probably killed or captured."

31. Edward Hallowell Report, November 7, 1863, *The War of the Rebellion: A Compilation of the Official Records of the Union and Confederate Armies*, 28, pt. 1, 362. Hereafter cited as *OR*.

32. McFeely, "Notes on Seeing History," 667.

33. Return of Casualties in the Union Forces, *OR*, 28, pt. 1, 210.

34. Beauregard to Cooper, July 21, 1863—9 p.m. *OR*, 28, pt. 2, 214.

35. Quincy Gillmore Report, *OR*, 28, pt. 1, 16; Truman Seymour Report, November 1, 1863, *OR*, 28, pt. 1, 348.

36. Cullen, *Civil War in Popular Culture*, 164. The author notes that despite his heroism Carney did not receive the Medal of Honor until thirty-seven years later.

37. Historians have pointed out the inconsistencies of positions taken by soldiers on both sides. In this instance, racism was certainly not omnipresent in soldiers who wore blue, but many expressed at a minimum concerns about blacks becoming soldiers alongside them and at maximum a stark refusal to accept that possibility as legitimate or acceptable. See, for example, Glathaar, *Forged in Battle*, 81, and Robertson, *Soldiers Blue and Gray*, 32.

38. Cullen, *Civil War in Popular Culture*, 163.

39. If anything, the mob threatened the shipyards and vessels rather than the other way around, but director Scorsese obviously wanted explosions to highlight the battle between Vallon and the Butcher. Spann, *Gotham at War*, 99.

40. Stout, *Upon the Altar of the Nation*, 246.

41. Spann, *Gotham at War*, 93.

42. Spann, *Gotham at War*, 94.

43. McPherson, *Battle Cry of Freedom*, 609.

44. McPherson, *Battle Cry of Freedom*, 608.

45. Spann, *Gotham at War*, 95–101. See also numerous reports, *OR*, 27, pt. 2, 875–940.

46. Spann, *Gotham at War*, 101.

Chapter 13: The Angels of Gettysburg

1. See Shaara, *Killer Angels*.

2. Gallagher, *Lee and His Generals*, 219.

3. Freeman, *Lee's Lieutenants*, 3:139.

4. *The War of the Rebellion: A Compilation of the Official Records of the Union and Confederate Armies*, 27, pt. 2, 321.

5. Thomas, *Bold Dragoon*, 255.

6. Reardon, *Pickett's Charge in History and Memory*, 211. She notes that Berenger had Trimble in the first line and Pettigrew in the second when it should have been in the reverse. For an examination of Pettigrew's brigade, see Hess *Lee's Tar Heels*.

7. Ladd and Ladd, *Bachelder Papers*, 1192.

8. Quoted in Sword, *Southern Invincibility*, 181.

9. *Gods and Generals* is also populated with a daunting number of roles, including those filled by prominent political figures such as U.S. senators George Allen, Robert Byrd, and Phil Gramm. In one sense, this inclusion of nonactors carries on in the tradition that Ron Maxwell began with the inclusion of Ken Burns and Ted Turner in *Gettysburg*, but the presence of such individuals does little to advance the story. Of course, sometimes the device works. Alfred Hitchcock, for instance, loved to slip himself into his films to see if anyone would notice.

10. Biographer Emory Thomas records Lee as writing on January 11, 1865: "I think we must decide for ourselves whether slavery shall be extinguished by our enemies, and the slaves used against us, or use them ourselves at the risk of the effects which may be produced upon our social institutions. My own opinion is that we should employ them without delay." Thomas, *Robert E. Lee*, 347. It is not known how "Stonewall" felt about arming slaves and adding them to the Confederate armies. Of the "peculiar institution" itself, Bud Robertson notes, "Jackson neither apologized for nor spoke in favor of the practice of slavery." Robertson, *Stonewall Jackson*, 191.

11. Jackson and Gregg almost had a running feud with each other over Stonewall's treatment of the South Carolinians' regimental commanders and his troops. The stern Jackson frequently chided Gregg's command for its lax discipline, including behavior that ranged from taking fence rails and apples without authorization to moving too slowly to suit the commanding general. Yet Stonewall was extremely solicitous of Gregg when the latter fell mortally wounded at Fredericksburg. Robertson, *Stonewall Jackson*, 545, 585, 594, 639, 658, and 663. Bud Robertson's biography is the most thorough study of the general's life and career. Others include Farwell, *Stonewall*, and Vandiver, *Mighty Stonewall*.

12. Quoted in Robertson, *Stonewall Jackson*, 633.

13. Robertson, *Stonewall Jackson*, 234.

14. Stout, *Upon the Altar of the Nation*, 73.

15. Sears, *Chancellorsville*, 231.

16. The time of the attack varies according to different sources. Sears puts the advance at 5:30 p.m. Sears, *Chancellorsville*, 272. Ferguson sets it at 5:15 and points out that the range covered the period of 4:00 to 6:00. Ferguson, *Chancellorsville 1863*, 171.

17. Ferguson, *Chancellorsville 1863*, 178.

18. According to Krick, the sun had set at 6:49, but a full moon illuminated the night. Krick, *Smoothbore Volley That Doomed the Confederacy*, 7. He also notes the presence of Union riders in close proximity to the Southern lines, which created a sense of confusion and anxiety among the North Carolinians who held the section of the lines as Hill's and Jackson's parties approached them (16–17).

19. Krick, *Smoothbore Volley That Doomed the Confederacy*, 1. Krick notes, "Despite the conventional wisdom about Jackson's wounding, no Confederate initially opened fire directly on the general's party by mistake" (18).

20. Krick, *Smoothbore Volley That Doomed the Confederacy*, 39.

21. Quoted in Robertson, *Stonewall Jackson*, 748, 750.

22. Quoted in Robertson, *Stonewall Jackson*, 752.
23. Toplin, *Reel History*, 55–57.
24. Robertson, *Stonewall Jackson*, 746–47. Freeman also suggests that Lee felt that "there was no one in whose hands he would feel safe in leaving the army," a justification that Robertson reasonably dismisses. Freeman, *R. E. Lee*, 2:561. Nearly a decade later, in examining the high command of the Army of Northern Virginia, Freeman is silent on the issue. Freeman, *Lee's Lieutenants*, Vol. 2.
25. Thomas, *Robert E. Lee*, 288.
26. Farwell, *Stonewall*, 529.

Chapter 14: The Plight of the Prisoners of War

1. Speer, *Portals to Hell*, xiv. The author notes that of the total of 150 prisoner-of-war facilities, only about ten on each side "attained major notoriety," and that these twenty camps and compounds accounted for the vast number of deaths among their populations (16).
2. Comparisons of these prisons can be a sensitive subject. Benton McAdams bristles at the label for Rock Island Prison in Illinois as the "Andersonville of the North." "The comparison is unjust," he explains; "the death rate at Andersonville exceeded 30 percent; mortality at Rock Island was 16 percent." He concludes, "Rock Island deserves censure perhaps; it does not deserve the legend." McAdams, *Rebels at Rock Island*, xi–xii.
3. Benjamin Franklin Cooling notes that the thousands of Confederate prisoners gathered at Dover Landing for transportation on steamers continued to experience "trauma" on their way north. Cooling, *Forts Henry and Donelson*, 217–19.
4. Long, *Civil War Day by Day*, 399.
5. Hesseltine, *Civil War Prisons*, 182.
6. Walker, "Rock Island," in Hesseltine, ed., *Civil War Prisons*, 48–49.
7. Walker, "Rock Island," in Hesseltine, ed., *Civil War Prisons*, 49.
8. Hesseltine, *Civil War Prisons*, 192.
9. Walker, "Rock Island," in Hesseltine, ed., *Civil War Prisons*, 50.
10. Walker, "Rock Island," in Hesseltine, ed., *Civil War Prisons*, 55.
11. Walker, "Rock Island," in Hesseltine, ed., *Civil War Prisons*, 58; McAdams, *Rebels at Rock Island*, 158–59.
12. McAdams, *Rebels at Rock Island*, 159.
13. Steedman Papers, Civil War Times Illustrated Collection, U.S. Military Institute, Carlisle, Pennsylvania. The same source indicates that prisoners who accepted the offer received better treatment than those who did not.
14. Walker, "Rock Island," in Hesseltine, ed., *Civil War Prisons*, 55.
15. Some of Stuart's men were at Mechanicsville, but they were raiding the Union supply base at White House when the other Peninsula campaign engagements mentioned occurred. Sears, *To the Gates of Richmond*, 195, 255–58. Sears notes, "Jeb Stuart and the cavalry experienced few of war's hardships on the Peninsula" (258).
16. Hyams, *Life and Times of the Western Movie*, 167.
17. Speer, *Portals to Hell*, 292–93.

18. Mays, *Saltville Massacre*, 59, 71. Wirz died on the same gallows as the Lincoln conspirators. Speer, *Portals to Hell*, 292.

19. Marvel, *Andersonville: The Last Depot*, 26–27.

20. Futch, *Andersonville*, 17.

21. Futch, *Andersonville*, 31.

22. Marvel, *Andersonville: The Last Depot*, ix.

23. McPherson, *Battle Cry of Freedom*, 796.

24. McPherson, *Battle Cry of Freedom*, 797.

25. Two of the accounts of prison life in Andersonville by John McElroy and John Ransom were produced and have been reprinted with wide distribution and introductions by well-known historians.

26. Salecker, *Disaster on the Mississippi*, 206, puts the total number of deaths at between 1,700 and 1,750. He notes that the government's official toll for the disaster was 1,238 (1,101 soldiers and 137 civilians and crew).

27. Wade, *Titanic*, 13, sets the deaths by drowning or hypothermia at 1,522 souls. Of the sinking of the two vessels, Gene Eric Salecker makes comparisons in number of passengers, victims, and percentages with the *Titanic*, before observing, "The paroled prisoners who had been shoe-horned onto the *Sultana*, along with her forgotten civilian passengers and crew, were not important enough to be remembered. No Astors or Strauses or Guggenheims were on the *Sultana*," 216.

Chapter 15: The War and the Waves

1. For a full treatment of this important naval confrontation, see Davis, *Duel between the First Ironclads*. The ironclad *Virginia*, as well as its historic engagement with the *Monitor* and its fate, is the subject of Quarstein, *C.S.S. Virginia*.

2. See Kloeppel, *Danger Beneath the Waves*, and Ragan, *Hunley* and *Submarine Warfare*.

3. Decatur's full quotation was: "Our country! In her intercourse with foreign nations may she always be right; but our country, right or wrong!"

4. See Flanders, "Night They Burned the Yard," and Long, "Gosport Affair, 1861."

5. Symonds, *Confederate Admiral*, 161.

6. Symonds, *Confederate Admiral*, 167–68.

7. James Keenan, Norfolk Barracks, March 11, 1862, in Bell I. Wiley Papers, Box 1, Woodruff Library, Emory University, Atlanta.

8. Richmond *Sentinel*, August 26, 1863.

9. Hasker told the tale of his experiences with the *Hunley* and his narrow escape, as well as his military service, many times following the war in a stereoopticon show. Hasker was the great-great grandfather of the author. Hasker, "Great Naval Battles," Personal Papers in the author's possession; "Battle of Hampton Roads," *Farmville Herald*, February 21, 1896; Charles H. Hasker Obituary, *Richmond Times-Dispatch*, July 9, 1898. See also Fort, "First Submarine in the Confederate Navy," 459; Kloeppel, *Danger Beneath the Waves*, 39; Ragan, *Hunley*, 52.

10. Author Clive Cussler and divers of the National Underwater and Marine Agency helped to make it possible to raise the *Hunley* by locating her in May 1995. Ragan, *Hunley*, 180, 184–85; Ragan, *Submarine Warfare*, vi.

11. Douglas Fairbank's *The Black Pirate* (1926); Errol Flynn's *Captain Blood* (1935), *The Sea Hawk* (1940), and *Against All Flags* (1952); Tyrone Power's *The Black Swan* (1942); Burt Lancaster's *The Crimson Pirate* (1952); and Yul Brynner's *The Buccaneer* (1958) are examples. Laurence Olivier and Gregory Peck play more conventional roles in *That Hamilton Woman* (1941) and *Captain Horatio Hornblower* (1951), respectively. See also Jeffrey Richards, *Swordsmen of the Screen*.

Epilogue: Screening the "Real War"

1. Aaron, *Unwritten War*, 66.

2. Carnes, "Hollywood History," 78

3. Quoted in Carnes, *Past Imperfect*, 22.

4. Quoted in Blatt et al., eds., *Hope and Glory*, 224.

5. Carnes, "Hollywood History," 83.

6. Vidal, *Screening History*, 81. Vidal recognizes the futility of determining the "truth" when it comes to history in whatever medium. "I often upset professional keepers of the national myths with the phrase 'the agreed-upon facts.' I would have thought that this was a reasonably careful way of saying that there are not many facts of any kind that we can ever be sure of. . . . Naturally, some agreed-upon facts are more agreed-upon than others. But these imprecise consensuses are all that we have" (87).

BIBLIOGRAPHY

Primary Sources

Confederate Letter about Bascom Home Guards, Bess to Miss Katie. Bascom, Georgia. May 10, 1861. Bell I. Wiley Papers. Box 1, Folder 26. Woodruff Library, Emory University, Atlanta.

Fort, W. B. "First Submarine in the Confederate Navy. *Confederate Navy* 26 (October 1918): 459–60.

Gooding, James Henry. *On the Altar of Freedom. Corporal James Henry Gooding: A Black Soldier's Letters from the Front.* Edited by Virginia Matzke Adams. Amherst: University of Massachusetts Press, 1991.

Gorgas, Josiah. *The Journals of Josiah Gorgas 1857–1878.* Edited by Sarah Woolfolk Wiggins. Tuscaloosa: University of Alabama Press, 1995.

Grant, Ulysses S. *Personal Memoirs of U.S. Grant.* New York: Webster, 1886.

Guerrant, Edward O. *Bluegrass Confederate: The Headquarters Diary of Edward O. Guerrant.* Edited by William C. Davis and Meredith L. Swentor. Baton Rouge: Louisiana State University Press, 1999.

Hasker, Charles H. Papers of Charles H. Hasker. In author's possession.

Heston, Charlton. *The Actor's Life: Journals 1956–1976.* Edited by Hollis Alpert. New York: Dutton, 1976.

———. *In the Arena: An Autobiography.* New York: Simon & Schuster, 1995.

Jones, John Beauchamp. *A Rebel War Clerk's Diary at the Confederate States Capital.* Edited by Earl Schenck Miers. New York: Barnes, 1961.

Keenan, James. Letter. Norfolk Barracks, March 11, 1862. Bell I. Wiley Papers. Box 1. Woodruff Library, Emory University, Atlanta.

Ladd, David L., and Audrey J. Ladd, eds. *The Bachelder Papers: Gettysburg in Their Own Words.* Dayton, OH: Morningside House, 1994.

Lincoln, Abraham. *The Fiery Trial: The Speeches and Writings of Abraham Lincoln.* Edited by William E. Gienapp. Oxford: Oxford University Press, 2002.

McElroy, John. *Andersonville: A Story of Rebel Prisons.* Toledo, OH: Locke, 1879.

Ransom, John L. *Andersonville.* Philadelphia: Douglas Brothers, 1883.

Richmond *Sentinel.*

Richmond *Times–Dispatch.*

Scott, Robert N. *War of the Rebellion: A Compilation of the Official Records of the Union and Confederate Armies.* U.S. Government Printing Office.

Shaw, Robert Gould. *Blue-Eyed Child of Fortune: The Civil War Letters of Colonel Robert Gould Shaw.* Edited by Russell Duncan. Athens: University of Georgia Press, 1992.

Stanton, C. L. "Submarines and Torpedo Boats." *Confederate Veteran* 22 (September 1914): 398–99.

Steedman, Isaiah W. Papers. Civil War Times Illustrated Collection. U.S. Military History Institute, Carlisle, Pennsylvania.

Watkins, Sam. "Co. Aytch," Maury Grays. First Tennessee Grays, or a Side Show of the Big Show. Nashville: Presbyterian Printing House, 1882. Reprint, New York: MacMillan, 1962.

Wilson, Woodrow. The Papers of Woodrow Wilson. Edited by Arthur S. Link. Princeton, NJ: Princeton University Press, 1966–1994.

Other Works

Crane, Stephen. The Red Badge of Courage. New York: Appleton and Co., 1895.

Mitchell, Margaret. Gone with the Wind. New York: Macmillan, 1936.

Shaara, Michael. The Killer Angels: A Novel. New York: McKay, 1974.

Secondary Sources

Books

Aaron, Daniel. The Unwritten War: American Writers and the Civil War. New York: Knopf, 1973.

Angle, Craig. The Great Locomotive Chase. Rouzerville, PA.: Published by the author, 1992.

Ashdown, Paul, and Edward Caudill. The Mosby Myth: A Confederate Hero in Life and Legend. Wilmington, DE: Scholarly Resources, 2002.

———. The Myth of Nathan Bedford Forrest. Lanham, MD: Rowman & Littlefield, 2005.

Ballard, Michael B. U.S. Grant: The Making of a General, 1861–1863. Lanham, MD: Rowman & Littlefield, 2005.

———. Vicksburg: The Campaign That Opened the Mississippi. Chapel Hill: University of North Carolina Press, 2004.

Barton, Michael. Goodmen: The Character of Civil War Soldiers. University Park: Pennsylvania State University Press, 1981.

Bearss, Edwin Cole. The Campaign for Vicksburg. 3 vols. Dayton, OH: Morningside, 1985–1986.

Bernstein, Iver. The New York City Draft Riots: Their Significance for American Society and Politics in the Age of the Civil War. New York: Oxford University Press, 1990.

Black, Robert C., III. Railroads of the Confederacy. Chapel Hill: University of North Carolina Press, 1952.

Blair, William. Virginia's Private War: Feeding Body and Soul in the Confederacy, 1861–1865. New York: Oxford University Press, 1998.

Blatt, Martin H., Thomas J. Brown, and Donald Yacovone, eds. Hope and Glory: Essays on the Legacy of the Fifty-Fourth Massachusetts Regiment. Amherst: University of Massachusetts Press, 2001.

Blight, David W. Race and Reunion: The Civil War in American Memory. Cambridge: Harvard University Press, 2001.

Bluchard, Peter. One Gallant Rush: Robert Gould Shaw and His Brave Black Regiment. New York: St. Martin's, 1965.

Bowers, Claude G. The Tragic Era: The Revolution after Lincoln. Cambridge, MA: Houghton-Mifflin, 1929.

Boykin, Edward C. *Beefsteak Raid.* New York: Funk and Wagnalls, 1960.

Brown, D. Alexander. *Grierson's Raid: A Cavalry Adventure of the Civil War.* Urbana: University of Illinois Press, 1954.

Brown, Dee. *The Galvanized Yankees.* Urbana: University of Illinois Press, 1963.

Burchard, Peter. *"We'll Stand by the Union:" Robert Gould Shaw and the Black 54th Massachusetts Regiment.* New York: Facts on File, 1993.

Burgoyne, Robert. *Film Nation: Hollywood Looks at U.S. History.* Minneapolis: University of Minnesota Press, 1997.

Bynum, Victoria E. *The Free State of Jones: Mississippi's Longest Civil War.* Chapel Hill: University of North Carolina Press, 2001.

Campbell, Edward D. C., Jr. *The Celluloid South: Hollywood and the Southern Myth.* Knoxville: University of Tennessee Press, 1981.

Cassidy, John M. *Civil War Cinema: A Pictorial History of Hollywood and the War between the States.* Missoula, Mont.: Pictorial Histories, 1986.

Castel, Albert. *Decision in the West: The Atlanta Campaign of 1864.* Lawrence: University Press of Kansas, 1992.

———. *William Clarke Quantrill: His Life and Times.* New York: Fell and Co., 1962.

Castel, Albert, and Thomas Goodrich. *Bloody Bill Anderson: The Short Savage Life of a Civil War Guerrilla.* Mechanicsburg, PA: Stackpole, 1998.

Cavanaugh, Michael Arthur, and William Marvel. *Petersburg Campaign: The Battle of the Crater: "The Horrid Pit," June 25–August 6, 1864.* Lynchburg, VA: Howard, 1989.

Chadwick, Bruce. *The Reel Civil War: Mythmaking in American Film.* New York: Knopf, 2001.

Cisco, Walter Brian. *Wade Hampton: Confederate Warrior, Conservative Statesman.* Washington, DC: Brassey's, 2004.

Clark, John E., Jr. *Railroads in the Civil War: The Impact of Management on Victory and Defeat.* Baton Rouge: Louisiana State University Press, 2001.

Clinton, Catherine. *Tara Revisited: Women, the War and the Plantation Legend.* New York: Abbeville, 1995.

Colton, Ray C. *The Civil War in the Western Territories, Arizona, Colorado, New Mexico and Utah.* Norman: University of Oklahoma Press, 1959.

Connelly, Thomas Lawrence. *Army of the Heartland: The Army of Tennessee, 1861–1862.* Louisiana State University Press, 2001 (rpt.).

Connelly, Thomas Lawrence. *Autumn of Glory: The Army of Tennessee, 1862–1865.* Louisiana State University Press, 2001 (rpt.).

Cook, Adrian. *The Armies of the Streets: The New York City Draft Riots of 1863.* Lexington: University of Kentucky Press, 1974.

Cooling, Benjamin Franklin. *Forts Henry and Donelson: The Key to the Confederate Heartland.* Knoxville: University of Tennessee Press, 1987.

Crook, D. P. *The North, the South, and the Powers, 1861–1865.* New York: Wiley & Sons, 1974.

Cullen, Jim. *The Civil War in Popular Culture: A Reusable Past.* Washington: Smithsonian Institution Press, 1995.

Daniel, Larry J. *Shiloh: The Battle That Changed the Civil War.* New York: Simon & Schuster, 1997.

Davis, Ronald L. *John Ford: Hollywood's Old Master.* Norman: University of Oklahoma Press, 1995.

Davis, William C. *Battle at Bull Run: A History of the First Major Campaign of the Civil War*. Garden City, NY: Doubleday, 1977.

———. *The Battle of New Market*. Garden City, NY: Doubleday, 1975.

———. *The Cause Lost: Myths and Realities of the Confederacy*. Lawrence: University Press of Kansas, 1996.

———. *Duel between the First Ironclads*. Garden City, NY: Doubleday, 1975.

Dean, Eric T., Jr. *Shook Over Hell: Post-Traumatic Stress, Vietnam, and the Civil War*. Cambridge, MA: Harvard University Press, 1997.

Donald, David Herbert. *Lincoln*. New York: Simon & Schuster, 1995.

Dunnavant, Robert, Jr. *The Railroad War: N. B. Forrest's 1864 Raid Through Northern Alabama and Middle Tennessee*. Athens, AL: Pea Ridge, 1994.

Eyman, Scott. *Print the Legend: The Life and Times of John Ford*. New York: Simon & Schuster, 1999.

Farwell, Byron. *Stonewall: A Biography of General Thomas J. Jackson*. New York: Norton, 1992.

Faust, Patricia L., ed. *Historical Times Illustrated Encyclopedia of the Civil War*. New York: HarperCollins, 1986.

Fellman, Michael. *Inside War: The Guerrilla Conflict in Missouri during the American Civil War*. New York: Oxford University Press, 1989.

Ferguson, Ernest B. *Chancellorsville 1863: The Souls of the Brave*. New York: Knopf, 1992.

Finch, L. Boyd. *Confederate Pathway to the Pacific: Major Sherod Hunter and Arizona Territory, CSA*. Tucson: Arizona Historical Society, 1996.

Fishel, Edwin C. *The Secret War for the Union: The Untold Story of Military Intelligence in the Civil War*. Boston: Houghton-Mifflin Company, 1996.

Fisher, Noel C. *War at Every Door: Partisan Politics and Guerrilla Violence in East Tennessee, 1860–1869*. Chapel Hill: University of North Carolina Press, 1997.

Foner, Eric. *Reconstruction: America's Unfinished Revolution, 1863–1877*. New York: Harper & Row, 1988.

Foster, Gaines. *Ghosts of the Confederacy: Defeat, the Lost Cause and the Emergence of the New South, 1865–1913*. New York: Oxford University, 1987.

Franklin, John Hope. *The Emancipation Proclamation*. Garden City, NY: Doubleday, 1963.

Freehling, William W. *The South vs The South: How Anti-Confederate Southerners Shaped the Course of the Civil War*. New York: Oxford University Press, 2001.

Freeman, Douglas Southall. *Lee's Lieutenants: A Study in Command*. New York: Scribner's Sons, 1942–1944.

———. *R. E. Lee: A Biography*. New York: Scribner's Sons, 1934–1935.

French, W. *The South and Film*. University Press of Mississippi, 1981.

Frye, Dennis E. *Gods and Generals: Photographic Companion*. Gettysburg, PA: Thomas, 2003.

Futch, Ovid L. *History of Andersonville Prison*. Jacksonville: University of Florida Press, 1968.

Gallagher, Gary W. *Lee and His Generals in War and Memory*. Baton Rouge: Louisiana State University Press, 1998.

Glathaar, Joseph T. *Forged in Battle: The Civil War Alliance of Black Soldiers and White Officers*. New York: Free Press, 1990.

Goodrich, Thomas. *Black Flag: Guerrilla Warfare on the Western Border, 1861–1865*. Bloomington: University of Indiana Press, 1995.

———. *Bloody Dawn: The Story of the Lawrence Massacre.* Kent, OH: Kent State University Press, 1991.

Graham, Allison. *Framing the South: Hollywood, Television, and Race during the Civil Rights Struggle.* Baltimore: Johns Hopkins University Press, 2001.

Grimsley, Mark. *The Hard Hand of War: Union Military Policy toward Southern Civilians 1861–1865.* New York: Cambridge University Press, 1995.

Groce, W. Todd. *Mountain Rebels: East Tennessee Confederates and the Civil War, 1860–1870.* Knoxville: University of Tennessee Press, 1999.

Hammen, Scott. *John Huston.* Boston: Twayne, 1985.

Hart, B. H. Liddell. *Strategy.* New York: Praeger, 1967.

Heider, David Stephen, and Jeanne T. Heidler (eds.). *Encyclopedia of the American Civil War: A Political, Social, and Military History.* Norton, 2002 (reissue).

Henderson, Robert M. *D. W. Griffith: His Life and Work.* New York: Oxford University Press, 1972.

———. *D. W. Griffith: The Years at Biograph.* New York: Farrar, Strauss, and Giroux, 1970.

Hess, Earl J. *Lee's Tar Heels: The Pettigrew–Kirkland–MacRae Brigade.* Chapel Hill: University of North Carolina Press, 2002.

Hesseltine, William Best. *Civil War Prisons: A Study in War Psychology.* Columbus: Ohio State University Press, 1920.

Hoy, Claire. *Canadians in the Civil War.* Toronto: McArthur, 2004.

Hyams, Jay. *The Life and Times of the Western Movie.* Columbus, 1983.

Inscoe, John C., and Gordon B. McKinney. *The Heart of Confederate Appalachia: Western North Carolina in the Civil War.* Chapel Hill: University of North Carolina Press, 2000.

Jordan, David M. *Winfield Scott Hancock: A Soldier's Life.* Bloomington: Indiana University Press, 1988.

Jordan, Weymouth T., comp. *North Carolina Troops, 1861–1865: A Roster.* 14 vols. Raleigh: Division of Archives and History, 1966–97.

Josephy, Alvin M., Jr. *The Civil War in the American West.* New York: Knopf, 1992.

Kerby, Robert L. *Kirby Smith's Confederacy: The Trans-Mississippi South, 1863–1865.* New York: Columbia University Press, 1972.

Kinard, Jeff. *The Battle of the Crater.* Fort Worth, TX.: Ryan Place, 1995.

Kinchen, Oscar A. *Confederate Operations in Canada and the North: A Little-Known Phase of the American Civil War.* North Quincy, MA: Christopher, 1970.

Kinnard, Roy. *The Blue and the Gray on the Silver Screen: More Than 80 Years of Civil War Movies.* Secaucus, NJ: Birch Lane, 1996.

Kirby, Jack Temple. *Media-Made Dixie: The South in the American Imagination.* Baton Rouge: Louisiana State University Press, 1978.

Kloeppel, James E. *Danger Beneath the Waves: A History of the Confederate Submarine H. L. Hunley.* Orangeburg, SC: Sandlapper, 1992.

Krick, Robert K. *The Smoothbore Volley That Doomed the Confederacy: The Death of Stonewall Jackson and Other Chapters on the Army of Northern Virginia.* Baton Rouge: Louisiana State University Press, 2002.

Lang, Robert, ed. *The Birth of a Nation.* New Brunswick, NJ: Rutgers University Press, 1994.

Langman, Larry, and David Ebner. *Hollywood's Image of the South: A Century of Southern Films.* Westport, CT: Greenwood, 2001.

Leckie, William H. *The Buffalo Soldiers: A Narrative of the Negro Cavalry in the West.* Norman: University of Oklahoma Press, 1967.

Leckie, William H., and Shirley A. Leckie. *Unlikely Warriors: General Benjamin Grierson and His Family.* Norman: University of Oklahoma Press, 1984.

Leslie, Edward E. *The Devil Knows How to Ride: The True Story of William Clarke Quantrill and His Confederate Raiders.* New York: Random House, 1996.

Linderman, Gerald F. *Embattled Courage: The Experience of Combat in the American Civil War.* New York: Free Press, 1987.

Link, Arthur S. *Wilson: The New Freedom.* Princeton, NJ: Princeton University Press, 1956.

Long, E. B. *The Civil War Day by Day: An Almanac 1861–1865.* Garden City, NY: Doubleday, 1971.

Longacre, Edward G. *From Union Stars to Top Hat: A Biography of the Extraordinary General James Harrison Wilson.* Harrisburg, PA: Stackpole, 1972.

———. *Gentleman and Soldier: A Biography of Wade Hampton III.* Nashville, TN: Rutledge Hill, 2003.

McAdams, Benton. *Rebels at Rock Island: The Story of a Civil War Prison.* DeKalb: Northern Illinois University Press, 2000.

McBride, Joseph. *Searching for John Ford: A Life.* New York: St. Martin's, 2001.

McCague, James. *The Second Rebellion: The Story of the New York City Draft Riots.* New York: Dial, 1968.

McCarthy, Todd. *Howard Hawks: The Grey Fox of Hollywood.* New York: Grove, 1997.

McCrisken, Trevor B., and Andrew Pepper. *American History and Contemporary Hollywood Film.* New Brunswick, NJ: Rutgers University Press, 2005.

McDonough, James Lee. *Shiloh—In Hell before Night.* Knoxville: University of Tennessee Press, 1977.

McFeely, William S. *Frederick Douglass.* New York: Norton, 1991.

McKnight, Brian D. *Contested Borderland: The Civil War in Appalachian Kentucky and Virginia.* Lexington: University of Kentucky Press, 2006.

McLemore, Richard Aubrey, ed. *A History of Mississippi.* Jackson: University and College Press of Mississippi, 1973.

McMurry, Richard M. *Atlanta 1864: Last Chance for the Confederacy.* Lincoln: University of Nebraska Press, 2000.

———. *Two Great Rebel Armies.* Chapel Hill: University of North Carolina Press, 1989.

McPherson, James M. *Battle Cry of Freedom: The Civil War Era.* New York: Oxford University Press, 1988.

———. *For Cause and Comrades: Why Men Fought in the Civil War.* New York: Oxford University Press, 1997.

———. *What They Fought For: 1861–1865.* Baton Rouge: Louisiana State University Press, 1994.

McWhiney, Grady. *Braxton Bragg and Confederate Defeat,* Vol. 1: *Field Command.* New York: Columbia University Press, 1969.

Maltin, Leonard. *Movie & Video Guide, 2001 Edition.* New York: Penguin, 2000.

Marszalek, John F. *Sherman: A Soldier's Passion for Order.* New York: Free Press, 1993.

Marvel, William. *Andersonville: The Last Depot.* Chapel Hill: University of North Carolina Press, 1994.

May, Robert E. *The Union, the Confederacy, and the Atlantic Rim.* West Lafayette, IN: Purdue University Press, 1995.

Mays, Thomas D. *The Saltville Massacre*. Fort Worth, TX: Ryan Place, 1995.

Mitchell, Reid. *Civil War Soldiers: Their Expectations and Their Experiences*. New York: Viking, 1988.

Monaghan, Jay. *Civil War on the Western Border, 1854–1865*. Boston: Little Brown, 1955. Reprint, Lincoln: University of Nebraska Press, 1984.

Morris, Roy, Jr. *Sheridan: The Life and Wars of General Phil Sheridan*. New York: Crown, 1992.

Munn, Michael. *Charlton Heston: A Biography*. New York: St. Martin's, 1986.

Neely, Mark E., Jr. *The Fate of Liberty: Abraham Lincoln and Civil Liberties*. New York: Oxford University Press, 1991.

Noe, Kenneth W., and Shannon H. Wilson, eds. *The Civil War in Appalachia: Collected Essays*. Knoxville: University of Tennessee Press, 1997.

Paludan, Philip Shaw. *Victims: A True Story of the Civil War*. Knoxville: University of Tennessee Press, 1981.

Papanek, John L. (ed.). *Spies, Scouts and Raiders: Irregular Operations*. Alexandria, Va.: Time-Life Books, 1985.

Place, J. A. *The Western Films of John Ford*. Secaucus, NJ: Citadel Press, 1974.

Pressly, Thomas J. *Americans Interpret Their Civil War*. Princeton: Princeton University Press, 1954.

Pugh, David G. *Sons of Liberty: The Masculine Mind in Nineteenth Century America*. Westport, Conn.: Greenwood, 1983.

Quarstein, John V. *C.S.S. Virginia: Mistress of Hampton Roads*. Lynchburg, VA: Howard, 2000.

Rable, George C. *Fredericksburg! Fredericksburg!* Chapel Hill: University of North Carolina Press, 2002.

Ragan, Mark K. *The Hunley: Submarines, Sacrifice, and Success in the Civil War*. Charleston, SC: Narwhal, 1995.

——. *Union and Confederate Submarine Warfare in the Civil War*. Mason City, IA: Savas, 1999.

Ramage, James A. *Rebel Raider: The Life of General John Hunt Morgan*. Lexington: University Press of Kentucky, 1986.

Reardon, Carol. *Pickett's Charge in History and Memory*. Chapel Hill: University of North Carolina Press, 1997.

Richards, Jeffrey. *Swordsmen of the Screen: From Douglas Fairbanks to Michael York*. London: Routledge & Kegan Paul, 1977.

Robertson, James I., Jr. *General A. P. Hill: The Story of a Confederate Warrior*. New York: Random House, 1987.

——. *Soldiers Blue and Gray*. Columbia: University of South Carolina Press, 1988.

——. *Stonewall Jackson: The Man, the Soldier, the Legend*. New York: Macmillan, 1997.

Roland, Charles P. *Albert Sidney Johnston: Soldier of Three Republics*. Austin: University of Texas Press, 1964.

——. *An American Iliad: The Story of the Civil War*. Lexington: University Press of Kentucky, 1991.

——. *Reflections on Lee: A Historian's Assessment*. Mechanicsburg, PA: Stackpole, 1995.

Roquemore, Joseph. *History Goes to the Movies*. New York: Main Street, 1999.

Rovin, Jeff. *The Films of Charlton Heston*. Secaucus, NJ: Citadel, 1977.

Salecker, Gene Eric. *Disaster on the Mississippi: The Sultana Explosion, April 27, 1865*. Annapolis, MD: Naval Institute Press, 1996.

Schickel, Richard. *Clint Eastwood: A Biography*. New York: Knopf, 1996.

———. *D. W. Griffith: An American Life*. New York: Simon & Schuster, 1984.

Schultz, Duane. *Quantrill's War: The Life and Times of William Clarke Quantrill 1837–1865*. New York: St. Martin's, 1997.

Sears, Stephen W. *Chancellorsville*. Boston: Houghton-Mifflin Company, 1996.

———. *To the Gates of Richmond: The Peninsula Campaign*. New York: Ticknor & Fields, 1992.

Shea, William L., and Terrence J. Winschel. *Vicksburg Is the Key: The Struggle for the Mississippi River*. Lincoln: University of Nebraska Press, 2003.

Shirley, Glenn. *Belle Starr and Her Times: The Literature, the Facts, and the Legend*. Norman: University of Oklahoma Press, 1982.

Silber, Nina. *The Romance of Reunion: Northerners and the South, 1865–1900*. Chapel Hill: University of North Carolina Press, 1993.

Silverman, Joan L. "The Birth of a Nation: Prohibition Propaganda," in *The South and Film*, edited by Warren French, 23-30. Jackson: University Press of Mississippi, 1981.

Simpson, Brooks D. *Ulysses S. Grant: Triumph Over Adversity, 1822–1865*. Boston: Houghton-Mifflin, 2000.

Slotkin, Richard. *Gunfighter Nation: The Myth of the Frontier in Twentieth-Century America*. New York: Atheneum, 1992.

Smith, Timothy B. *The Untold Story of Shiloh: The Battle and the Battlefield*. Knoxville: University of Tennessee Press, 2006.

Spann, Edward K. *Gotham at War: New York City, 1860–1865*. Wilmington, DE: Scholarly Resources, 2002.

Speer, Lonnie R. *Portals to Hell: Military Prisons of the Civil War*. Mechanicsburg, PA: Stackpole, 1997.

Stern, Philip Van Doren. *Secret Missions of the Civil War*. New York: Bonanza, 1959.

Stiles, T. J. *Jesse James: Last Rebel of the Civil War*. New York: Knopf, 2002.

Stout, Harry S. *Upon the Altar of the Nation: A Moral History of the Civil War*. New York: Penguin, 2006.

Sword, Wiley. *Shiloh: Bloody April*. New York: Morrow, 1974.

———. *Southern Invincibility: A History of the Confederate Heart*. New York: St Martin's, 1999.

Symonds, Craig L. *Confederate Admiral: The Life and Wars of Franklin Buchanan*. Annapolis, MD: Naval Institute Press, 1999.

———. *Joseph E. Johnston: A Civil War Biography*. New York: Norton, 1992.

Thomas, Emory M. *Bold Dragoon: The Life of J. E. B. Stuart*. New York: Harper & Row, 1986.

———. *The Confederacy as a Revolutionary Experience*. Englewood Cliffs, NJ: Prentice-Hall, 1971.

———. *The Confederate Nation: 1861–1865*. New York: Harper & Row, 1979.

———. *The Confederate State of Richmond: A Biography of the Capital*. Austin: University of Texas Press, 1971.

———. *Robert E. Lee: A Biography*. New York: Norton, 1995.

Toplin, Robert Brent. *History by Hollywood: The Use and Abuse of the American Past*. Urbana: University of Illinois Press, 1996.

———. *Reel History: In Defense of Hollywood*. Lawrence: University Press of Kansas, 2002.

Trulock, Alice Rains. *In the Hands of Providence: Joshua L. Chamberlain and the American Civil War*. Chapel Hill: University of North Carolina Press, 1992.

Turner, George Edgar. *Victory Rode the Rails: The Strategic Place of Railroads in the Civil War*. Indianapolis: Bobbs-Merrill, 1953.

Urwin, Gregory J. W. *Custer Victorious: The Civil War Battles of General George Armstrong Custer*. Rutherford: Fairleigh Dickinson University Press, 1983.

Vandiver, Frank E. *Mighty Stonewall*. New York: McGraw-Hill, 1957.

Vidal, Gore. *Screening History*. Cambridge, MA: Harvard University Press, 1992.

Wade, Wyn Craig. *Titanic: End of a Dream*. New York: Penguin, 1980.

Warner, Ezra J. *Generals in Blue: Lives of the Union Commanders*. Baton Rouge: Louisiana State University Press, 1964.

———. *Generals in Gray: Lives of the Confederate Commanders*. Baton Rouge: Louisiana State University Press, 1959.

Waugh, John C. *The Class of 1846. From West Point to Appomattox: Stonewall Jackson, George McClellan and Their Brothers*. New York: Warner, 1994.

Weaver, Jeffrey C. *The Civil War in Buchanan and Wise Counties Bushwhackers' Paradise*. Lynchburg, VA: Howard, 1994.

Wellman, Manly Wade. *Giant in Gray: A Biography of Wade Hampton of South Carolina*. New York: Scribner's Sons, 1949.

Welsh, Jack D. *Medical Histories of Confederate Generals*. Kent, OH: Kent State University Press, 1995.

Wert, Jeffry, D. *Custer: The Controversial Life of George Armstrong Custer*. New York: Simon & Schuster, 1996.

———. *General James Longstreet, The Confederacy's Most Controversial Soldier: A Biography*. New York: Simon & Schuster, 1993.

———. *Gettysburg: Day Three*. New York: Simon & Schuster, 2001.

———. *Mosby's Rangers*. New York: Simon & Schuster, 1990.

Wiley, Bell Irvin. *The Life of Billy Yank: The Common Soldier of the Union*. Indianapolis: Bobbs-Merrill, 1952.

———. *The Life of Johnny Reb: The Common Soldier of the Confederacy*. Indianapolis: Bobbs-Merrill, 1943.

Williams, Martin. *Griffith: First Artist of the Movies*. New York: Oxford University Press, 1980.

Williams, T. Harry. *P. G. T. Beauregard: Napoleon in Gray*. Baton Rouge: Louisiana State University Press, 1954.

Wills, Brian Steel. *A Battle from the Start: The Life of Nathan Bedford Forrest*. New York: HarperCollins, 1992.

———. *The War Hits Home: The Civil War in Southeastern Virginia*. Charlottesville: University Press of Virginia, 2001.

Wilson, Charles Reagan. *Baptized in Blood: The Religion of the Lost Cause, 1865–1920*. Athens: University of Georgia Press, 1980.

Winks, Robin W. *Canada and the United States: The Civil War Years*. Baltimore: Johns Hopkins Press, 1960.

Winschel, Terrence J. *Triumph and Defeat: The Vicksburg Campaign*. Mason City, IA: Savas, 1999.

York, Neil Longley. *Fiction As Fact: The Horse Soldiers and Popular Memory*. Kent, OH: Kent State University Press, 2001.

Essays and Unpublished Manuscripts

Adams, Michael C. C., "Seeking Glory: Our Continuing Involvement with the 54th Massachusetts." *Studies in Popular Culture* 14 (1992): 11–19.

Biggs, Gregg. Review of the Film *The Horse Soldiers*. *Blue and Gray Magazine* (June 1993): 46.

Brooksher, William R., and David K. Snider. "A Piece of Rebel Rascality." *Civil War Times Illustrated* 23 (June 1984): 10–18.

Carnes, Mark C. "Hollywood History." *American Heritage* (September 1995): 74–79, 81–84.

Clinton, Catherine. "Gone with the Wind." In *Past Imperfect: History According to the Movies*, edited by Mark C. Carnes, 132–35. New York: Holt, 1995.

Conti, Gerald. "Seeing the Elephant," *Civil War Times Illustrated* 23 (June 1984): 19.

Davis, Stephen. "Joel Chandler Harris' Version of the Andrews Raid: Writing History to Please the Participant." *Georgia Historical Quarterly* 74, no. 1 (Spring 1990): 99–116.

Flanders, Alan B. "The Night They Burned the Yard." *Civil War Times Illustrated* 8 (February 1980): 30–39.

Frye, Dennis, ed. *Gods and Generals*. Leesburg, VA: Primedia History Group, 2003.

Gaughan, Anthony. "Woodrow Wilson and the Legacy of the Civil War." *Civil War History* 43 (September 1997): 225–42.

Jorgensen, C. Peter. "Gettysburg: How a Prize-Winning Novel Became a Motion Picture." *Civil War Times Illustrated* 32 (November–December 1993), 40–49, 92–93, 113.

Lindberg, Kip, and Matt Matthews. "'It Haunts Me Night and Day': The Baxter Springs Massacre." *North and South* 4 (June 2001): 42–53.

Litwack, Leon. "The Birth of a Nation." In *Past Imperfect: History According to the Movies*, edited by Mark C. Carnes, 136–41. New York: Holt, 1995.

Long, John S. "The Gosport Affair, 1861." *Journal of Southern History* 23 (1957): 155–172.

Lykes, Richard W. "The Great Civil War Beef Raid." *Civil War Times Illustrated* 5 (February 1967): 5–12, 47–49.

McFeely, William S. "Notes on Seeing History: The Civil War Made Visible." *Georgia Historical Quarterly* 76 (Winter 1990): 666–71.

McKnight, Brian D. "To Perish by the Sword: Champ Ferguson's Civil War," Unpublished manuscript.

McPherson, James M. "Glory." In *Past Imperfect: History According to the Movies*, edited by Mark C. Carnes, 128–31. New York: Holt, 1995.

Neely, Mark E., Jr. "Abraham Lincoln." In *The American Civil War: A Handbook of Literature and Research*, edited by Steven E. Woodworth, 189–202. Westport, Conn.: Greenwood, 1996.

Nofi, Alfred A., "Johnny Shiloh—the Drummer Boy of Chickamauga." *North & South* (2006): 10–11.

Sharp, Arthur. "The Spirit of Christian Warfare?" *Civil War Times Illustrated* 23 (November 1984): 32–37.

Spears, Jack. "The Civil War on the Screen." *The Civil War on the Screen and Other Essays*. South Brunswick: Barnes, 1977, 11–116.

Steiger, Janet, "*The Birth of a Nation*: Reconsidering Its Reception." In *The Birth of a Nation*, edited by Robert Lang. New Brunswick, NJ: Rutgers University Press, 1994.

Thomas, Emory M. "The Richmond Bread Riot." *Virginia Cavalcade* (1986): 41–44.

Walker, T. R., "Rock Island Prison Barracks." In *Civil War Prisons*, edited by William E. Hesseltine. Kent, OH: Kent State University Press, 1972.

Wills, Brian Steel. "Films and Television." In *The American Civil War: A Handbook of Literature and Research*, edited by Steven E. Woodworth, 613–19. Westport, Conn.: Greenwood, 1996.

Wilson, Charles Morrow. "The Hit-and-Run Raid." *American Heritage* 12 (August 1961): 28–31 and 90–93.

INDEX

ABOUT THE AUTHOR

Brian S. Wills is Kenneth Asbury Professor of History at the University of Virginia's College at Wise. He is the author of *The Confederacy's Greatest Cavalryman: Nathan Bedford Forrest*, *The War Hits Home: The Civil War in Southeastern Virginia*, and *No Ordinary College: A History of the University of Virginia at Wise*.